Instructor's Solutions Manual
for

Moore, McCabe, Duckworth, and Sclove's
The Practice of Business Statistics

Lori Seward

University of Colorado at Boulder

W. H. Freeman and Company
New York

Printed in the United States of America

ISBN: 0-7167-9692-9

First printing 2003

CONTENTS

Introduction
To the Instructor

This Instructor's Manual tries to make it easier to teach from the first edition of *The Practice of Business Statistics* (PBS). This manual contains some helpful teaching tools, such as an updated review of Internet resources, and suggestions for using the *Against All Odds* and *Decisions Through Data* videos. I have also included a suggested course outline. I have written the solutions to all chapter problems and selected chapter cases.

David Moore and Darryl Nester wrote the instructor guide for David Moore's *The Basic Practice of Statistics* (BPS). For those of you unfamiliar with BPS I'd like to explain that while BPS was written for a more general student population with a wider range of quantitative skills than the PBS text, the fundamental approaches in the two textbooks are the same. The guide that David and Darryl wrote contains invaluable advice for instructors, whether they are teaching in a business college or other discipline. I have kept as much of their advice as I could and added comments where I thought appropriate. (My comments are preceded with *LS* to keep them separate from David and Darryl's original advice.) I have kept the portions of David's discussions of the BPS approach for each chapter that apply to PBS. This means that most of David's original comments are included in this manual as well.

I welcome any suggestions or comments on the solutions. In particular, please notify me of any errors that may have escaped my notice at the time of publication. I can be reached at:

Lori Seward
Systems Division
Leeds School of Business
University of Colorado at Boulder
Boulder CO 80309-0419
303/492-0284   lori.seward@colorado.edu

Applicable excerpts from *Instructor's Guide with Solutions for Moore's The Basic Practice of Statistics* by Darryl K. Nester and David S. Moore.

- There is more attention to data analysis. Chapters 1 and 2 give quite full coverage. It is now becoming common to emphasize data in a first course, but many texts still begin with a too-brief treatment of "descriptive statistics."
- There is more attention to designing data production. It is surprising to a practicing statistician how little attention these ideas (among the most influential aspects of statistics) receive in many first courses. Chapter 3 discusses sampling and experimental design, with attention to some of the practical issues involved.
- *LS:* One of the ways PBS differs from BPS is with the treatment of probability, random variables, and with the addition of the Poisson distributions. I had added them to my course when using BPS. Business processes are often modeled using these additional distributions and it would be a mistake to leave them out of a business statistics course. Furthermore, as students move on to their upper level courses in operations and quality issues they need the probability foundation.
- There is more discussion of the ideas of inference. Chapter 6 (with the introduction to sampling distributions in Chapter 4) is the core of the presentation of inference. The ideas aren't easy, but are the key to an understanding that is more than mechanical.
- The presentation of significance tests emphasizes *P*-values rather than probabilities of Type I and Type II errors and tests with fixed   . This reflects common practice and helps students understand the output of statistical software. The alternative approach appears in the optional Section 6.4.
- *LS:* The discussion of the power of a significance test should also be a requirement in any complete business statistics course. It is a difficult concept for the students to grasp but seeing it at this introductory level will make it easier to understand the next time they encounter the idea of power.
- There is more attention to statistics in practice. Realism may be too much to claim in a book that is genuinely elementary. Nonetheless, Chapter 3 describes the practical difficulties of producing good data and the exposition and examples in Chapters 7 to 11 raise many issues that arise in applying inference methods to real problems.

Upon completion of a course based on PBS, students should be able to think critically about data, to select and use graphical and numerical summaries, to apply standard statistical inference procedures, and to draw conclusions from such analyses. They are ready for more specialized statistics courses (such as applied regression or quality control), for "research methods" courses in many fields of study, and for projects, reports, or employment that require basic data analysis.

Calculators and Computers

The practice of statistics requires a good deal of graphing and numerical calculation. Doing some graphing and calculating "by hand" may build understanding of methods. On the other hand, graphics and calculations are always automated in statistical practice. Moreover, struggling with computational aspects of a procedure often interferes with a full understanding of the concepts. Students are easily frustrated by their inability to complete problems correctly. Automating the arithmetic greatly improves their ability to complete problems. We therefore favor automating calculations and graphics as much as your resources and setting allow.

All students should have a calculator that does "two-variable statistics," that is, that calculates not only x and s but the correlation r and the least-squares regression line from keyed-in data. PBS is written so that a student with such a calculator will not often be frustrated by the required calculations. Even if you use computer software, students should have a calculator for use during class, at home, and on exams.

Two-variable statistics calculators are inexpensive (generally available for less than $20). PBS does not present anachronistic "computing formulas" that presuppose a four-function calculator.

LS: Based on my experience with large classes, it is almost a "must" for the students to have the same type of calculator. Business students will most likely find some type of financial calculator useful for future courses. I give my students a choice between two calculators in two different price ranges so that during class we don't have to struggle with many different types of keypads. While some freshmen have graphing calculators from high school,1 I've found the majority of these students spend more time learning their calculator than learning statistics. Small classes (less than 30 students) can take advantage of graphing calculators.

Graphing calculators now automate almost all procedures discussed in a first statistics course, including basic graphs. Calculators have the great advantage that students own them, carry them around, and take them home. If everyone in the classroom has a graphing calculator, class discussions can take on new dimensions: pose a problem and let everyone work on it. Students who took advanced math in high school are often familiar with graphing calculators when they arrive in our classes. If your circumstances favor use of a specific type of graphing calculator, by all means do it.

Software retains some clear advantages in entering and editing data and in graphics not constrained by the small window of a graphing calculator. Almost all students now have some familiarity with personal computers, so that the learning curve for menu-driven software is short and steep. Use software, even a spreadsheet such as Excel, if you can. A good deal of computer output appears in PBS, from several different packages. Separate student guides keyed to PBS are available for most of these options. The output is deliberately varied because any statistics student should become accustomed to looking at computer output and should be able to recognize terms and results familiar from her study.

LS: The solutions included in this manual were solved with both Excel and Minitab. The emphasis is on Excel output. I use Excel in my courses. Although some professionals view Excel as less sophisticated and more cumbersome than other software packages, it is a great teaching tool. I have found that many students are expected to use Excel in future course work and while interning in industry jobs. Students who can use Excel for statistical analysis are capable of learning to use more sophisticated software very quickly. Students who learn a more sophisticated software package may not be able to step back down to Excel if they need to in a future course or during their initial employment.

Using Video

One of the most effective ways to convince your students that statistics is useful is to show them real people (not professors) employing statistics in a variety of settings. Video allows you to do this in the classroom. Two related video series that contain many short documentaries of statistics in use "on location" are:

- *Against All Odds: Inside Statistics.* This telecourse, consisting of 26 half-hour programs, was prepared by COMAP for the Annenberg Corporation for Public Broadcasting Project. It is available in the United States at a subsidized price. Call 1-800-LEARNER for information or to order a copy.
- *Statistics: Decisions Through Data.* This set of 21 shorter modules (5 hours total) is intended for use as a classroom supplement in secondary schools. It was prepared by COMAP for the National Science Foundation and draws on the location segments of *Against All Odds*. It is available from COMAP. Call 1-800-77-COMAP for information. If you are outside the United States, you can obtain information about both video series from
COMAP Inc.
Suite 210
57 Bedford Street

Lexington, MA 02173 USA
Fax 1-617-863-1202

Because David Moore was the content developer for these video series, they fit the style and sequence of PBS well. We do not recommend showing complete programs from *Against All Odds* in the classroom. The shorter modules from *Decisions Through Data* are more suitable for classroom use. Video is a poor medium for exposition, and it leaves viewers passive. It is therefore generally not a good substitute for a live teacher. We suggest regular showing of selected on-location stories from AAO or DTD in most classrooms, rather than full programs. If you have a very large lecture (several hundred students), however, full DTD video modules along with computer demonstrations will help hold an audience too large for personal interaction.

Video has several strengths that make short segments an ideal supplement to your own teaching. Television can bring real users of statistics and their settings into the classroom. And psychologists find that television communicates emotionally rather than rationally, so that it is a vehicle for changing attitudes. One of our goals in teaching basic statistics is to change students' attitudes about the subject. Because video helps do this, consider showing video segments regularly even if you don't think they help students learn the specific topic of that class period. You can find more discussion of the uses of video, and references, in (Moore, 1993).

Here are some specific suggestions for excerpts from *Against All Odds* and *Decisions Through Data* that work effectively in class. The parenthetical comments in each case state what section of BPS the video illustrates.
- The 14-minute video *What is Statistics?* is a good way to start a course. This collage of examples from *Against All Odds* forms part of the first unit of AAO and is the first module of DTD. It is available separately (and inexpensively) from
The American Statistical Association
1429 Duke Street
Alexandria, VA 22314 USA
(703) 684-1221 or www.amstat.org
- *Lightning Research* from Program 2 of AAO, Module 3 of DTD. A study of lightning in Colorado discovers interesting facts from a histogram. (Section 1.1. BPS Figure 1.3 comes from this study.)
- *Calories in Hot Dogs* from Program 3 of AAO and Module 5 of DTD. The five number summary and box plots compare beef, meat, and poultry hot dogs. (Section 1.2. Exercise 1.39 concerns these data and Exercise 2.9 is based on the same article from *Consumer Reports*.)
- *The Boston Beanstalk Club* from Program 4 of AAO, Module 7 of DTD. This social club for tall people leads to discussion of the 68–95–99.7 rule for normal distributions. (Section 1.3.)
- *Saving the Manatees* from Program 8 of AAO, Module 11 of DTD. There is a strong linear relation between the number of power boats registered in Florida and the number of manatees killed by boats. (The manatees can illustrate any of Sections 2.1 [scatterplots], 2.3 [least-squares regression], or Chapter 11 [regression inference] in BPS.
- *Obesity and Metabolism* from Program 8 of AAO and Module 12 of DTD looks at the linear relationship between lean body mass and metabolic rate in the context of a study of obesity. (Sections 2.1, 2.2, and 2.3. Data appear in Exercise 2.7 and are also used for Exercise 2.22.)
- *Sampling at Frito-Lay* from Program 13 of AAO or Module 17 of DTD illustrates the many uses of sampling in the context of making and selling potato chips. (Section 3.1.) A student favorite.
- *The Physicians' Health Study* from Program 12 of AAO (Module 15 in DTD) is a major clinical trial (aspirin and heart attacks) that introduces design of experiments. (Section 3.2. Data from the

Physicians' Health study appear in Exercise 2.100 and Exercise 3.48 asks a simplified version of the design.)

• *Sampling Distributions* are perhaps the single most important idea for student understanding of inference. Module 19 of DTD presents the general idea, the basic facts about the sampling distribution of the sample mean x, and the application of these ideas to an x control chart. The setting is a highly automated AT&T electronics factory. (Sections 4.3 and 4.4.)

• *Battery Lifetimes* from Program 19 of AAO lead to an animated graphic that illustrates the behavior of confidence intervals in repeated sampling. Module 20 in DTD is a presentation of the reasoning of confidence intervals using the same setting that can be shown in its entirety. (Section 6.1.)

• *Taste Testing of Colas* is the setting for an exposition of the reasoning of significance tests in Module 21 of DTD. This treatment is preferable to that in AAO. (Section 6.2 uses the same example [6.8] to introduce tests; Example 7.2 in the following chapter applies the t procedures to the cola data.)

• *Welfare Reform* in Baltimore, from Program 22 of AAO, is a comparative study of new versus existing welfare systems that leads to a two-sample comparison of means. (Section 7.2. Exercise 7.62 concerns some data from this study.)

• *The Salem Witchcraft Trials*, revisited in Program 23 of AAO, show social and economic differences between accused and accusers via comparison of proportions. (Section 8.2.)

• *Medical Practice*: Does the treatment women receive from doctors vary with age? This story in Program 24 of AAO produces a two-way table of counts. (Chapter 9.)

• *The Hubble Constant* relates velocity to distance among extra-galactic objects and is a key to assessing the age of the expanding universe. A story in Program 25 of AAO uses the attempt to estimate the Hubble constant to introduce inference about the slope of a regression line. (Chapter 11. Figure 2.13 is a scatterplot of Hubble's data, which is used in Examples 2.10 and 2.11 to illustrate some descriptive facts about regression and correlation.)

Here is a complete list of the documentary segments in AAO, with timings for use if your VCR measures "real time," along with ratings from one to four stars. Professor Edward R. Mansfield of the University of Alabama prepared this handy guide. We are grateful to him for permission to reproduce it here. Start your VCR timer when the first signal on the tape appears. Remember that AAO programs are packaged two to a tape; the timings for the even-numbered programs may need some adjustment because the gap between programs seems to vary a bit.

Program 1: What is Statistics?
4:48 Domino's Pizza ***
13:15 The "What is Statistics?" collage of later examples
Program 2: Picturing Distributions (no timings/ratings available for Program 2)
—:— When does lightning strike?
—:— TV programming and demographics
—:— Diagnostic-related groups
Program 3: Describing Distributions
5:55 Comparable worth in Colorado Springs *
16:07 Calories in hot dogs **
21:00 Musical analysis of urine data **
Program 4: Normal Distributions
33:50 Age distributions and Social Security *
46:07 Boston Beanstalk social club for tall people *
50:38 Why don't baseball players hit .400 any more? ***
Program 5: Normal Calculations
7:07 Auto emissions at GM Proving Ground *
14:10 Cholesterol values **

19:50 Sizes of military uniforms **
Program 6: Time Series
34:50 The body's internal clock *
43:48 Psychology: reaction time study *
Program 7: Models for Growth
3:00 Children's growth rates and hormone treatment ***
14:00 Gypsy moth infestations **
Program 8: Describing Relationships
32:25 Manatees vs. motor boats in Florida ***
37:55 Cavities vs. fluoride levels
39:31 1970 draft lottery ***
44:04 Obesity: metabolic rate vs. lean body mass *
Program 9: Correlation
5:42 Identical twins raised apart ***
16:22 Baseball players' salaries **
20:53 The Coleman Report (education in the 1960s) *
Program 10: Multidimensional Data Analysis
32:28 Chesapeake Bay pollution **
47:42 Bellcore graphics **
Program 11: The Question of Causation
5:42 Simpson's paradox ****
12:47 Smoking and cancer (historical survey) ***
Program 12: Experimental Design
32:46 Observational study of lobster behavior *
36:14 Physicians' Health Study: aspirin and heart attacks ****
43:39 Is Ribavirin too good to be true? ***
47:22 Police response to domestic violence *
Program 13: Blocking and Sampling
4:45 Strawberry field research *
13:28 Undercounting in the Census ***
20:48 Sampling potato chips at Frito Lay ****
Program 14: Samples and Surveys
41:21 National Opinion Research Center ****
Program 15: What Is Probability?
10:50 Persi Diaconis on randomness *
17:49 Traffic control in New York (simulation model) **
Program 16: Random Variables
33:36 Cheating on AP Calculus *
34:33 Space Shuttle *Challenger* disaster ****
43:02 Points in a professional basketball game
49:10 Earthquakes in California *
Program 17: Binomial Distributions
3:46 The "hot hand": free throws in basketball ***
9:45 A finance class experiment **
17:22 Sickle cell anemia *
24:25 Quincunx: falling balls **
Program 18: The Sample Mean and Control Charts
33:45 Roulette
35:04 Interviews with gamblers **
40:44 The casino always wins ****
47:03 Control charts at Frito-Lay ***

53:41 W. Edwards Deming ****
Program 19: Confidence Intervals
11:35 Duracell batteries **
18.25 Rhesus monkeys in medical studies *
21:21 Feeding behavior of marmosets
Program 20: Significance Tests
34:18 Is this poem by Shakespeare? **
49:06 Discrimination within the FBI ***
Program 21: Inference for One Mean
5:55 National Institute of Standards and Technology **
13:30 Taste testing of cola ***
21:08 Autism *
Program 22: Comparing Two Means
33:32 Welfare programs in Baltimore **
45:05 Product development at Union Carbide ***
51:00 SAT exams: can coaching help?
Program 23: Inference for Proportions
3:03 Measuring unemployment (Bureau of Labor Statistics) *
11:58 Safety of drinking water ***
20:15 The Salem witch trials
Program 24: Inference for Two-Way Tables
34:11 Ancient humans (markings on teeth) **
43:30 Does breast cancer treatment vary by age? **
52:02 Mendel's peas **
Program 25: Inference for Relationships
3:32 How fast is the universe expanding (Edwin Hubble)? ****
Program 26: Case Study
35:49 How AZT for treatment of AIDS was tested ***

Resources on the Internet

The WorldWide Web has made great amounts of information—of varying degrees of usefulness—easily available. Here are some worthwhile sites with resources for use in conjunction with BPS. Some of these sites have links to other interesting locations. Do remember that URLs change much more often than this Guide is reprinted. First, some general collections:

• Carnegie-Mellon University maintains *StatLib*, an electronic repository of things of statistical interest, including data sets. To get started, visit lib.stat.cmu.edu. Note in particular the "Data and Story Library," an on-line source related to the EESEE collection of case studies that is included on the BPS CD-ROM.

• The *Journal of Statistics Education*, an electronic journal of the American Statistical Association, contains much of interest to teachers of statistics. For more information, visit www.amstat.org/publications/jse/.

• The Chance web site, hosted by Dartmouth College, provides timely "current events" material to supplement a statistics course. Find it at www.dartmouth.edu/~chance/.

• If you want to find some examples of "bad statistics," visit these sites, whose names are self-explanatory: www.junkscience.com and www.mathmistakes.com.

It is very useful for students to visit "real statistics" sites to get a glimpse of the richness of the subject:

• Ask students to locate facts about their home county at the Census Bureau, www.census.gov.

• Or read the latest press release about employment and unemployment from the Bureau of Labor Statistics at stats.bls.gov. Look under "News Releases" and then under "Employment & Unemployment" for releases with the title "Employment Situation." Also, the unified gateway to federal statistical agencies at www.fedstats.gov is comprehensive but a bit overwhelming.

•   Find current Gallup Poll press releases and Gallup's explanations of how sample surveys work at www.gallup.com. The National Council on Public Polls (www.ncpp.org) has statements on "Principles of Disclosure" and "20 Questions for Journalists" that make interesting reading. Nielsen Media Research, provider of the usual TV program ratings, has a writeup on "What TV Ratings Really Mean" that includes an explanation of why sampling works: www.nielsenmedia.com/FAQ.

•   The abstracts of current medical research in the *New England Journal of Medicine* (www.nejm.org) demonstrate that you must know some statistics to read medical literature. Choose a clinical trial and an observational study from the available abstracts, then ask students to search for them by subject and to write a description of the design, the explanatory and response variables, and the conclusions.

Applets deserve separate mention. You can find a large number of attractive interactive animated simulations that demonstrate important facts about probability and statistics. We recommend these for class demonstrations as well as for student work, particularly if you are not using software in your course. Most are at university locations, and their URLs change often. And, despite its claims, Java is quite machine- and browser-dependent. Test applets on the machines your students will use to be certain that they will run. Here are some sources that were attractive in mid-1999:

•   David Lane of Rice University has an excellent collection of Java applets, and also links to other similar sites: www.ruf.rice.edu/~lane/stat_sim/.

•   Also look at the collection by Todd Ogden and R. Webster West at the University of South Carolina: www.stat.sc.edu/rsrch/gasp/.

•   Another nice applet collection, from the University of Newcastle in Australia, is www.anu.edu.au/nceph/surfstat/surfstat-home/surfstat.html. This URL seems to change often, so you may need to search for "surfstat."

•   A collection emphasizing probability, by Charles Stanton of California State University at San Bernardino: www.math.csusb.edu/faculty/stanton/m262/probstat.html.

•   Another that is especially strong in probability (look at the poker hand applet) is by Kyle Siegrist of the University of Alabama at Huntsville: www.math.uah.edu/stat/.

•   Want to select an SRS or do experimental randomization, even for large samples, and bypass the table of random digits? Visit the Research Randomizer at www.randomizer.org.

Planning a Course

In preparing to teach from PBS, look at the **STATISTICS IN SUMMARY** sections that conclude each chapter. There you will find a detailed list of the essential skills that students should gain from study of each chapter. These learning objectives appear at the end of the chapters because they would make little sense to students in advance. You can use them for advance planning as you decide what to emphasize and how much time to devote to each topic.

Also look at the **APPLY YOUR KNOWLEDGE** exercises, short sets of exercises that cover the specific content of the preceding exposition. Their location tells students "You should be able to do this right now." They also show the instructor what students can be expected to do at each step. The longer sets of **SECTION EXERCISES** at the end of each section ask students to integrate their knowledge, if only because their location doesn't give as clear a hint to the skills required. The **CHAPTER REVIEW EXERCISES** add another level of integration. You can help students by judicious selection of exercises from all three locations.

One of the emphases of the movement to reform teaching in the math sciences is that we should make our classrooms as interactive as possible by involving students in discussion, reaction, problem-solving and the like. Those who try this find that course outlines cover a bit less material—but that the students master more of it. The outlines below reflect this; your mileage may vary. Mature students who have learned how to learn can create their own interaction with text and lecture, and so progress much faster. Reformers tend to undervalue lectures for mature students.

Course Outline

LS: The outline below is intended for undergraduate business students and should be used as a guide only. Experience has shown me that the size of the class has more to do with the pace than the quantitative skills of the students. I teach a "mega" section with over 400 students. While this is clearly an undesirable way to teach a statistics course, it is a reality with which instructors at large universities are now faced. Rather than fighting the administrators I have had to develop a method that works in spite of the conditions.

After teaching my "mega" section without recitations for three semesters I was finally given the funding to add recitations. The level of understanding of conceptual issues rose dramatically. I attribute this improvement to having time in a "safe" environment to work examples. I try to break our class time up so that I lecture for 2/3 of the time and they work on examples together for the other third. The recitations are the times for the students to work on problems together. Someone is there in the classroom to answer questions and correct their mistakes. My TAs and I walk around the room while the students are working. I have found they ask questions when we are standing next to their desks that they simply won't ask when we are standing at the blackboard or overhead.

In the smaller classes I try to provide the same proportion of lecture time to work time 2/3 to 1/3. In these classes, however, the work time is each class period. I typically select problems from the text or put together examples on my own for them to work in class. Again, walking around the room while they work brings out more questions than I would ever get in front of the class.

I have taught the following outline from three different perspectives:
- A sixteen-week semester meeting twice each week for 50 minutes with a recitation meeting for 50 minutes each week to supplement the lectures. This is a good solution for the "mega" sections. If you aren't successful in convincing the college to offer smaller classes, they might be open to recitations. I try to keep the recitations to around 40 or 50 students each. This gives the students opportunities to ask questions and spend more time working problems during class.
- A sixteen-week semester meeting twice each week for 75 minutes each class. This works well for classes that are less than 100 students. Fifty students is a very manageable group.
- This outline can be adapted for a five-week summer course that meets for one hour and 35 minutes each day. This also works best for classes less than 50 students.

Week One:

      Introduction and Describing Data   PBS sections 1.1 and 1.2

      I show the film *What is Statistics?* on the first day of class.

Week Two:

      The Normal Curve   PBS section 1.3

I give time to master the calculators and software this week. When I have a class that is less than 50 students I try to take them into a computer lab for one day to give a hands-on learning experience for the software.

Week Three:
      Two variable relationships   PBS sections 2.1, 2.2, begin 2.3
      Regression
Week Four:
      Regression cont., Categorical Data   PBS sections 2.3, 2.4, and 2.5
Week Five:
      Sampling and Randomness   PBS Chapter 3 and section 4.1
Week Six:
      Review for **Exam I**   One day
      Exam I   One day

I find that most students can comfortably finish a 40-question MC test that is evenly distributed with calculations and concepts in less than 90 minutes.

Some of you might ask why include the start of chapter four at the end of the first section of material. What I have found with business students is that the material in Chapters 1-3 is quite manageable while chapters 4, 5, and 6 are daunting. This short foray into new material gives them an idea of what is to come. The students are more likely to link the material between Chapters 1-3 and the rest of the textbook when I organize the course this way.

Week Seven:
      Probability, Sampling Distributions   PBS sections 4.2, 4.3 and 4.4

We can start to move faster at this point in the semester. Most students are now familiar with the routine of class and the vocabulary. Many of the homework problems can be done with pencil and paper and the answers to questions often take on specific numerical values, which was not always the case in chapters 1-3. Students get satisfaction out of solving for the "right" answer.

Week Eight:
      Probability, Binomial Distribution   PBS sections 5.1 and 5.2
Week Nine:
      Poisson Distribution, Conditional   PBS sections 5.3 and 5.4
      Probability
Week Ten:
      Estimation and Significance   PBS sections 6.1 and 6.2
Week Eleven:
      Significance, Testing Errors (define)   PBS section 6.3 and start 6.4
Week Twelve:
      Review for **Exam II**   One Day
      Exam II   One Day

I find that most students need more time to work the problems on this exam. I use approximately 30 MC questions with an even mix between calculations and conceptual questions.

Week Thirteen:
      Calculating Power   PBS section 6.4
Week Fourteen:
      Inference for Mean, Comparing   PBS sections 7.1 and 7.2
      Means
Week Fifteen:
      Inference for Proportions   PBS Chapter 8
Week Sixteen:
      Inference for Two-Way Tables   PBS Chapter 9
Comprehensive Final Exam

Chapter Comments

The comments below contain brief discussions of philosophy, teaching suggestions, and additional data and examples for use in teaching.

Part I: Understanding Data

One of the most noteworthy changes in statistics instruction in the past decade is the renewed focus on helping students learn to work with data. The change in instruction follows a change in research emphases. Statistics research has pulled back a bit from mathematics (though, as the wise saying goes, you can never be too rich or too thin or know too much mathematics) in favor of renewed attention to data analysis and the problems of scientific inference. It is no longer thought proper to devote a week to "descriptive statistics" (means, medians, and histograms) before plunging into probability and probability-based inference.

Contemporary introductions to statistics include a substantial dose of "data analysis." In addition to reflecting statisticians' consensus view of the nature of their subject, working with data has clear pedagogical advantages. Students who may be a bit anxious about the study of statistics can begin by learning concrete skills and exercising judgment that amounts to enlightened common sense.

Chapters 1 and 2 present the principles and some of the tools of data analysis. For teachers whose training is primarily mathematical, effective teaching of data analysis requires some reorientation. Here are four principles.

1. Emphasize the strategy, not just the skills. It is easy to treat data analysis as a longer stretch of descriptive statistics. Now we present stemplots, boxplots, the 5-number summary, . . . , in addition to means, medians, and histograms. There is a larger strategy for looking at data which these tools help implement. The STATISTICS IN SUMMARY figures at the end of Chapters 1 and 2 stress some elements of this strategy, such as

- Begin with a graph, move to numerical descriptions of specific aspects of the data, and (sometimes) to a compact mathematical model. *Which* graphs, numerical summaries, and mathematical models are helpful depends on the setting.

- Look for an overall pattern and for striking deviations from that pattern. Deviations such as outliers may influence the choice of descriptive summaries, and the presence and clarity of the overall pattern suggests what mathematical models may be useful.

2. Don't import inferential ideas too soon. The point of view of data analysis is to let the data speak, to examine the peculiarities of the data in hand without at first asking if they represent some wider universe or answer some broader question. The distinction between sample and population, which is central to inference, is deliberately ignored in data analysis.

John Tukey of Bell Labs and Princeton, who shaped the subject, refers to "bunches" of data. PBS doesn't go that far, but does delay the sample-population distinction until Chapter 3, where it is essential to the discussion of designs for producing data. One aspect of successful teaching is to resist the temptation to tell students everything at once. Let them grasp the strategy and tools of basic data analysis first. These will be under control and very helpful when we come to inference.

3. Use real data. Remember the mantra: data are not just numbers; they are numbers with a context. The context enables students to communicate conclusions in words and to judge whether their conclusions are sensible. Data come with at least a bit of background, though for beginning instruction that background may not fully reflect the complexities of the real world. I'm willing to oversimplify for the sake of clarity, but not to ask empty operations with mere numbers. PBS provides small and moderate-size data sets in more than adequate number for basic instruction. You should want more.

- Two general compilations are *A Handbook of Small Data Sets* (Hand et al., 1994) and *A Casebook for a First Course in Statistics and Data Analysis* (Chatterjee et al., 1995). Both contain data with background and are accompanied by data disks. Specialized texts now often contain more data disks. For example, Thi´ebaux (1994) and McBean and Rovers (1998) have data on the subjects of their titles.

• Mine the electronic terrain. Many data sets and other resources are available on the WorldwideWeb and through other electronic means. Check the Internet sites listed earlier in this guide for some good sources.

• Amass your own collection of data. Data about the states, with $n = 50$ or $n = 51$, are a convenient size for simple data analyses. The *Statistical Abstract of the United States* is a good place to start. The *Information Please Environmental Almanac*, which includes the provinces of Canada as well as the states, has much data of interest to students. Consider the percent of solid waste output that is recycled (Minnesota is an outlier), toxic chemical releases (Louisiana and Texas are outliers), or per capita energy use in Canada (Alberta is an outlier). The "Almanac" issue of the *Chronicle of Higher Education*, published each year around September 1, contains much data on students and education.

• The students themselves are another source of data. You should consider starting the term with a survey asking a variety of questions. Assure students that responses are anonymous. Try to get both quantitative and categorical data, and ask students' gender to allow two-sample comparisons. You can use these data for in-class illustrations throughout the course. For example, you might ask some of these items:

– Are you MALE or FEMALE?
– To the nearest inch, how tall are you?
– On a typical school day, how much time do you spend watching television?
(Answer in minutes. For example, 2 hours is 120 minutes or 1 and 1/2 hours is
90 minutes.)
– On a typical school day, how much time do you spend outside of class studying and doing homework?
(Answer in minutes.)
– How much money in coins are you carrying right now? (Don't count any paper money, just coins).
– How old [tall, heavy] do you think Dr. X is?
– How many siblings do you have?
– How large was your high school graduating class?
– What is your favorite type of cheese?
– How many credit cards do you have? How high is your balance?

• Encourage students to look carefully at the data they encounter *outside* of class. You might ask students to collect examples of statistics used poorly or in a misleading way, and to comment on the context of the data they find. If they gain nothing else from this course, they at least should become more intelligent consumers of data. Far too many people give only slight attention to the numbers they read or hear. For example:
– A home security company, hoping to sell its services, placed an ad in a Sunday newspaper stating that: "When you go on vacation, burglars go to work. . . .
According to FBI statistics, over 26% of home burglaries take place between Memorial Day and Labor Day. . . . " Is that a convincing reason to install a security system?
– Shortly before O.J. Simpson was found not guilty in his criminal trial, a poll in the Los Angeles area found that 27% of whites, and 73% of blacks, believed he was innocent. Asked their impressions of this result, quite a few students observed only that the two percentages add to 100%. This is true, but completely coincidental (they are percentages of two separate groups!). An informed citizen should find much more interesting issues to consider here.

4. Communicating results is important. If we could offer just one piece of advice to teachers using PBS, it would be this: *A number or a graph, or a magic phrase such as "Reject H0," is not an adequate answer to a statistical problem.* Insist that students state a brief conclusion in the context of the specific problem setting. We are dealing with data, not just with numbers.

Chapter 1: Examining Distributions

Students taking a first course in statistics often do not know what to expect. Some may view statistics as a field where the major task is to tabulate large collections of numbers accurately. Others have heard that statistics is more like mathematics with a lot of complicated formulas that are difficult to use. Few are expecting a course where they need to use their common sense and to think.

Your presentation of the material in Chapter 1 sets the tone for the entire course. We would like students to see that they can succeed and to become accustomed to making judgments and discussing findings rather than just solving problems. Try to use selected examples or exercises as a basis for class discussion. Presenting new data of special interest to your students is useful. Don't speed through the descriptive material because it seems simple—students don't always find the mechanics simple, and are not accustomed to "reading" graphics. And they are certainly not used to talking about what the data show.

Section 1.1 Displaying distributions with graphs. Be flexible in assessing student graphs and interpretations: It isn't always clear whether to split stems in a stemplot or how to choose the classes for a histogram. Try by your flexibility to help students not to get hung up on minor details of graphing. Similarly, how symmetric a histogram or stemplot must be to warrant calling the distribution "symmetric" is a matter for judgment. So is singling out outliers. Be flexible, but discourage students from, for example, calling the largest observation an outlier regardless of whether it is isolated from the remaining observations. Flexibility may also help students live with software. In making stemplots, for example, some software packages truncate long numbers and others round; some put the larger stems on top and others put the smaller stems there. These variations have little effect on our picture of the distribution.

Section 1.2 Describing distributions with numbers. The common descriptive measures summarize things we can see graphically, but they summarize only part of what we can see. The graphical presentation is primary for data analysis. Students should have a calculator that gives them $\bar{x}$ and s from keyed-in data. Do warn them that many calculators offer a choice between dividing by n and dividing by $n-1$ in finding the standard deviation s. We want $n-1$. (What is worse, many calculators label their choices as n and $n-1$. We haven't met yet, but we want to use s to denote the standard deviation of a set of data.) Use a data set in class and let students check their calculator skills. If you use software, you may find versions of a boxplot and rules for calculating quartiles that differ slightly from those in BPS. Encourage students to ignore this and to work with what the software reports. Do remember that no single numerical summary is appropriate for all sets of data, and that any numerical summary may miss important features such as gaps or multiple peaks.

Section 1.3 The normal distributions. Note that normal distributions are introduced here as models for the overall pattern of some sets of data, not in the context of probability theory. Although this ordering of material is unusual, it has several advantages. The normal distributions appear naturally in the description of large amounts of data, so that the later assumption for inference that "the population has a normal distribution" becomes clearer. Moreover, mastering normal calculations at this point reduces the barrier posed by the material on probability and sampling distributions (Chapter 4). If the students already know how to compute normal "probabilities" and have some understanding of the relative frequency interpretation from this section, the transition to ideas about probability is easier.

It is also true that meeting normal distributions early explains the otherwise mysterious affection of statisticians for the standard deviation. The organizing idea is that we can sometimes use a mathematical model as an approximation to the overall pattern of data. Normal distributions are one example; a linear regression line (next chapter) is another. The 68–95–99.7 rule is a useful device for interpreting μ and for normal distributions. It also makes it possible to think about normal distributions without a table. Many distributions are nonnormal, so don't make this into the so-called "empirical rule" for distributions in general.

Chapter 2: Examining Relationships

Having dealt with methods for describing a single variable, we turn to relationships among several variables. At the level of PBS, that means mostly relationships between two variables. That a relationship between two variables can be strongly affected by other ("lurking") variables is, however, one of the chapter's themes. Note the new vocabulary (explanatory and response variables) in the chapter Introduction, as well as the reiteration of basic strategies for data analysis. Correlation and regression are traditionally messy subjects based on opaque "computing formulas" based on sums of squares. PBS asks that students have a "two-variable statistics" calculator that will give them the correlation and the slope and intercept of the least-squares regression line from keyed-in data. This liberates the instructor—we can give reasonably realistic problems and concentrate on intelligent use rather than awful arithmetic. The computing formulas are anachronistic and don't appear in the text. Do remember that data input and editing can be frustrating on a calculator, so reserve large problems for computer software.

The descriptive methods in this chapter, like those in Chapter 1, correspond to formal inference procedures presented later in the text. Many texts delay the descriptive treatment of correlation and regression until inference in these settings can also be presented. There are, we think, good reasons not to do this. By carefully describing data first, we emphasize the separate status and greater generality of data analysis. There are many data sets for which inference procedures do not apply—data for the 50 states, for example. Fitting a least squares line is a general procedure, while using such a line to give a 95% prediction interval requires additional assumptions that are not always valid. In addition, students become accustomed to examining data *before* proceeding to formal inference, an important principle of good statistical practice. Finally, correlation and regression are so important that they should certainly appear in a first course even if you choose not to discuss formal inference in these settings.

Section 2.1 Scatterplots. Using graphs should be comfortable by now. Constructing scatterplots is a relatively easy task (but tedious without software for all but small data sets.) Interpreting the plots takes some practice. In the classroom, build instruction on examples and stress that common sense and some understanding of the data are necessary to do a good job of description. Computers can make the plots, but people are needed to describe them. Again, the general rule is to look for overall patterns and deviations from them. Patterns such as clusters and positive and negative association are useful in many cases but can lead to distorted descriptions when imposed in situations where they do not apply.

Section 2.2 Correlation. Correlation is presented before regression in part because it does not require the explanatory-response distinction. This also allows us to give a meaningful formula for the regression slope, using the correlation. Students should have a calculator that gives r from keyed-in data. You can therefore use the somewhat messy formula for r as a basis for explaining how correlation behaves (fit this to your students' ability to read algebra), but avoid using it for computation.

Section 2.3 Least-squares regression. The background to regression isn't always clear to students, so don't skip over it: We'd like to draw the *best* line through the points on our scatterplot; to do this, we need an explicit statement of what we mean by "best." The least squares idea gives such a statement, one that assumes we want to use the line to predict y from x. Least squares isn't terribly natural. At this point, just say that it's the most common way to fit a line. (Least squares is easily influenced by extreme observations, but it has many nice properties that have kept it the standard method even though computers have reduced its ease-of-computation advantage.) The concepts of "outlier" and "influential observation" are important. An observation is influential if removing it would move the regression line. This is clearly a matter of degree. More advanced statistical methods include numerical measures of influence. I've defined "outlier" broadly to keep things simple for students—they only have to look for isolated extreme points in any direction. That's a matter of degree also. Outliers in y have large residuals; outliers in x are often influential.

Section 2.4 Interpreting correlation and regression. For now at least, computers can't do anything in this section. As calculations are automated, interpretive ideas become a more important part of even basic instruction.

Section 2.5 Relations in categorical data.* This is "applied arithmetic" but students don't find it trivial. There is no recipe (I do give guidelines) for deciding what percents to calculate and compare in describing a relationship between two categorical variables.

Chapter 3: Producing Data

This is a relatively short chapter with a lot of ideas and little numerical work. Students find the essentials quite easy, but they are very important. This chapter isn't mathematics, but it is core content for statistics. Weaknesses in data production account for most erroneous conclusions in statistical studies. The message is that production of good data requires careful planning. Random digits (Table B) are used to select simple random samples and to assign units to treatments in an experiment. There are numerous examples that can serve as the basis for classroom discussion.

The chapter also has a secondary purpose: the use of chance in random sampling and randomized comparative experiments motivates the study of chance behavior in Chapter 4. I have tried to motivate probability by its use in statistics, and to concentrate on the probabilistic ideas most directly associated with basic statistics. This chapter starts that process.

Section 3.1 Designing samples. The deliberate use of chance to select a sample is the central idea. Many of the inference procedures in later chapters assume that the data are a simple random sample. Others require several independent SRSs or another simple model. In this section we learn what an SRS is, and also get a glimpse of the practical difficulties that can damage a sample to the point that formal inference is of little value.

Section 3.2 Designing experiments. The randomized comparative experiment may be the single greatest contribution of statistics to the advance of knowledge. Since Fisher introduced randomization in the 1920s, these ideas have revolutionized the conduct of studies in fields from agriculture to medicine. No student should leave a first statistics course without understanding the distinction between experiments and observational studies and understanding why properly designed experiments are the gold standard for evidence of causation. When experiments can't be done, causation is a slippery subject, and statistical methods that claim to give evidence for causation are not for beginners and are often debated by experts. Good experiments allow relatively clean conclusions.

Part II: Understanding Inference

The reasoning of classical statistical inference is built on asking, "What would happen if I used this method many times?" Confidence limits, *P*-values, and error probabilities answer that question in varied settings. All of these answers utilize the *sampling distribution* of a statistic, which addresses the underlying question by displaying the distribution of the statistic in repeated samples or experiments carried out under the same circumstances. Sampling distributions are a tough idea to convey to students, but they are central to inference and can't be avoided without loss of conceptual mastery.

Distributions are the big idea of probability for understanding the reasoning of basic statistical inference. The goal of Chapter 4 is to efficiently convey the probability ideas needed to understand inference, in particular sampling distributions. Chapter 6 is (apart from the optional Chapter 5) the most difficult in the book. There is no hiding the fact that the reasoning of confidence intervals and (more so) significance tests isn't easy. But if all the calculations are done by software, as is now the case in practical applications of statistics, students must carry away this reasoning if our presentation of inference is to have much lasting value. Chapters 7 and 8 present the simplest inference procedures of interest in practice, for inference about means (Chapter 7) and proportions (Chapter 8). Chapter 7 is essential, because in it we meet many issues relevant to applying statistical methods to real problems. Chapter 8 is not essential, but it is short and easy. You can shorten your path through this part of PBS by omitting Chapter 8 if you wish. Chapters 10 and 11, but not Chapter 9, are accessible by this route.

Chapter 4: Probability and Sampling Distributions
Section 4.1 Randomness. Much evidence shows that even students who can do formal probability exercises have little conceptual understanding of random behavior. We therefore start very informally. Do take the time to do some of the simulation exercises in this section. If you have the capability to automate simulations, use it here. Most statistical software packages and many graphing calculators will, for example, simulate the Bernoulli and binomial distributions. That allows you to have students actually do simulations. Perhaps they will see that coin tossing, Shaq's free throws, and the results of a "Yes/No" opinion poll question are instances of the same setting. We think that's a more profound "mathematical" insight than learning the binomial formula.

Section 4.2 Probability models. This section introduces the simplest facts about probability—all we need to use the language of probability to discuss statistical inference. A probability model is a set of possible outcomes plus a way of assigning probabilities that satisfies some basic rules. There are two common ways to assign probabilities: assign a number to each of a finite set of outcomes, or assign a number as the area under a density curve. That's it. If you find it necessary to do more, you can jump to Section 5.1, but don't do that out of mere habit. Probability is a high barrier to students, and this is a statistics course.

Yes, we know discrete distributions can take infinitely many values. That's not very helpful to students without a math background that includes infinite series. Recall the saying of the physicist Richard Feynman that "The real problem in speech is not precise language. The problem is clear language." He was talking about mathematics textbooks when he said that. We need not tell students everything we know.

Section 4.4 Sampling distributions. Section 4.2 gave us a language to use. Now we continue the main track, following up on the discussion of sampling in Chapter 3. Sampling distributions are of course one of the big ideas of statistics. We also get in context some important probability facts, the law of large numbers and the central limit theorem. Do simulations here.

LS: An easy one to do in class is to pass around dice to the students. Have them roll the dice any number of times (but at least five times) and record their individual rolls and then calculate their average. If you have a computer in class you can easily create a picture of the two distributions: one of the individual rolls and one of their means. I also use this opportunity to calculate the mean and standard deviation from the probability distribution and then look at the sample means and standard deviations. This is a great hands-on illustration of the idea of sampling variability and the Central Limit Theorem.

Chapter 6: Introduction to Inference
This chapter contains many fundamental ideas. We introduce confidence intervals and tests along with some cautions concerning the use and abuse of tests. Throughout, the setting is inference about the mean μ of a normal population with known standard deviation σ. As a consequence, the z procedures presented are not applicable to most real sets of data. They introduce ideas in a setting where students can do familiar normal calculations, and they pave the way for the more useful t procedures presented in the next chapter. Experience shows that many students will not master this material upon seeing it for the first time. Fortunately, they will meet the key ideas again in the next chapter. By the time they have completed both chapters and worked many exercises, they should grasp the fundamentals. Be patient, and remember that understanding the reasoning of inference is more important than the number of procedures learned.

Section 6.1 Estimating with confidence. Figures 6.3 and 6.4 display the big idea: the recipe for a 95% confidence interval produces intervals that hit the true parameter in 95% of all possible samples. (In formal language, the recipe has probability 0.95 of producing an interval that catches the true parameter.) Simulation can help students understand this central idea.

Section 6.2 Tests of significance. The reasoning of significance tests is conceptually the hardest point in a first course in statistics. *LS:* I try to appeal to the students' common sense when working with these types of problems. It helps to bring published results of real studies to show what the language is and how the results are used. I give many examples of conclusion statements along with business actions to get their minds thinking in this way.

Section 6.3 Making sense of statistical significance. In discussing z confidence intervals, PBS offers a "warning label" reminding users of conditions for proper use. That label applies to the z tests also. Tests are, however, more difficult to interpret than are confidence intervals. Many statisticians feel that tests are overused, or at least over-interpreted. Hence this short section. The discussions of "choosing a level of significance" and "statistical significance and practical significance" offer some cautions about the interpretation of statistical significance. "Statistical inference is not valid for all sets of data" and "beware of multiple analyses" apply to confidence intervals as well, but abuses seem more common in the setting of tests.

Section 6.4 Error probabilities and power.* Some instructors stress P-values in teaching beginners; others stress the two types of error and their associated error probabilities. We are in the former camp. Why begin with P-values? First, "assessing the strength of evidence" is a better description of practical inference than is "making decisions." Second, P-values are prominent in the output from statistical software, so users of statistics must understand them. The fact that there is an elegant mathematical theory (Neyman-Pearson) based on the fixed- approach should not be allowed to sway practical instruction for beginners. That said, P-values are not sufficient for a full account of statistical tests. The idea of *power*- how likely is this test to detect an alternative you really want to detect if it is true- is certainly important in practice.

LS: For business students that will go on to study business process design and improvement, understanding that decisions involve risk and being able to quantify those risks are important concepts. Power is a way to quantify the risks involved in making business decisions. I don't believe it should be left out of a business statistics course. Be warned however that the material is difficult. I try to stick with one or two examples and spend extra time asking the students to consider the consequences of their business decisions.

Chapter 7: Inference for Distributions
The one- and two-sample t procedures are among the most-used methods of inference. One sample t confidence intervals and significance tests are a short step from the z procedures of Chapter 6. The two-sample procedures present a complication: the "textbook standard" method assumes equal variances in the population, an assumption that is hard to verify and often not justified. PBS ignores that method in favor of two alternatives that work even if the population variances differ: a reasonably good conservative approximation for hand use, and a very accurate approximation that is implemented in almost all statistical software packages. Another deviation from the "textbook standard" occurs in the optional Section 7.3, where the basic recommendation concerning inference about population spread is "Don't do it without expert advice." This choice is also well justified by literature citations. The exposition in this chapter pays at least some attention to the problems of applying statistical inference to real data.

Section 7.1 Inference for the mean of a population. If you want to do inference about μ but don't know σ, just replace the unknown σ by its sample estimate s in the z procedures. That's the driving idea. It leads to the t distributions and to the use of all of Table C. Because the mechanics are so similar to those of Chapter 6, you can replay the reasoning of inference and pay more attention to interpreting the results.

The section calls attention to the use of one-sample methods for matched pairs data and to the conditions needed to use the methods in practice.

Section 7.2 Comparing two means. Students now need to distinguish one-sample, matched pairs, and two-sample settings. That's how this section opens. For inference about the difference $\mu 1 - \mu 2$ of two population means, we start with the natural sample estimator $x1 - x2$ and its sampling distribution. The distribution is (at least approximately) normal, so standardize the estimator and replace the unknown σi by the sample standard deviations si. You may not wish to emphasize this intuitive "derivation," depending on your students' capacities for generalization, but it repeats the logic of earlier settings. We then come to the actual two-sample t procedures: just use the smaller of $n1 - 1$ and $n2 - 1$ as the degrees of freedom. Everything else is optional, but if you are using software you will want students to read the section headed "more accurate levels."

Section 7.3 Inference for population spread. The contrast in the practical usefulness of the t procedures for means and the chi-square and F procedures for standard deviations is a good argument for not allowing theoretical statistics to set the agenda for a first course in statistical methods. These tests are all (at least approximately) likelihood ratio tests for normal distributions. They therefore share a widely accepted general principle and some large-sample optimality properties. But they are vastly different in their actual usefulness. The t tests (and their extension to ANOVA for comparing many means) are relatively little affected by deviations from normality. Tests for standard deviations, on the other hand, are so sensitive to deviations from normality that I do not believe they should be used in practice.

What then should we do about the standard tests for standard deviations in the context of a first statistics course? PBS allows three choices. You can ignore the issue altogether—this section is optional. You can discuss the issue and also present the most common of the questionable procedures, the F test for comparing two standard deviations. Or you can discuss the first subsection in Section 7.3, bluntly titled "Avoid inference about standard deviations," and omit the actual F test on the grounds that we have explained why it is not of much value. I usually take the third approach.

Chapter 8: Inference for Proportions
This chapter presents the z procedures for one-sample and two-sample inference about population proportions. The procedures are approximate, based on the large-sample normal approximation. Note that we avoid a common source of confusion by giving only the normal approximation for $\hat{p}$, rather than starting with the normal approximation for binomial counts. By now the students should be comfortable with the general framework for confidence intervals and significance tests. Those who have not yet mastered these concepts get an additional opportunity to learn these important ideas.

Section 8.1 Inference for a population proportion. Here are confidence intervals and significance tests for a single proportion. Students will just follow the recipes given, but you may want to point out why the basic ideas are reasonable. *LS:* Evidence in the literature is overwhelmingly in favor of the "add two successes and two failures" approach to estimating proportions. This is the approach taken in PBS.

Section 8.2 Comparing two proportions. This section presents confidence intervals and significance tests for comparing two population proportions. Students should be able to distinguish two-sample from one-sample settings from their work in Chapter 7. As in the previous section, we use different standard errors for confidence intervals and tests. Pooling the two samples in the test statistic, while making the test inconsistent with the confidence interval, keeps the two-sample test consistent with the 2×2 case of the chi-square test for two-way tables in Chapter 9.

Part III: Topics in Inference

The concluding three chapters of PBS present independent accounts of inference in three more advanced settings: two-way tables of count data (Chapter 9), simple linear regression (Chapter 10) and multiple regression (Chapter 11).

Chapter 9: Inference for Two-Way Tables

The Pearson chi-square test is one of the most common inference procedures and, because it tests the existence of a relationship between two categorical variables under several sampling models, one of the most versatile. Do note the stress that the overall test ("Yes, these variables are related") is not a full analysis of the data. The descriptive analysis of the nature of the relationship is essential.

The chi-square test, like the tests in Chapter 8, is an approximate test whose accuracy improves as the cell counts increase. There is an "exact" test for two-way tables, called the Fisher exact test. For example, this test reports $P = 0.0071$ rather than the chi-square test's $P = 0.0052$ for the data of Example 9.1 of BPS. This test treats *both sets of marginal totals* as fixed in advance. In Example 9.1, only one set was fixed by the design of the study. Some statisticians prefer to always do inference "conditional" on the observed marginal totals, as Fisher's test does. This is a debate that you don't want to reveal to your students! You can find a description of the Fisher test in, e.g., Agresti (1990) and a more advanced survey in Agresti (1992).

Chapter 11: Inference for Regression

There are many interesting problems in which the relationship between two variables can be summarized graphically and numerically with a least squares line. Not all of these can be analyzed using the methods presented in this chapter. Inference for linear regression is based on a statistical model that expresses the assumptions underlying the inference procedures. The section headed "The regression model" is therefore essential to understanding regression inference. This section also introduces s, the "standard error about the line," as the key measure of sample variability in the regression setting. You will sometimes find s called "residual standard error" or "root MSE" in computer output or other texts.

The calculations required for regression inference, even after the least squares line is in hand, are quite unpleasant without software. Most exercises in this chapter therefore give the output from a regression program. If your students are using software, you can ask them to produce the equivalent output from the data. If your students lack software access, you can give them the results of key calculations (see the exercise solutions).

References

1. Agresti, Alan (1990), *Categorical Data Analysis*, Wiley, New York.
2. Agresti, Alan (1992), A survey of exact inference for contingency tables, *Statistical Science*, 7, pp. 131–177.
3. Chatterjee, Samprit, Handcock, Mark S., and Simonoff, Jeffrey S. (1995), *A Casebook for a First Course in Statistics and Data Analysis*, Wiley, New York.
4. Hand, D. J., F. Daly, A.D. Lunn, K. J. McConway, and E. Ostrowski (1994), *A Handbook of Small Data Sets*, Chapman and Hall, London.
5. McBean, Edward A. and Rovers, Frank A. (1998), *Statistical Procedures for Analysis of Environmental Monitoring Data & Risk Assessment*, Prentice Hall, Upper Saddle River, New Jersey.
6. Moore, David S. (1993), The place of video in new styles of teaching and learning statistics, *The American Statistician*, 47, pp. 172–176.
7. Moore, David S. and discussants (1997), New pedagogy and new content: the case of statistics, *International Statistical Review*, 65, pp. 123–165.

8. Thi´ebaux, H. Jean (1994), *Statistical Data Analysis for Ocean and Atmospheric Sciences*, Academic Press, San Diego, California.

Chapter 1
Examining Distributions
Solutions

1.1 a) Vehicles **b)** Variables: vehicle type (categorical), transmission type (categorical, number of cylinders (quantitative), city MPG (quantitative), and highway MPG (quantitative).

1.2 a) Gender is categorical. **b)** Age is quantitative. **c)** Race is categorical. **d)** Smoker is categorical. **e)** Blood pressure is categorical. **f)** Calcium level is quantitative.

1.3 a) The columns in the chart to the left display nominal data and therefore can be shown in any order desired. **b)** No, a pie chart would not be appropriate since the categories do not make up a whole (or 100%).

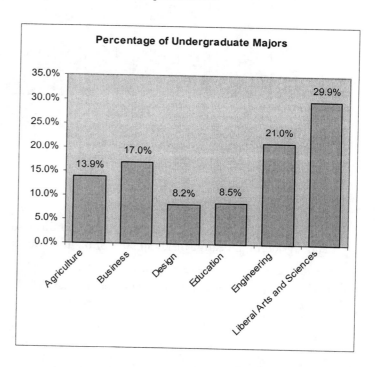

1.4 a)

Occupational deaths	Count	Percent of total
Agricultural	807	13%
Mining	121	2%
Construction	1190	20%
Manufacturing	719	12%
Trans and utilities	1006	17%
Wholesale	237	4%
Retail	507	8%
Finance	105	2%
Service	732	12%
Government	562	9%
Other occupations	37	1%

The "other" category represents occupational deaths not found in the 10 specified categories. This percentage is 1%.

b)

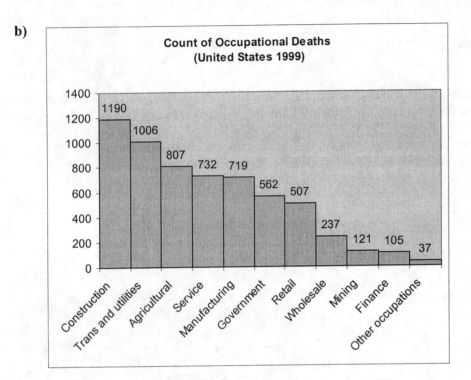

c) We can see that the first three categories, Construction, Transportation and Public Utilities, and Agricultural deaths, make up 50% of the total occupational deaths in 1999.

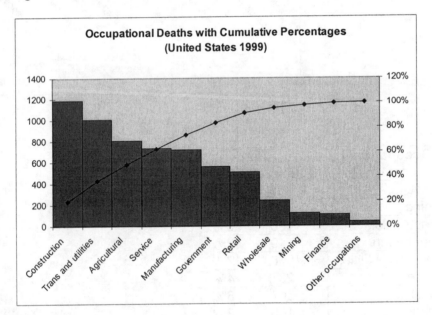

d) Yes, we could use a pie chart to display the data because we know the total number of occupational deaths.

1.5

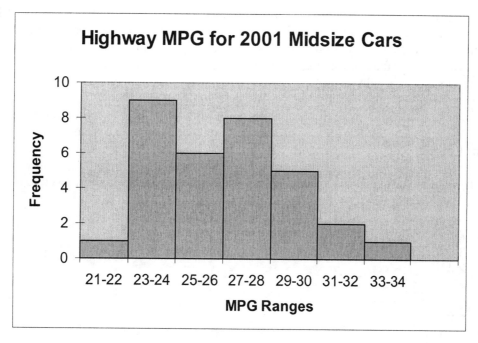

1.6

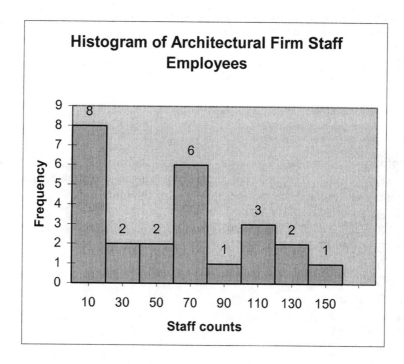

1.7 a) The distribution of mileage is roughly symmetric about the point 27, with a range of 11 (33-22). There do not appear to be any outliers. (Refer to the histogram shown in problem 1.5.) **b)** The Jaguar S/C and the BMW 740I are the two lowest mileages and should be subject to the "gas guzzler" tax. Notice that all three Jaguar models fall in the two lowest classes.

1.8 The average salaries in figure 1.3 appear to have a somewhat symmetric distribution with a center at 2.25 or 2.5 million. The range of average salaries is 4 million. Figure 1.4 shows the average salaries of the Cincinnati Reds. The distribution is not symmetric, is skewed to the right, with a wide range of 10 million. The center is hard to describe. One could say the distribution is centered at 1 million since this class has approximately half of the observations. One could also say that the average may be close to 4 million since the distribution is skewed right.

1.9 a) The distribution of monthly returns appears fairly symmetric. **b)** The center of the distribution is close to zero or slightly greater than zero. **c)** The range of returns is –15% to 18%. **d)** Roughly 35-40% of the monthly returns were less than zero.

1.10 The stemplot of staff counts is shown below. The distribution is strongly skewed to the right, which   we also observed in the histogram shown in problem 1.6,

```
 0 | 7
 1 | 3 4 5 5 5 7 7
 2 | 2 4
 3 |
 4 |
 5 | 2 7
 6 | 1 2 8
 7 | 0 0 2
 8 |
 9 | 6
10 |
11 | 0 1 5
12 | 6
13 | 1
14 |
15 | 5
```

1.11 The stemplot is shown below. The center of the distribution is near 28. There do not appear to be any clear outliers although the distribution appears skewed to the right. The range of values is 3 to 93. The split stemplot is also shown below.

```
0 | 3  9  9
1 | 1  3  4  5  6  7  7  8  8  9
2 | 0  0  0  1  2  3  4  5  5  6  6  8  8  8  8
3 | 2  5  6  9  9
4 | 1  3  4  5  5  7  9
5 | 0  3  5  9
6 | 1
7 | 0
8 | 3  6  6
9 | 3
```

Split Stemplot

```
0 | 3
0 | 9 9
1 | 1 3 4
1 | 5 6 7 7 8 8 9
2 | 0 0 1 2 3 4
2 | 5 5 6 6 8 8 8
3 | 2
3 | 5 6 9 9
4 | 1 3 4
4 | 5 5 7 9
5 | 0 3
5 | 5 9
6 | 1
6 |
7 | 0
7 |
8 | 3
8 | 6 6
9 | 3
9 |
```

1.12 a)

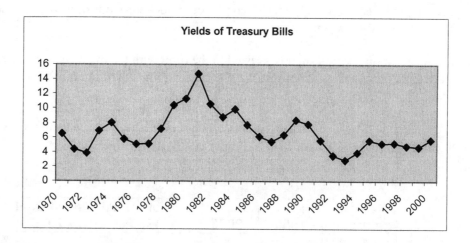

b) The temporary peaks in rates can be seen in years 1974, 1981, 1984, 1989, and 1995. (Note: 1984 is not an obvious peak.) **c)** The highest rate occurred in 1981 and since that time there has been a noticeable downward trend in rates.

1.13 a) The individuals described by this data set are Mutual Funds. **b)** In addition to the name of the fund there are four other variables. The "category" and "largest holding" variables are categorical and the "net assets" and "year-to-date return" variables are quantitative. **c)** The unit of measurement for "net assets" is millions of dollars and for "year-to-date return" it is percentage.

1.14 a)

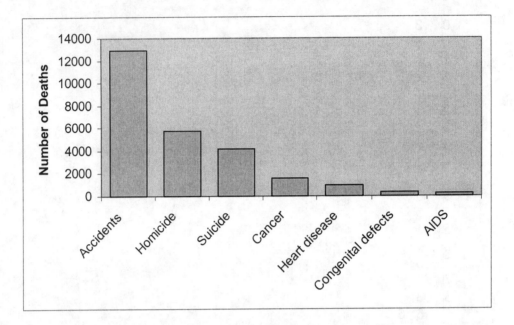

b) To make a pie chart we need to know the total number of deaths in this age group in 1997.

1.15 Obviously reasons will vary. Reasonable suggestions include: market potential for their business, availability of employees, tax benefits from municipality, accessibility to an airport, public education system (for employees relocating), housing costs, construction costs, predicted growth in the area.

1.16 The distribution appears slightly skewed to the right with the majority of years seeing no more than 4 hurricanes. It appears that the center of the distribution is between 3 and 4 per year.

1.17 Sketches should vary. The distribution will be skewed left because there are more new coins in students' pockets than old coins.

1.18 a)

Age group	1950	2075	% of total 1950	% of total 2075
Under 10 yrs	29.3	34.9	19.42%	11.29%
10-19	21.8	35.7	14.45%	11.55%
20-29	24	36.8	15.90%	11.91%
30-39	22.8	38.1	15.11%	12.33%
40-49	19.3	37.8	12.79%	12.23%
50-59	15.5	37.5	10.27%	12.14%
60-69	11	34.5	7.29%	11.17%
70-79	5.5	27.2	3.64%	8.80%
80-89	1.6	18.8	1.06%	6.08%
90-99	0.1	7.7	0.07%	2.49%
100-109		1.7		0.55%

b) The highest percentage age group is the under 10 age group with almost 20%.

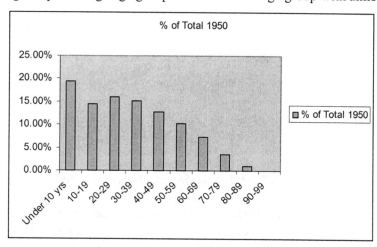

c) The most obvious changes between 1950 and 2075 is the more uniform distribution observed in 2075. There are also observations in a new category, the 100-109 age group.

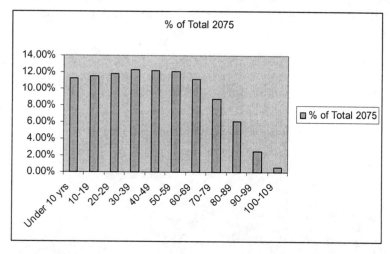

1.19 a) The count of service calls is not an appropriate measure to report when comparing reliability between Brand A and Brand B dishwashers. The total number of owners of Brand A and Brand B included in the study are very different (13,376 vs. 2942). **b)** A better measure of reliability might be the percentage of owners of each brand that requested a service call. Comparing these percentages shows that 22% (2942/13,376) of Brand A owners requested a service call while 40% of Brand B owners requested a service call. It appears that Brand B has a much lower reliability than Brand A.

1.20 a)

```
1  0  4  4  4  5
2  0  2  2  6  6  7
3  4  6
4  2  8
```

Split Stemplot

```
1 | 0   4   4   4
1 | 5
2 | 0   2   2
2 | 6   6   7
3 | 4
3 | 6
4 | 2
4 | 8
```

The split stemplot shows the skewness of the distribution much more clearly.

b) The distribution of percentage decline is skewed to the right. **c)** The center appears to be at 22. The range of values is 10 to 48. It makes sense to explain that during a bear market stocks fall around 22% but can fall close to 50% during some markets. It would be interesting to look at the duration of the decline for those years with a very high percentage decline in stock prices.

1.21 Other variables that might indicate "size" of a company include: market share in their particular market, number of employees, number of facilities, profit (not simply revenue).

1.22

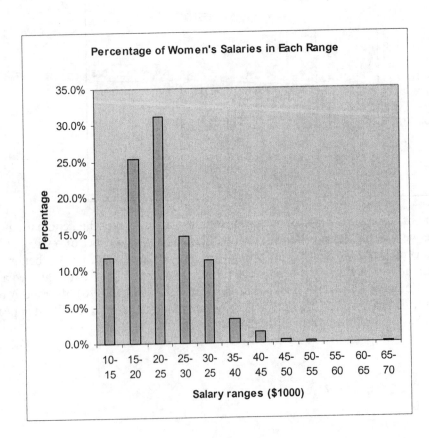

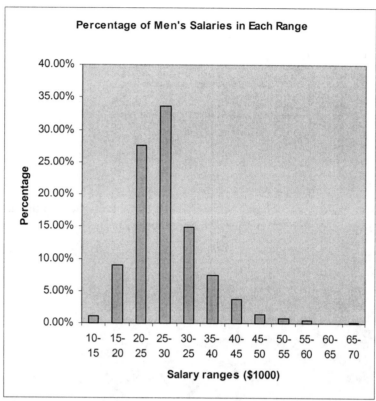

The overall shape for both distributions is similar: both are heavily skewed to the right. The distributions also have the same spread. The difference between the two is the center of the distribution. The center for women's salaries appears to be in the $20,000-$25,000 range whereas the men's salaries appear to center in the $25,000-$30,000 range. An interesting observation is that almost 70% of the women in this factory earn less than $25,000 and only 40% of the men earn less than $25,000.

1.23

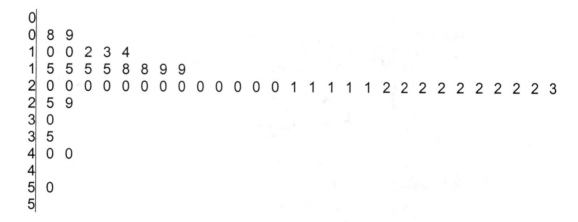

The distribution does not appear heavily skewed although the majority of monthly fees are less than $23. The $50 monthly charge may be an outlier. Most ISPs were charging around $20 a month in August 2000. The charges in the high end of the distribution may have been early subscribers. ISPs offered their services at a fairly high premium in the beginning and subscription rates tended to drop as more subscribers signed up. (Although it may be possible that early subscribers were offered low rates to initially sign on.)

1.24

Engineers		Architects

```
                                              Engineers                                                    Architects

4  4  3  2  1  1  1  1  0  0  0  0  0  0  0  0  0   0 | 0 |  2  2  3  3  3  4  4
                                                  7 | 0 |  5  5  5  5  5  5  6  8  9
                                       4  3  2  2 | 1 |  0  2  2
                                                    1 |  9  9
                                             3  3  1 | 2 |  1  4
                                                    2 |  9
                                                    3 |  1
                                                  5 | 3 |
```

The distribution of engineers is much more heavily skewed to the right than the distribution of architects. There appears to be an outlier of 53 engineers for one firm.

1.25

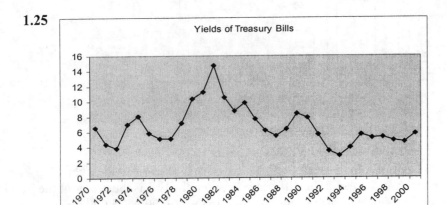

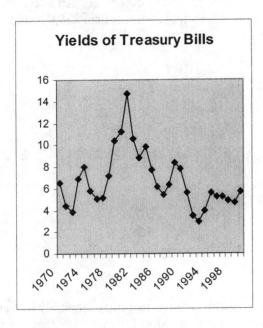

1.26

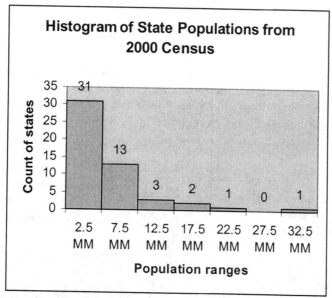

The distribution of state populations is skewed to the right. This makes sense because we expect there to be a small number of states with very large populations such as California and Texas. More than half of the states fall into the smallest range. The center appears to be around 5 million and the spread is approximately 20-25 million. I would consider California to be an outlier.

1.27 a) Household income includes all people living under one roof. You would expect a household to have a greater income than an individual.

b)

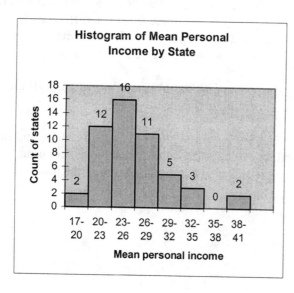

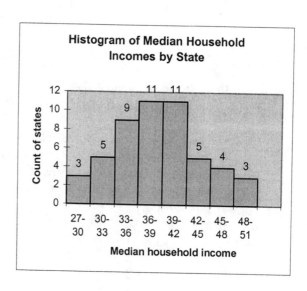

c) The mean personal income distribution is skewed to the right with two states possibly being outliers. This makes sense because we would expect more variability in personal income than household income. If we looked at the distribution of personal income within each state we would probably see that they are heavily skewed to the right also. The median household income is greater for most states, which is what we explained in part (a). The shape is more symmetrical because we are looking at the distribution of medians, rather than means. (Medians are resistant to outliers whereas means are not.)

1.28 a) Two states with the same number of doctors may not offer the same level of health care if their populations are very different.
b) This histogram does not give a clear look at the distribution because of the outlier. The outlier is for Washington, DC and can be taken out of the data set since DC is not technically a state. The resulting histogram, without the outlier, shows a skewed distribution. States average close to 200 doctors per 100,000 people with the range being from 100-450.

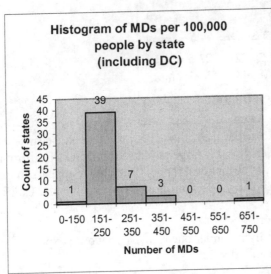 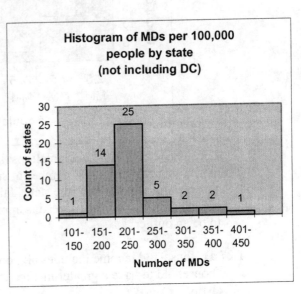

1.29 The mean earnings for Black males is $19,804.17, for White females is $21,484.80, and for White males is $21,839.93. The mean values suggest that there may be a difference in earnings between black and white employees and between black male and female employees. The more striking difference appears between black and white employees.

1.30 a) The mean amount spent by a grocery shopper is $34.70. **b)** The trimmed mean of the lowest 46 observations is $30.15. The outliers inflate the mean.

1.31 The median earnings for Black males is $18,383.50, for White females is $19,960, and for White males is $19,977. The median values do show the same difference as the mean values. In each case, however, the median is less than the mean indicating the distribution on salaries may be skewed to the right.

1.32 a)

```
1 | 3
2 | 3 9
3 | 9
4 | 1 2
5 | 1 6 9
6 | 2 4
7 |
8 | 8
```

b) The mean and median with the outlier are: 4.725 and 4.65. The mean and median without the outlier are 4.355 and 4.2.

1.33 The mean income is $675,000 and the median income is $330,000. When a distribution is skewed to the right the mean is greater than the median.

1.34 The five number summary for the four different groups are as follows:

	Black females	**White females**	**Black males**	**White males**
Low	$12,641	$14,698	$16,576	$15,100
Q₁	16,555	17,879.50	17,018.50	18,245
Median	17,516	19,960	18,383.50	19,977
Q₃	19,090	25,014.50	21,268.50	23,531
High	20,788	31,176	29,347	30,383

The box plots created from the sample data in table 1.8 do show the same distributions of salary data as shown in figure 1.11.

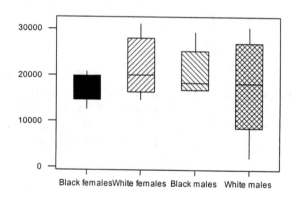

1.35 a) The five-number summary is shown in the table below:

	Asian countries	Eastern European countries
Low	1.3	-12.1
Q₁	3.4	-1.6
Median	4.65	1.4
Q₃	6.05	4.3
High	8.8	7

b) The box plot on the following page shows the distribution of growth of consumption for the two groups of countries. We can see that the growth for the Asian countries was much stronger over this time period than for the Eastern European countries.

Growth of Per Capita Private Consumption

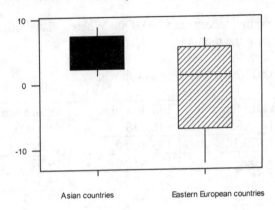

Asian countries   Eastern European countries

1.36 a)

```
2  | 8 9
3  | 0 2 6
4  | 6 7 9
5  | 2 2 2 3 4 8 8 9
6  | 0 3 3
7  | 2
```

b) We would expect the median to be greater than the mean. The distribution appears slightly skewed to the left. **c)** The mean is 49.65 and the five-number summary is 28, 41, 52, 58.5, and 72. The median is greater than the mean (52 > 49.65) as anticipated. **d)** The range of the middle half of managerial and administrative average annual wages is 17.5 (58.5 – 41).

1.37 a) 983.5 **b)** 347.23

1.38 a) Refer to problem 1.28 (b). The second graph shows the distribution of MDs without DC. **b)** The five-number summary is 402, 241.25, 220, 196.25, and 150. The mean and standard deviation are as follows: $\bar{x} = 228.34$, $s = 55.34$. Based on the histogram, the five-number summary shows that the distribution is skewed to the right. (Note the small distance between the median and the minimum compared to the median and the maximum.) **c)** The graph shows that 40 of the states have less than 250 MDs per 100,000 people. This is 80% of all states.

1.39 The median is 27.86. The median is less than the mean, which was 34.70. This is because the distribution is skewed to the right.

1.40 The distribution appears skewed to the right; therefore, a five-number summary would be a better numerical description of the distribution. The five-number summary for this distribution is: 1.5, 2.7, 3.4, 4, 8.9. ($\bar{x} = 3.58, s = 1.24$)

1.41 a) $\bar{x} = 28.77$, $s = 17.77$ **b)** $\bar{x} = 31.71$, $s = 14.15$ The outlier inflates the values of the mean and standard deviation. **c)** The advertiser means that the vehicles are similar in make, model, year. The objective is to remove any variation due to different vehicle sizes, ages, or any other performance related issues.

1.42 – 1.44 Applet

1.45 a)

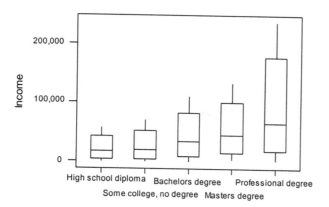

b) From the box plots it appears that income increases as education level increases. The average income level does not increase as much as the range of income within each educational category. For example, the range of income in the first category, high school diploma, is $56,294 whereas the range of income in the last category, professional degree, is $233,967.

1.46 For the category "high school diploma" the fifth percentile is at position 1598, the first quartile is at position 7993, the median is between positions 15985 and 15986, the third quartile is at position 23978, and the 95th percentile is at 30371. For the category "professional degree" the fifth percentile is at position 61, the first quartile is between positions 307 and 308, the median is at position 615, the third quartile is between positions 922 and 923, and the 95th percentile is at position 1167.

1.47 The mean number of violent crime incidents per 100,000 people is 523 and the standard deviation is 320. The histogram on the following pages shows that the distribution is skewed to the right. There is also a clear outlier. This happens to be DC again.

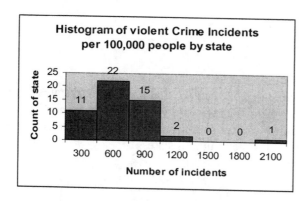

1.48   Northern states $\bar{x} = 361.89, \ s = 216.45$

```
 0  |
 1  | 13 20 21
 2  |
 3  | 34 91
 4  |  3 42
 5  |
 6  | 44 89
 7  |
 8  |
 9  |
10  |
```

Southern states $\bar{x} = 621.5, \ s = 259.07$

```
 0  |
 1  |
 2  | 19
 3  | 17 45
 4  | 69
 5  | 65
 6  |  7  7 78
 7  | 90
 8  | 47
 9  | 90
10  | 24
```

Midwestern states $\bar{x} = 419, \ s = 204.35$

```
 0  | 87
 1  | 97
 2  | 71
 3  | 10 38
 4  |  9 35 38
 5  | 15 77 90
 6  |
 7  |
 8  | 61
 9  |
10  |
```

Based on the stem plots and numerical summaries one can see that the Southern states have a higher incidence of violent crime than the Northeastern or Midwestern states. When comparing small data sets both pictures and numerical summaries help us see the differences. Note the higher mean and standard deviation for the Southern states.

1.49 $\bar{x} = 7.5$, $s = 2.03$ for both data sets. The stemplot below shows that data set A is skewed left and data set B is skewed right. Both data sets have outliers as well.

```
        Data A                    Data B
                  1|  3
                74|  4
                  |  5  | 25  56  76
                26|  6  | 58  89
                  |  7  |  4  71  91
  77  74  14  10|  8  | 47  84
      26  14  13|  9  |
                  | 10 |
                  | 11 |
                  | 12 | 50
```

1.50 The mean wealth is $2.2 million and the median wealth is $800,000. One would expect the distribution on average wealth to be skewed heavily to the right.

1.51 a) The five-number summary is 9, 30, 49.5, 66, and 142. **b)** The distribution appears to be skewed to the right therefore the median is less than the mean.

1.52 a) The mean salary is $62,500. All the employees earn less than the mean. The median salary is $25,000. **b)** The mean increases to $87,500. This increase in the owner's salary does not affect the median.

1.53 a)

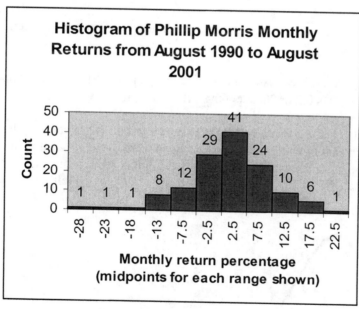

I chose a histogram because the data set was very large.

b) The two outliers on the low end of the distribution have values –26.6 and –22.9. The distribution appears symmetric about a center of 2.5 with a spread of approximately 40 (25-15). **c)** If the two outliers are included the mean is 1.55 and the standard deviation is 8.22. If one invested $100 and realized the mean return, they would have 101.55 at the end of the month. **d)** If one invested $100 and realized a return of –26.6% they would have $73.40 left at the end of the month. The mean and standard deviation without the two low outliers are 1.95 and 7.60. The mean increased and the standard deviation decreased after removing the outliers. Leaving out these outliers should not substantially affect the median and quartiles because they are resistant to outliers.

1.54 It makes sense that the mean change in price was a positive 111% while the median change in price was a negative 31%. One would expect the distribution on stock price change of IPOs to be skewed to the right.

1.55 The *mean* of all salaries in the NBA is $2.36 million. If this were the *median* then half of all players would be making less than this amount.

1.56 a) You should use the mean in this case. Even though income would be heavily skewed to the right, the mean will give the government a better estimate of the tax base because it will be greater than the median. **b)** The median should be used in this case. Again, the distribution is likely to be skewed to the right and the median will more accurately reflect the center of the distribution.

1.57 a) Choose all four numbers the same. **b)** The numbers 0, 0, 10, and 10, give a standard deviation of 5. **c)** There is more than one choice in part (a) but only one choice in part (b). The standard deviation measures the variation about the mean. Choosing numbers all the same gives a standard deviation of zero. Choosing an equal set of numbers as far from the mean as possible will give the largest standard deviation.

1.58 a) The IQR for black females is 2535 (see problem 1.34). Q_1 minus the low observation is 3914. 3914 > 1.5(2535); therefore, the low observation can be considered an outlier. **b)** No.

1.59 Sketches will vary but check to see that students understand the difference between *symmetric* and *skewed left*.

1.60 a) This is a 1×1 square and the area inside this square is equal to 1. **b)** The area under the square between 0.8 and 1.0 is 0.2 or 20%. **c)** 60%. **d)** 50%. **e)** $\mu = 0.5$.

1.61 a) The mean is at point C and the median is at point B. The mean is greater than the median because the distribution is skewed right. **b)** The mean and median are equal at point A because the distribution is symmetric. **c)** The mean is at point A and the median is at point B. The mean is less than the median because the distribution is skewed left.

1.62

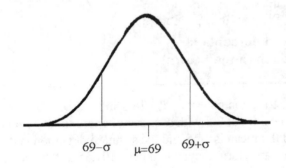

1.63 a) 2.5%. **b)** 64 – 74 inches. **c)** 16%.

1.64 a) 50%. **b)** 2.5%. **c)** 60-160.

1.65 The Z score for Eleanor is 1.8 and the Z score for Gerald is 1.5. Eleanor scored higher based on her standardized score.

1.66 a) .9978. **b)** .0022. **c)** .9515. **d)** .9978 - .0485 = .9493.

1.67 a) Z = 1.64. The area above 1.64 is 0.0505; therefore, 5.05% of vehicles have an MPG rating of 30 or greater. **b)** The area between 30 and 35 equals the area above 1.64 minus the area above 2.57. 4.54% of vehicles have an MPG rating between 30 and 35. **c)** 5.05%.

1.68 a)

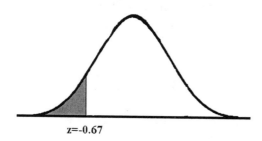

z=-0.67

b)

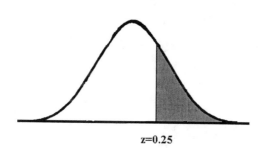

z=0.25

1.69 a) 59.48%. **b)** 452. **c)** 711.

1.70 The measurements are taken to the nearest hundredth of an inch and as we can see on the vertical axis there are many observations with the same values. (In essence the data have been *made discrete* which means that the distances are forced to take on values in the set (.01, .02, .03, .04, .05, .06, .07, .08). This results in the odd runs at each point.)

1.71 It appears that less than 5% of the observations are beyond two standard deviations from the mean. One might conclude that the density curve has a very steep middle with most points clustered around the mean.

1.72 The taller curve has an approximate standard deviation of 0.2 and the shorter curve has an approximate standard deviation of 0.5. Answers will vary.

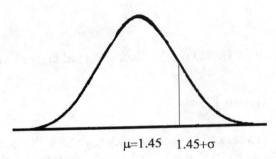

1.73

(0.65, 2.25)

1.74 a) Between 234 and 298 days. **b)** 234 days or less. **c)** It is unlikely. 218 is three standard deviations below the mean, which tells us only 0.15% of all women give birth in 218 days or less.

1.75 a)

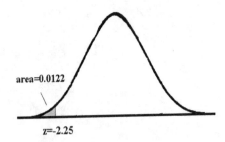

b)

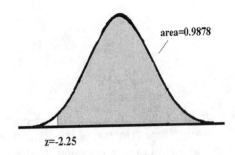

c)

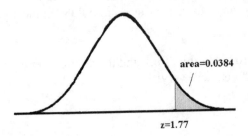

d)

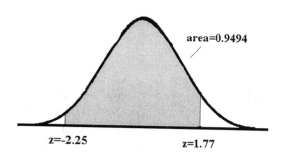

1.76 a) z = 0.84. **b)** z = 0.39.

1.77 17.11%

1.78 7.64%

1.79 a) –21% - 47%. **b)** 22.36%. **c)** 23.89%.

1.80 a) 5.16%. **b)** 54.71%. **c)** 279.44 days.

1.81 a) .25, $Q_1 = -0.67$, $Q_3 = 0.67$. **b)** $Q_1 = 255.28$, $Q_3 = 276.72$.

1.82 a) –1.28 and 1.28. **b)** 8.93 oz. and 9.31 oz.

1.83

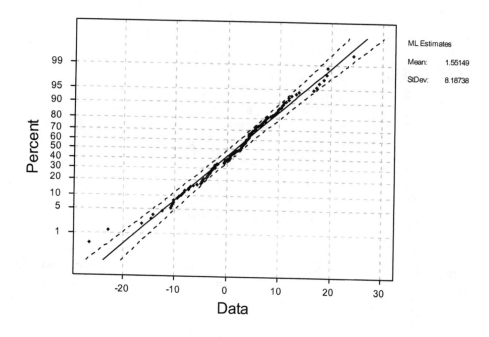

The distribution on the previous page appears fairly normal. One can see the two low outliers that fall above the line.

1.84 The histograms and quantile plots will differ for each student. Check to see that the student can use the software package correctly.

1.85 As in problem 1.84, the histograms will all look different since random data is being generated. The uniform density curve should look different than the bell curve. There may be some slight deviations but overall the curve should take on the shape of a rectangle. The normal plot will have an s-shaped curve rather than a straight line. The low values will fall below the normal line and the high values will lie above the normal line.

1.86 a) For each pair the smaller value is the median and the larger value is the mean. It makes sense that incomes are skewed to the right; therefore, the mean would be greater than the median. **b)** Households may contain more people than are included in a family. There may also be greater variation within a single household than within a single family if there are more than two wage earners. This would lead to households having a smaller income than families.

1.87 The categorical variables are gender and automobile preference. The quantitative variables are age and household income.

1.88 a) I would expect the number of patients admitted with heart attacks to be roughly the same for each day of the week because the occurrence of a heart attack would not be dependent on which day of the week it is. The data confirm this expectation. **b)** The distribution on the day on which patients are discharged shows that the number of discharges rises to Friday and dramatically drops off for Saturday and Sunday. It may be that patients want to be home for the weekend if possible.

1.89

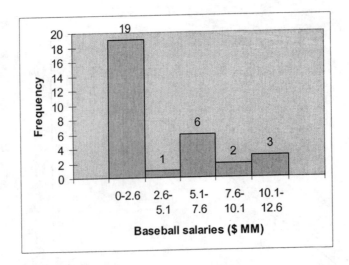

The mean and standard deviation are approximately $3.5 million and $4 million. The distribution is heavily skewed to the right. A better measure of central tendency would be the median. The median equals $1.6 million.

1.90

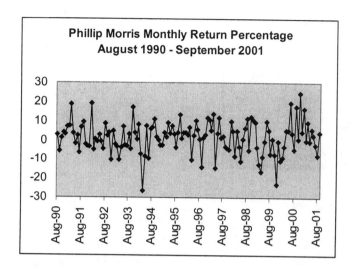

The time plot shows that the returns did not display any obvious trends up or down over this 10 year period. The two outliers discovered in problem 1.53 are shown as the low points on the plot. The two effects of action against smoking and sharp rises in stock prices may have produced this random-looking time plot.

1.91 a) The five-number summary for normal corn is 462, 400.5, 356, 337, and 272. The five-number summary for new corn is 477, 428.5, 404.5, 383.5, and 318. The box plots are shown below. We can see that the new corn has a more symmetrical distribution than the normal corn with a smaller spread and higher median. There is a higher weight gain overall for the new corn.

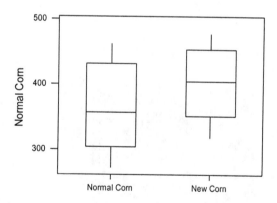

b) The mean and standard deviation of weight gain for the normal corn is 366.3 grams and 50.81 grams. The mean and standard deviation for the new corn is 402.95 grams and 42.73 grams. The mean weight gain of chicks fed the new corn is 36.65 grams higher than for chicks fed the normal corn.

1.92 a)

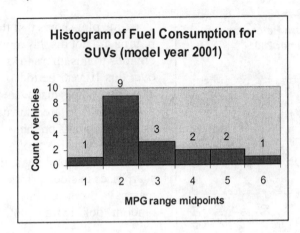

This histogram shows a distribution skewed to the right with a center at 18 MPG and a spread of 10 MPG.

b)

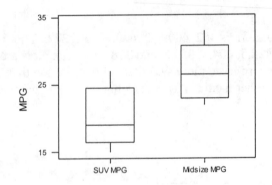

The box plots show that the MPG for Midsize cars is much greater than for SUVs. It also appears that the distribution of MPG for Midsize cars is more symmetrical than for SUVs.

1.93 a)

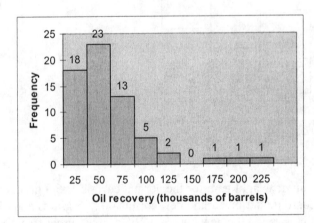

The distribution is heavily skewed to the right. **b)** The mean is 48.25 and the median is 37.9. Because the distribution is skewed to the right the mean is greater than the median. **c)** The five-number summary is 204.9, 59.45, 37.9, 21.6, and 2. Note the large range between the third quartile and the maximum value. This reflects the skewed nature of the data. (Note: quartiles were calculated using the Excel percentile command. The values may differ slightly than finding the quartiles by hand.)

1.94 The IQR is 37.85. The value 204.9 lies more than 1.5×IQR above the third quartile and is considered an outlier. There are five other values that would be considered high outliers using this criteria.

1.95 $\mu = 250$, $\sigma = 175.78$. Z scores of 1.28 and –1.28 are associated with an upper and lower tail area of 0.10, respectively. Setting each of these equal to the formula for the Z score results in two equations with two unknowns. One can solve for σ and then find the value of μ, or vice versa.

1.96 These graphs will vary from student to student. Check to see that graphs are properly labeled and that the student's written comments are consistent with the graphs shown.

1.97 The median value of California county populations is 156,000. The mean value is 427,230. The median is a better numerical summary measure since the distribution is so heavily skewed to the right. This histogram does not include Los Angeles since it was such a high outlier.

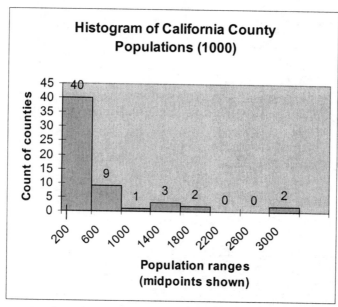

One possible division would be to set Los Angeles aside as one county. The population of Los Angeles makes up 28% of the population of California. The next group of counties might be Orange, San Diego, San Bernardino, Santa Clara, Riverside, Alameda, and Sacramento. These seven counties make up 39% of the state. The third division would be the remaining 50 counties. The populations of these counties are all under 1 MM people and they make up the remaining 33% of the state.

1.98

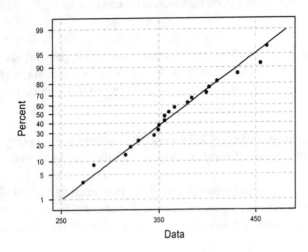

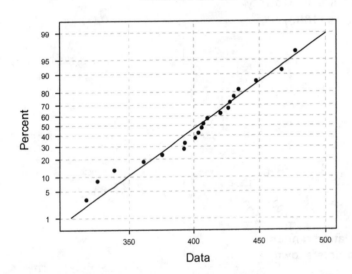

The normal plot for Normal Corn shows a fairly normal distribution. The use of the mean and standard deviation is justified. The normal plot for New Corn can be considered roughly normal although a few low points fall above the line.

1.99 Because the values and graphs will vary from student to student, the points to look for are an understanding of how to use a random number generator and recognizing that the values generated should follow a normal curve with a mean of 20 and standard deviation of 5. The distribution of the mean should look fairly symmetrical, have a bell shape curve, and the center should be close to 20. The distribution of *s* will not look like a bell curve. The normal plots will verify these observations.

Case Study 1.1

A. All Workers

The histograms below show the distribution of all salaries and the distribution of salaries after the top 1% was removed. The average of all 55,899 individuals was $37,864 and the average of those earning up to $210,000 was $35,233. Note the heavily right-skewed distribution. This is not surprising for a variable of this type.

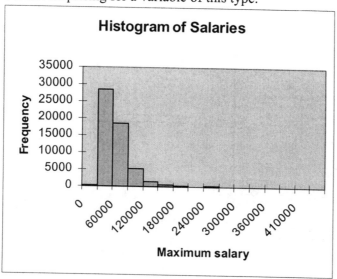

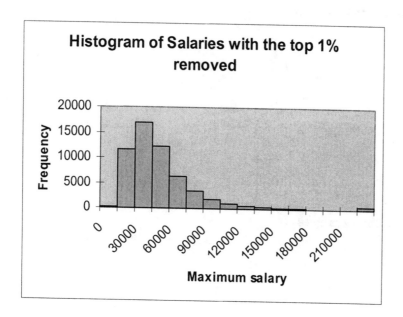

Case Study 1.2
The average salary for full-time employees is $21,292 and for part-time employees is $19,034. It appears from these numbers and the histograms below that there is a significant difference between the salaries of full-time employees and part-time employees.

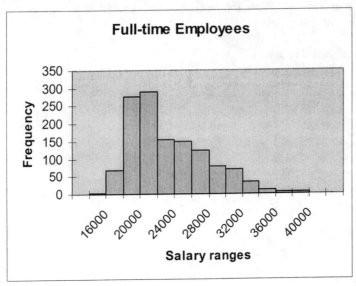

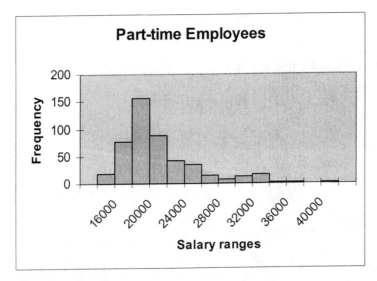

Average Full-time Salary for Blacks	$19,179
Average Part-time Salary for Blacks	$17,401
Average Full-time Salary for Whites	$22,315
Average Part-time Salary for Whites	$19,664

The differences between average full-time salaries and average part-time salaries for both blacks and whites show the same gap that was seen in the comparison without separating by race. Furthermore, the percentage of whites employed part-time is higher than the percentage of blacks employed part-time (28% compared to 23%). Histograms below show the salary distributions of the races by their job classification.

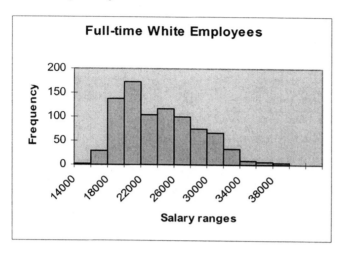

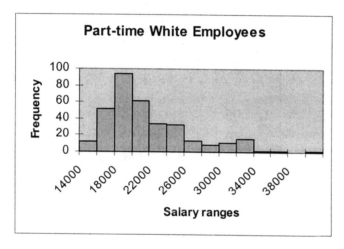

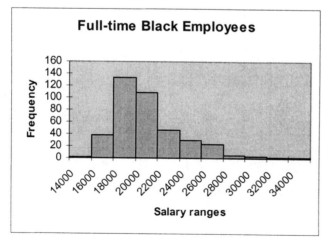

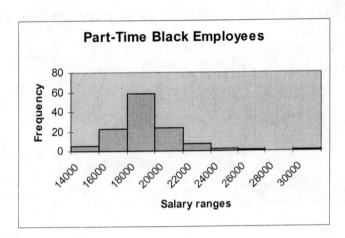

Chapter 2
Examining Relationships
Solutions

2.1 a) *Time studying* would be the explanatory variable and *grade* would be the response variable. **b)** Neither *weight* nor *height* is an obvious choice for an explanatory variable. **c)** *Amount of yearly rainfall* would be the explanatory variable and *yield* would be the response variable. **d)** It is not obvious which variable is the explanatory variable. One is probably more interested in identifying a relationship between *salary* and *sick days used* rather than predicting one from the other. **e)** Most people would choose *the economic class of a father* to be the explanatory variable and *the economic class of the son* to be the response variable because the father's class precedes the son's. This may not always be true.

2.2 *Price at beginning of year* would be the explanatory variable and *price at end of year* would be the response. These are quantitative variables.

2.3 The explanatory variable would be *type of hand wipe*. The response variable would be *level of skin irritation*. These are categorical variables.

2.4 a) Because the firm makes a decision on how many staff members to hire, I would choose *staff* as the explanatory variable and *billings* as the response variable.
b) The scatterplot below shows a linear relationship between *staff* and *billings*.

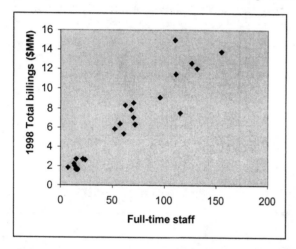

2.5 a) The Honda Insight gets approximately 62 MPG in the city and approximately 70 MPG on the highway. **b)** The relationship appears to be linear with highway MPG greater than city MPG. This is logical because city driving requires more stops and starts, thus reducing your gas mileage. **C)** Yes, the Insight fits the pattern.

2.6 a) The variables are positively related. **b)** The relationship is linear. **c)** Yes, billings can be predicted from staff levels, although there appears to be more variation in billings as staff levels increase. With a staff level of 75 members, I would predict the billings to be approximately $7 MM.

2.7 a) The explanatory variable is *speed*.

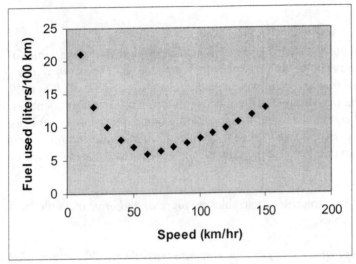

b) The relationship is curved, not linear. This makes sense because we've already observed that fuel consumption is higher for city driving (lower speeds) than highway driving (higher speeds). As speeds increase beyond normal highway driving one would expect the fuel consumption to go up also. **c)** It does not make sense to describe a nonlinear relationship as positive or negative because the relationship shows a negative trend up to 50 km/hr and an increasing trend above 50 km/hr. **d)** The relationship appears to be quite strong. The pattern is clearly shown on the scatterplot.

2.8 a) The explanatory variable is *lean body mass*.

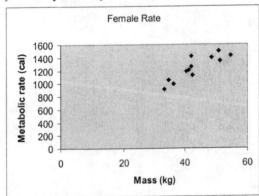

b) The association is a linear positive association and it appears strong.
c)

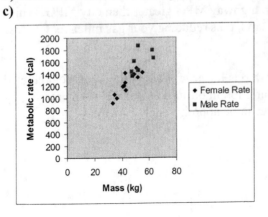

The pattern for the men is similar to that for the women in that we can see an increasing trend. The difference is that the linear pattern is not as strong and there appears to be more variation among the seven men observed.

2.9 a) A positive association means that the greater the duration, the longer the decline in earnings. Shorter durations resulted in shorter declines in earnings. **b)** The form of the relationship is roughly linear but not very strong. The scatterplot shows some variation at the lower durations, less than 10 months. As the durations increase to beyond 10 months the linear pattern appears stronger. **c)** The greatest decline is approximately 48% and lasted about 20 months.

2.10 The form of the relationship between GDP and life expectancy is nonlinear and displays an increasing trend, which is what we expected. The points on the scatterplot do show a strong pattern even though the pattern in not linear.

2.11 a) One would expect that if the household income increases, then the personal income would increase. Because household income includes more than one person it makes sense that this would be greater than personal income. **b)** In some states (or in DC) it is possible that there are a few extremely wealthy people that will skew the distribution of income. Because the mean is not resistant to outliers these few wealthy individuals will make the mean quite large. **c)** The overall pattern is positive linear. **d)** Both Connecticut and DC show up as outliers on the scatterplot. Connecticut is next to New York and many people who live in Connecticut work in New York; therefore, it makes sense that the mean personal income relative to median household income has a similar relationship to New York. Also, both DC and New York are political and financial capitals of the United States and would have a larger group of wealthy individuals than other states.

2.12

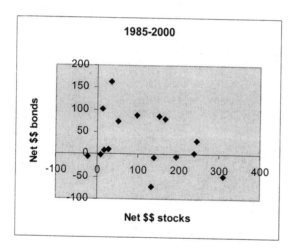

This scatterplot shows a negative trend with a weak linear relationship.

2.13

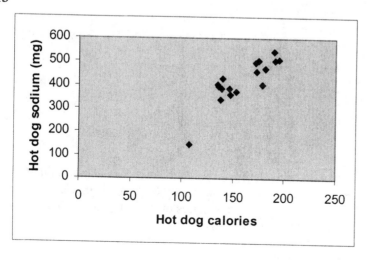

a) This scatterplot shows a strong linear relationship with a positive trend. Hot dogs that are high in calories tend to be high in sodium. **b)** The "Eat Slim Veal Hot Dog" is probably brand 13.

2.14 a) *Planting rate* is the explanatory variable.

b)

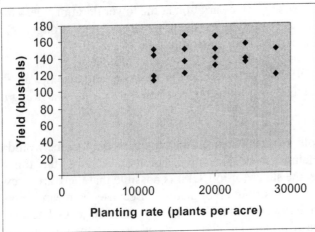

c) This scatterplot shows a slight nonlinear pattern. The yield increases from 12,000 plants per acres to 20,000 plants per acre and then starts to decrease beyond that level.

d) I would recommend a rate of 20,000 plants per acre. This resulted in the highest average yield.

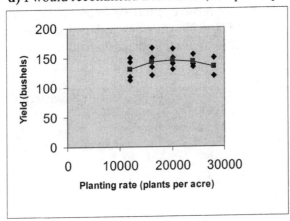

2.15 a)

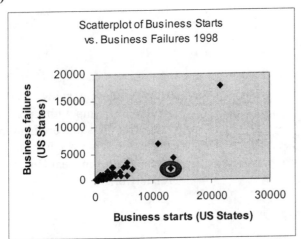

b) The association is said to be positive because as the variable *starts* increases, the variable *failures* also increases. **c)** See the scatterplot to find Florida. **d)** The outlier in the upper-right-hand corner is California with 21,582 starts and 17,679 failures. **e)** The four states outside the cluster in the lower-left-hand corner are California, Florida, New York, and Texas.

2.16 a) Crude oil production does not have a linear relationship with years. It does show an increasing trend as years go by but the shape of the relationship is nonlinear.

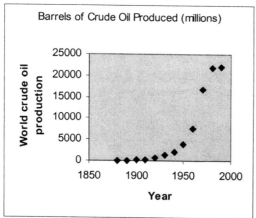

b) The overall pattern in this scatterplot is linear with a positive trend.

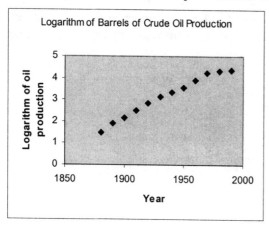

2.17 a)

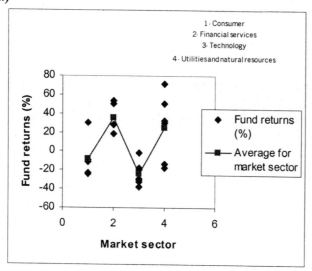

b) Financial Services and Utilities and Natural Resources were good sectors in which to invest. **c)** Because we cannot rank the sectors in increasing order we could not describe any relationship between the sector and a quantitative variable as positive or negative.

2.18 a)

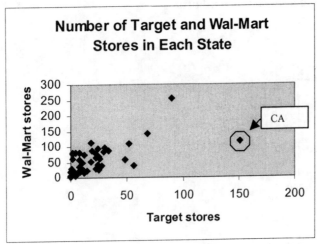

b) California stands out on the scatterplot because it has an unusually large number of Target stores compared to Wal-Mart stores. It appears that in most states the number of Wal-Mart stores is greater than Target stores. California does not follow this trend. **c)** This relationship is a weak positive relationship. It has a slight linear appearance.

2.19 a)

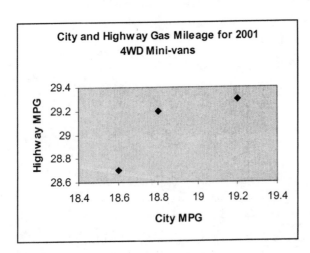

b) r = 0.849 **c)** The relationship is positive and appears to be a fairly strong linear relationship.

2.20 a) The relationship appears to be linear, positive, and fairly strong. **b)** r = 0.9792.

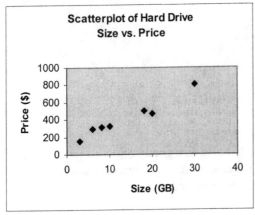

2.21 a) The correlation between duration of decline and magnitude of decline is positive but shows some scatter in the points. It would be safe to say that *r* is positive but not near 1, perhaps .75 or .80. **b)** The scatterplot in Figure 2.2 also shows a positive linear relationship but the points seem to fall closer to a straight line. The correlation coefficient is probably closer to 1 than in part (a).

2.22 a) The correlation coefficient should be exactly 1.0. Every point will fall on the same line. **b)** The correlation coefficient should be exactly 1.0. Every point will fall on the same line. These two examples should start the student thinking about having an equation for a line describe a set of paired data points.

2.23

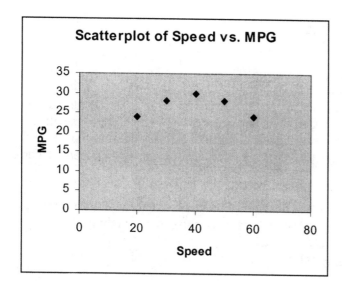

The correlation coefficient is 0. The relationship between speed and gas mileage is clearly not linear. Correlation measures the strength of *linear* relationships only.

2.24 Applet

2.25

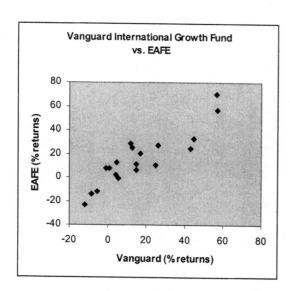

This scatterplot shows a clear positive linear relationship. The correlation coefficient is 0.898, which indicates a strong linear relationship. There do not appear to be any extreme outliers from the linear pattern.

2.26 a)

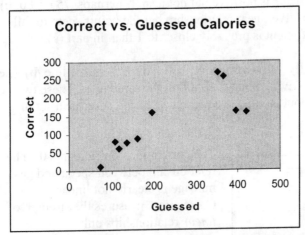

b) r = 0.825. This value of *r* makes sense based on the above scatterplot. The points show a fairly strong relationship but the two foods, spaghetti and snack cake; do not lie close to the other points. **c)** The fact that every guess was higher than the correct number of calories does not influence the correlation. If every guess were exactly 100 calories higher than the correct one then the correlation would be 1.0.

d) The correlation coefficient is now 0.984. The correlation increased because after removing the spaghetti and snack cake, the remaining eight points fall very close to a straight line.

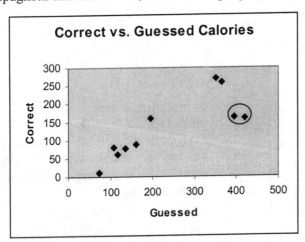

2.27 a) and b)

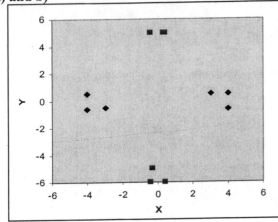

c) The correlation between *x* and *y* is 0.253. This is the same value for the correlation between *x** and *y**. Even though the values of *x* and *y* have changed, the *linear relationship* between the two variables has not changed. Correlation measures the strength of a linear relationship between two variables. As can be seen in the scatterplot, the points have shifted but how they appear in relation to each other has not.

2.28 a) r = 0.659. **b)** The correlation should increase. California is an outlier and does not fall on the linear pattern that the rest of the data do. *r* = 0.746. The correlation increased for the reason stated. **c)** The correlation for all fifty states will most likely decrease if Texas is removed. Texas helps define the linear pattern observed on the scatterplot. Without this data point, the linear relationship does not appear as strong. *r* = 0.584.

2.29 The study's conclusion means that there is no linear relationship between CEO compensation and company's stock performance. We cannot make a prediction about company performance from CEO compensation. The magazine must have misinterpreted the meaning of correlation. If high CEO compensation resulted in poor company stock performance, then the correlation would have been close to –1, not 0.

2.30 a) Rachel should choose small-cap stocks because that has a much smaller correlation with municipal bonds than large-cap stocks. **b)** Rachel should look for a negative correlation.

2.31 The outlier in Figure 2.2 helped define the linear pattern observed on the scatterplot. Removing that point left a group of points that did not have an obvious line to fall on. The outlier in Figure 2.8 did not fall in the pattern of the rest of the data points. By removing the outlier before calculating the correlation, we saw an increase in correlation.

2.32 See exercise 2.7 for the scatterplot. The correlation is –0.172. Because the relationship is linear the correlation is near zero.

2.33 a) Gender is a categorical variable. It does not make sense to calculate a correlation coefficient. **b)** Correlation cannot be greater than 1.0. **c)** Correlation has no units.

2.34 a) Standard deviations help explain variability in something. The fact that one fund has a standard deviation of only 9.94% and another fund 23.77% means that the first fund has much less spread or variability. **b)** Having a correlation of 0.85 with the S&P 500 means the Fidelity Magellan Fund more closely follows the stock market. A correlation of 0.55 means the Fidelity Small Cap Stock does not follow the stock market as closely. If an investor wants a fund whose performance he can predict based on the stock market, then the Fidelity Magellan Fund is his better choice.

2.35 a) The equation of the least-squares regression line is: $\hat{y} = 1.089 + 0.189x$. **b)** Using $r = 0.995$, $\overline{x} = 22.313$, $s_x = 17.738$, $\overline{y} = 5.306$, and $s_y = 3.368$, the slope is 0.189 and the y-intercept is 1.089.

2.36 a)

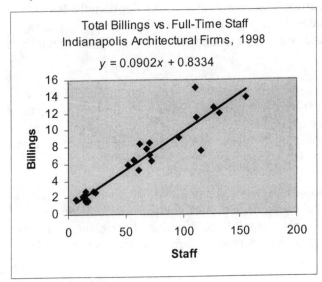

2.37 a) 35.5% of the variation in yearly changes is explained by the January change.   **b)** The equation of the regression line is: $\hat{y} = 6.083 + 1.707x$.   **c)** The prediction for the change in the year when the January change is 1.75% is 9.07%. We could have answered this without using the regression equation because we know that the point ($\bar{x}, \bar{y}$) will always fall on the regression line.

2.38 Applet

2.39 a)

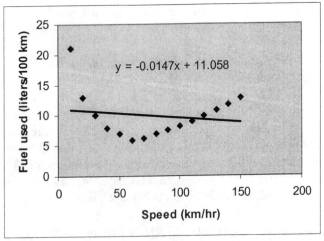

b) The scatterplot shows a definite curved pattern. I would not use the regression line to predict fuel used from speed. **c)** The sum of the residuals is –0.01. This is very close to zero.

d)

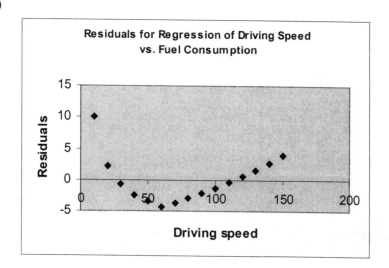

2.41 a) This outlier is in the upper right hand corner far away from the pattern of the other data points. It is pulling the regression line up towards it.

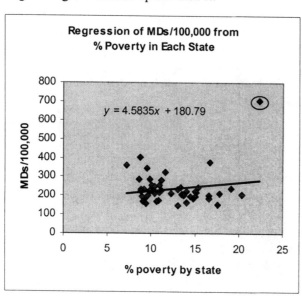

b) Now the regression line has a negative slope which means the number of MDs will decrease as poverty increases. The DC point was an influential point.

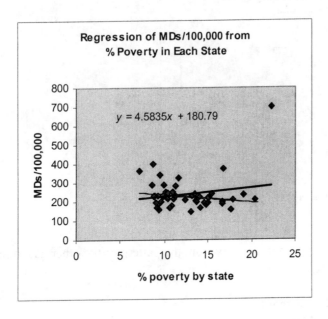

2.41 a)

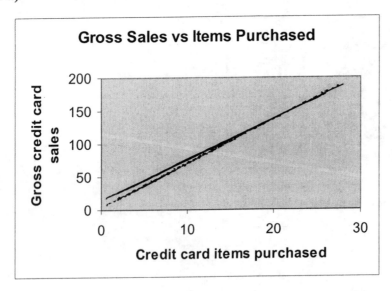

Yes, observation 1 does appear to influence the slope of the regression line. Gross sales estimates are much lower after observation 1 is removed from the analysis. **b)** After removing observation 1 the value of r^2 increases from .59 to .73. Because r^2 is not resistant to outliers, removing an outlier will increase its value.

2.42 a)

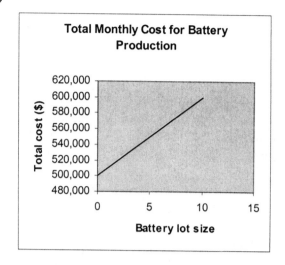

b) $700,000. **c)** $y = 500,000 + 20,000x$

2.43 a) $y = 96 - 4x$. **b)**

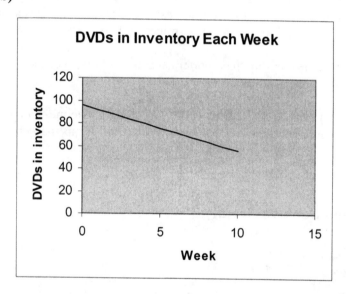

c) No, the initial inventory has only 96 DVDs. This inventory will last for 24 weeks.

2.44 a)

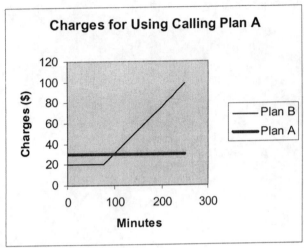

b) A user would need to talk almost 100 minutes a month to benefit from Plan B.

2.45 Because the correlation between American and European share prices is fairly high and positive, this means that when American share prices rise European share prices will rise as well. Unfortunately, when American share prices fall, European share prices will also fall.

2.46 No, this is not true. R^2 is the measure the reporter needed. Only 64% of the change in Wall Street will explain the change in European share prices.

2.47 a) $y = 15.46 + .8584x$. **b)** Approximately 40% of the variation in declines can be explained by this relationship. **c)** The predicted decline is 28.34%. The residual for this market is –14.34%.

2.48 a)

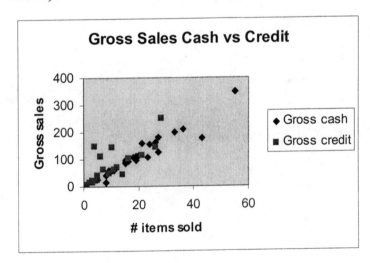

b)

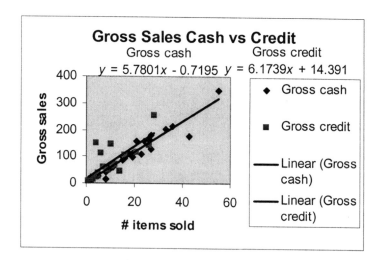

The slope for the gross cash sales regression line is: 5.7801. The slope for the gross credit sales regression line is: 6.1739. The larger slope for gross credit sales means that on average when people purchase with credit cards they tend to purchase more expensive items.

2.49 a) No, the calibration does not need to be redone. **b)** The least-squares line is $y = 1.6571 + .1133x$. For a specimen with 500 mg of nitrates, the expected absorbance would be 58.31. Yes, the prediction should be quite accurate.

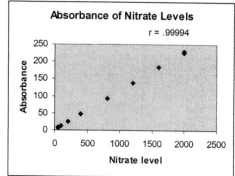

2.50 a)

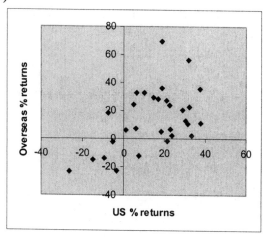

b) The correlation between US % returns and overseas % returns is .5043. This does not indicate a strong linear relationship. This can be seen in the scatterplot as well. Only 25.43% of the variation in overseas returns can be explained by US returns.

c) Predictions will not be accurate with this regression line because the relationship between US and Overseas returns is not strong.

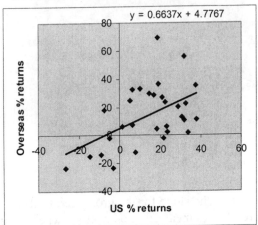

d) The circled point is year 1986. There do not seem to be any influential points.

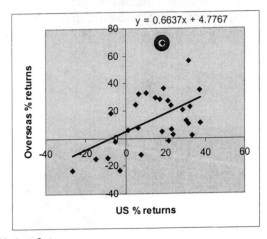

2.51 Applet

2.52 Applet

2.53 a)

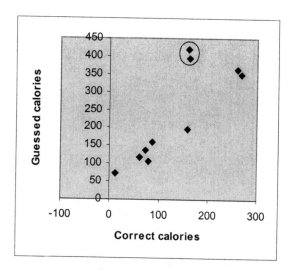

b) The regression line with all 10 data points is y = 58.59 + 1.3x. The regression line with spaghetti and snack cake removed is y = 43.88 + 1.15x.

c) Yes, it appears that the two points circled are influential observations because they influence the slope of the line. We can also see this in how the correlation coefficient increases in value after removing the two data points.

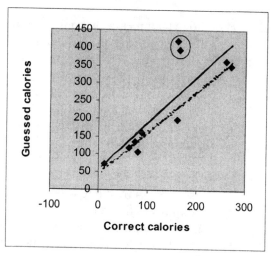

2.54 a) For data set A: y = 3.0001 + 0.5x and r = .816421. For data set B: y = 3.0009 + 0.5x and r = .816237. For data set C: y = 3.0025 + 0.4997x and r = .816287. For data set D: y = 3.0017 + 0.4999x and r = .816521. Notice that all values of r are very close and all the equations are close. With x = 10, the prediction for y is 8 for each regression line.

b)

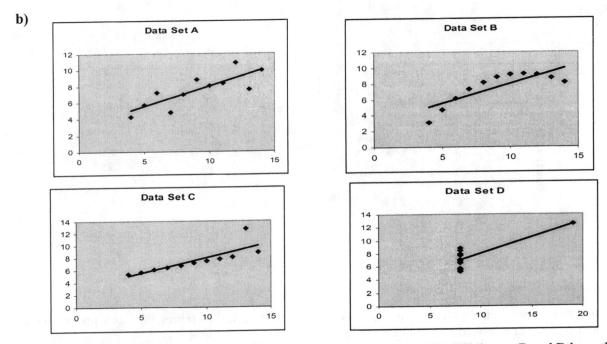

d) I would use the regression line for prediction with data sets A and C. While sets B and D have the same correlation coefficient, it is obvious from the scatterplots that they do not have a linear pattern. Data set C has one outlier but it does not appear to be influential.

2.55 a) The slope is 0.16 and the intercept is 30.2. **b)** 78.2. **c)** $r^2 = 0.36$, which means that only 36% of the variation in final exam scores can be explained by the total score before the exam. It is entirely possible that Julie scored higher on the final exam than Professor Friedman's prediction.

2.56 a)

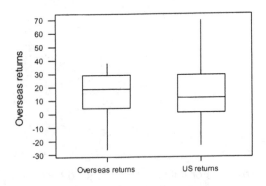

The five number summary for Overseas returns is: 37.6, 28.6, 18.4, 5.1, and −26.4. The five number summary for US returns is: 69.4, 28.5, 12, 2.1, and −3.2. **b)** Returns were about the same in the US and overseas as is shown by the IQR on the boxplots to the left. **c)** There was more variability in the US as can be seen by the length of the "whiskers" on the box plots. The US returns had a greater range than the overseas returns.

2.57 $r = -0.80$.

2.58 a) $y = -6.12 + 0.967x$. **b)** 93.5% of the variation in city MPG can be explained by highway MPG. **c)** City gas mileage for the Mercedes-Benz SL600 is predicted to be 12.25 MPG. Estimating city MPG to be 13 from figure 2.2, the residual for this car is approximately 0.75.

2.59 Since $\bar{y} = 46.6 + 0.41\bar{x}$, then $\bar{y} + \text{points} = 46.6 + 0.41(\bar{x} + 10)$. This results in points = 0.41(10) = 4.1. Octavio is predicted to score 4.1 points above average on the final exam.

2.60 a) The line would change to have a negative slope. The new equation would be: $y = 31.76 - 0.436x$. This is an influential observation because it changes the direction of the linear relationship from positive to negative. **b)** By adding the new data point, the original regression line stays almost the same, same slope and same intercept. The new data point is an outlier but is not influential. It is "anchored" by the three data points below.

2.61 a) $y = -0.525 + 0.38x$. **b)** 96 Target stores, residual = –6. **c)** $y = 30.31 + 1.13x$. **d)** 132 Wal-Mart stores, residual = 122.

2.62 a)

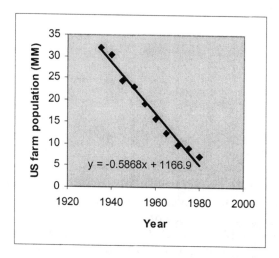

b) The regression line shows that population declined by approximately 580,000 people each year. 97.7% of the observed variation in population can be explained by time. **c)** Using this regression line one would predict that the farm population in 1990 would be –832,000. This is not a sensible result. The population cannot be negative.

2.63 The correlation would be lower because there would be much more variation in the individual stock prices than in their average. More scatter means more variation which leads to lower correlation.

2.64 The sketch should look similar to figure 2.20 with the cluster closest to the *x*-axis representing academia and the cluster closest to the *y*-axis representing businesses.

2.65 Large fires require many more firefighters than small fires. Large fires also cause more damage than small fires. The lurking variable is the size of the fire, not the number of firefighters at the fire.

2.66 It is possible the cause and effect relationship goes the other way: performing well at something causes individuals to feel good about themselves. Excellent teachers could be the lurking variable. An excellent teacher is usually excellent at instruction, which leads to high performance by an individual. An excellent teacher is also a wonderful encourager, which can help raise self-esteem for individuals.

2.67 No, larger hospitals most likely treat more seriously ill patients than smaller hospitals. Seriously ill patients tend to have longer hospital stays.

2.68 The regression line with the outlier is: $y = -91.2 + 3.212x$. The regression line without the outlier is: $y = 46.9 + 2.4x$. The scatterplot below shows the two lines. The outlier was not extremely influential. In fact the correlation coefficient was slightly higher with the outlier than without the outlier because the outlier point was part of the overall linear pattern.

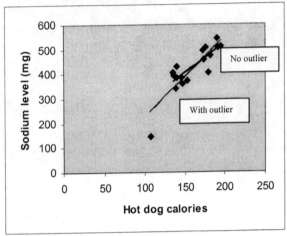

b) The sodium level would be between 390 and 406 mg.

2.69 The high school students that choose to take several math courses have most likely already made a decision to go to college. Once a decision is made to pursue an education beyond high school, it is likely an individual will be successful. Those students who choose not to take additional math classes in high school may not intend to attend college. If they decide later to attend college they may not be successful because they were not as prepared as if they had made the decision during high school. Another point to consider is that the better students tend to take harder classes such as math. The better students are also the ones that are likely to be successful in college.

2.70 A more plausible explanation is that heavier people tend to be on diets and try to reduce calories from sugar. Therefore they use artificial sweeteners.

2.71 a) The consumption has actually risen over this time period. This contradicts the economists' expectation.

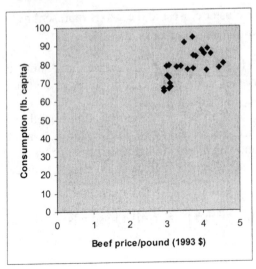

b) 35.8% of the variation in consumption can be explained by the price of beef.

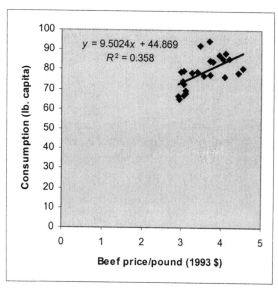

c) There do seem to be cycles. Consider the series from 1980 to 1988. As the residual values go from negative to positive this shows that the regression line is first underestimating beef consumption and then overestimating beef consumption. Prices during that time period were dropping steadily and yet consumption was declining also. There may be a time delay in the response to the price of beef.

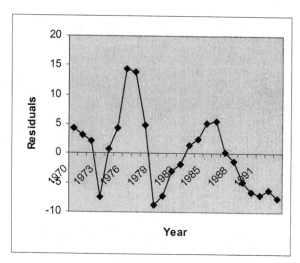

2.72 a)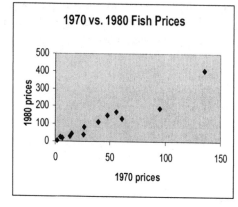

b) The overall pattern appears linear in the positive direction. It is difficult to say if the two points to the far right are outliers or not. They appear to follow the linear trend. **c)** $r = 0.967$, 93.5% of the variation in 1980 prices is explained by the 1970 prices. **d)** $r = 0.9538$. No, these observations do not have a strong effect on the correlation. The correlation decreased from 0.967 to 0.9538, not a significant decrease. **e)** Yes, the correlation does provide a good measure for the relationship between these variables because the scatterplot shows a strong linear pattern and there are no influential observations that heavily weight the correlation.

2.73 a) $r^2 = 0.910$ tells us the proportion of total daily sales explained by item count. In other words, the number of items sold explains 91% of the total daily sales. **b)** I would expect the correlation between the numbers of items sold and the transaction amount in an individual transaction to be less than the summary daily measure. There would be more variation in the individual transactions than in the daily totals.

2.74 The explanatory variable is herbal tea and the response variable is the residents' mood. The lurking variable that might explain a more cheerful mood could be simply the students' visits, not the tea itself.

2.75 A possible lurking variable could be that higher paying jobs carry with them an expectation that the employee will continue his education while employed. Also, social status may play a role. Affluent families can afford to pay for higher education. The men from these families also have access to higher paying jobs through their contacts.

2.76 It would be important to know family history of the children that have leukemia. It is also important to track the rate of leukemia in children who do not live near power lines so we can compare the rates.

2.77 a) The pattern seen on the residual plot is a funnel shape. As the salaries increase the residual values also increase. The regression model will predict lower salaries more accurately. **b)** The second residual plot does not show an increasing trend in error terms. Instead it appears that the new model will overestimate salaries during the first 3 years, underestimate from 5–10 years, and then even out up to around 15 years. From 15 years and beyond, the model will overestimate again.

2.78 4% are single, 94% are married, 1.5% are divorced, and 0.5% are widowed.

2.79 a) 5375 students. **b)** 18.7% of these students smoke **c)** Neither parent smokes: 1356, 25.2%. One parent smokes: 2239, 41.7%. Both parents smoke: 1780, 33.1%.

2.80

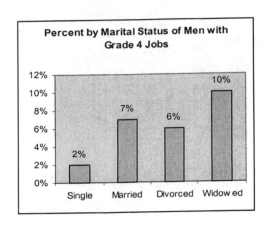

The graph shows that the group of widowed men has the largest percentage of men in the grade 4-job classification.

2.81 The percentages are as follows: 14% of students with neither parent smoking smoke, 19% of students who have one smoking parent smoke, and 22% of students with both parents smoking smoke. It appears there may be some validity to the claim that a parent who smokes might encourage their student to smoke.

2.82 The conditional distribution of marital status among men with grade 4 jobs is: 1.3% single, 96.7% married, 1.3% divorced, and 0.7% widowed.

2.83 a)

	Female	Male	Total
Accounting	68 (30.2%)	56 (34.8%)	124 (32%)
Administration	91 (40.4%)	40 (24.8%)	131 (34%)
Economics	5 (2.2%)	6 (3.7%)	11 (3%)
Finance	61 (27.1%)	59 (36.6%)	120 (31%)
Total	225 (58%)	161 (42%)	386

The conditional distribution for each major by gender is given in the table above. A column chart comparing the genders is given below.

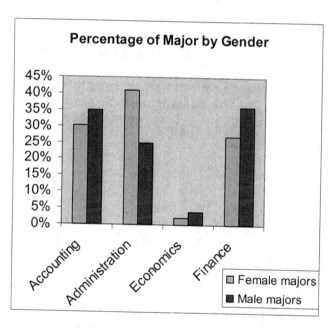

The percentages of men and women majoring in accounting, economics, and finance are close. Administration has a much higher percentage of women than men. **b)** The nonresponse rate is 53.5%.

2.84 First Count: 30   20   Second Count: 10   40
                        30   20   50   0

2.85 a) 3%, 2% **b)** 3.8%, 4%. Poor patients fare better in hospital A. **c)** 1%, 1.33%. **d)** Based solely on this data choose hospital A. **e)** There is a lurking variable: patient condition.

2.86 a) 14,340,000. **b)** 55.8%.

c)

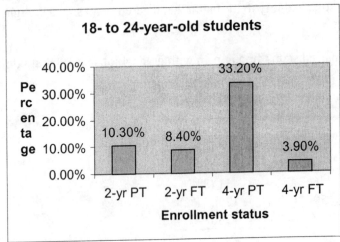

d) This age group makes up over half of the students enrolled in a college, and over 30% of the undergraduates enrolled as 4-year part-time students come from this age group.

2.87 a) 20.4%. **b)** 9.9%.

2.88 a) By age the counts of undergraduates are: Under 18–353,000, 18 to 24–8,001,000, 25 to 39–4,272,000, 40 and up–1,716,000.

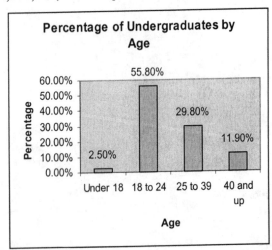 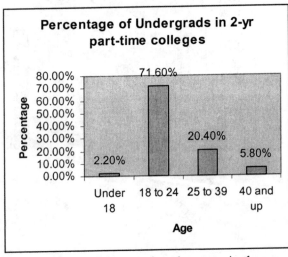

c) The main difference in the two age distributions is that while the majority of students are in the age group 18 to 24, almost 72% of 2-year part-time students are in this age group while only 56% of all undergraduates are in this group. **d)** The reason the total in this column is different than the actual sum is most likely due to round off error.

2.89 Older students (age 40 and up) make up almost 12% of all undergraduates. Of these older students 121,000 are enrolled as 2-year part-time students, 748,000 are enrolled as 2-year full-time students, 6,311,000 are enrolled as 4-year part-time students and 611,000 are enrolled as 4-year full-time students. The graph on the next page shows the distribution of this group of students in each of the four college types. What we see is that older students tend to enroll as full-time students more than part-time, whether it is in a 2-year college or a 4-year college.

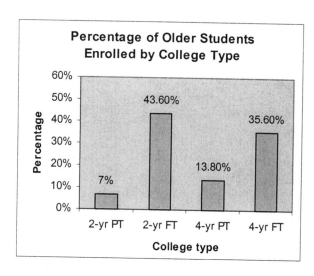

2.90 a) 55.8%. **b)** 48.5%. **c)** 74.5%.

2.91 a) P(Hired | age < 40) = .0644, P(Hired | age ≥ 40) = .0061
   b)

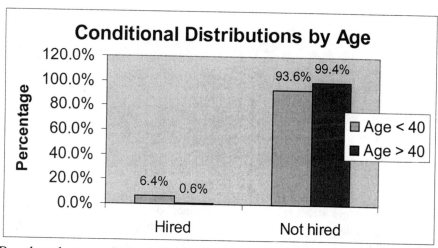

c) Based on these conditional distributions it does appear that the company is hiring young candidates more than older candidates. **d)** A lurking variable could be whether the candidates are equally qualified or not.

2.92 a) 59%. **b)** The nonresponse rate for each size company—small, medium, and large—is 37.5%, 59.5%, and 80% respectively. As the company size increases, it appears that the response rate decreases.

c)

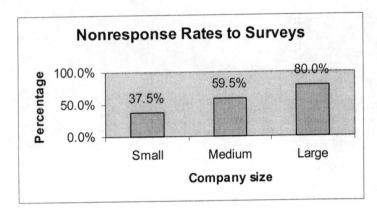

2.93 a)

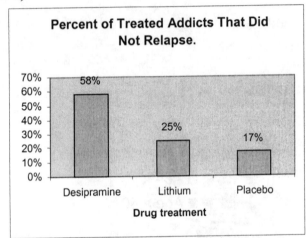

b) Yes, it appears that there is such a large reduction in relapses with the use of desipramine that this constitutes evidence of a cause and effect relationship. A placebo was used to discount the influence of simply being in the study. The placebo rate of relapse was much higher than either of the two anti-depressant drug treatments.

2.94 a) 7.7%. **b)**

c) From the evidence it appears that each employee is missing roughly the same percentage as the overall percentage. There appears no reason to single out a certain employee.

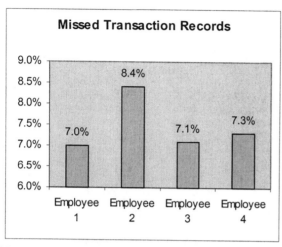

Note: Excel automatically sets the axis scales. See above. Pay careful attention to these because it can cause a distorted view of the differences in the percentages. The graph to the left shows more clearly that the percentages are actually quite close to each other.

2.95 a) The difference may be due to round off error.

b)

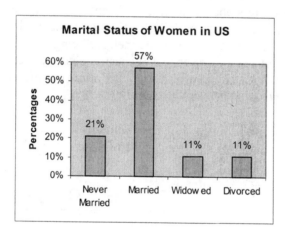

2.96 a)

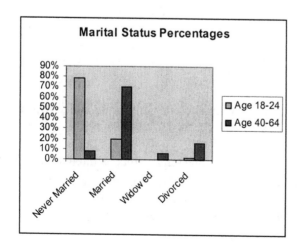

In the age group 18 to 24, almost 80% of women have never been married. This changes dramatically for the 40 to 64 age group. Over 70% of these women are married. **b)** The magazine should aim for 18 to 39.

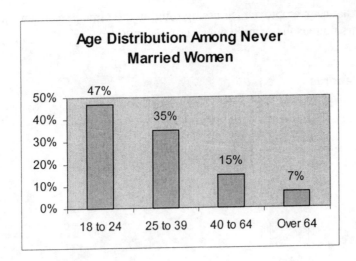

2.97 a)

	Admit	Deny
Male	490	210
Female	280	220

b) 70% of male applicants are admitted and 56% of female applicants are admitted. **c)** For the Business School: Male–80%, Female–90%. For the Law School: Male–10%, Female–33%. **d)** Without considering the variable of which professional school the applicant has applied to the percentages do not reflect a clear picture. More men apply to Wabash's professional schools overall, therefore, based solely on applications to professional school, more men are being admitted than women. Once we separate the data by type of school we see that Wabash is actually accepting a higher percentage of their women applicants. An important question for follow up study would be why there are so many more men than women applying to Wabash.

2.98

Smokers

	Overweight	Not
Early death	10	50
No	8	50

Nonsmokers

	Overweight	Not
Early death	20	10
No	30	20

Grouped Together

	Overweight	Not
Early death	30	60
No	38	70

2.99 The scatterplot does not show a strong pattern between Treasury bill return and stock return. It is reasonable to conclude that high interest rates do not greatly decrease returns on stocks.

2.100 $\hat{y} = 16.24 - 0.57x$. For x = 5%, y = 13.39%. **b)** The slope tells us that as interest rates increase, stock returns decrease. This supports the belief that in general high interest rates are bad for stocks. **c)** Knowing the return on Treasury bills for next year would not help predict the return on stocks. The scatterplot shows little relationship between the two variables and this is supported by the low value of R^2.

2.101 Removing this point would increase the correlation because the point lies outside the bulk of the data. This data point pulls the regression line down to the right. I don't believe it will strongly influence the regression line because the entire data set is heavily scattered and does not show a strong correlation to begin with.

2.102 a) $\hat{y} = .352 + 1.17x$, $r^2 = .276$ so approximately 28% of the change in Phillip Morris stock is explained by the S&P index. **b)** For every one unit change in the S&P index, Phillip Morris returns increase by 1.17. Their returns increase faster than the index. **c)** We want our individual stocks to rise faster than the market rises, but we want our stocks to drop more slowly than the market drops.

2.103 For two funds to be perfectly correlated their returns simply have to be proportional to each other. For every $1 fund A returns, fund B might return $0.50. Using fund A as the explanatory variable and fund B as the response variable means the slope of the line is less than 1. The graph below illustrates this point.

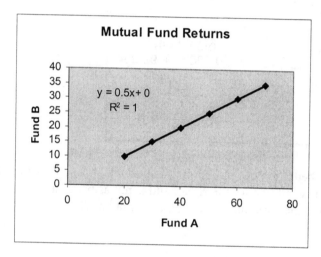

2.104 a)

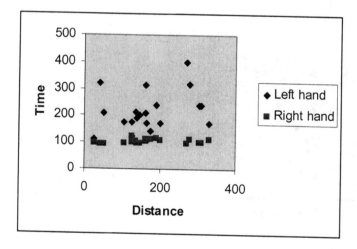

b) The data for the right hand shows a horizontal pattern. The data for the left hand is much more scattered.

c)

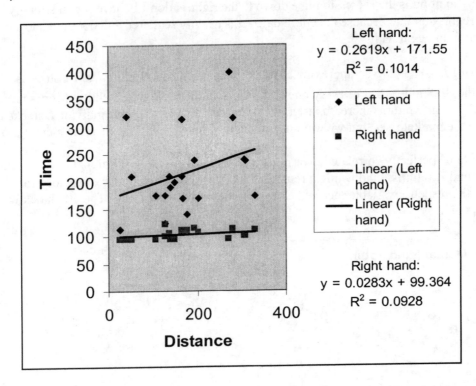

The regression line for the left hand does a better job of predicting time because it describes a little over 10% of the variation in time. The regression line for the right hand is not as predictive. Distance contributes less than 10% (9.3%) to the variation in time on the right hand.

d)

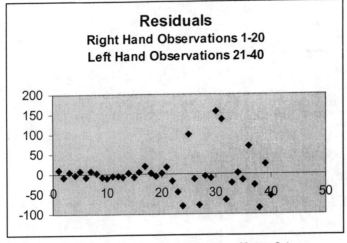

No, there does not appear to be a systematic effect of time.

2.105 a)

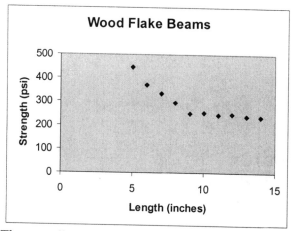

b) The overall pattern is nonlinear. There do not appear to be any outliers.

c) No, a straight line is not a good fit, even though the r-squared value might suggest otherwise. The scatterplot clearly shows a nonlinear pattern.

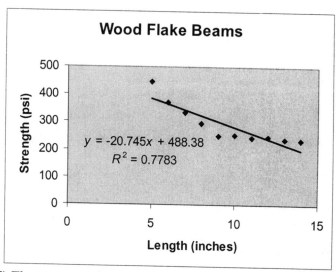

d) These two lines show a much better representation of the data. I would ask the experts why the strength levels out after 9 inches.

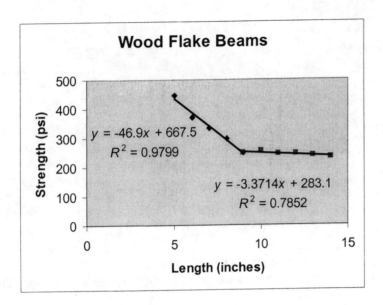

2.106 a)

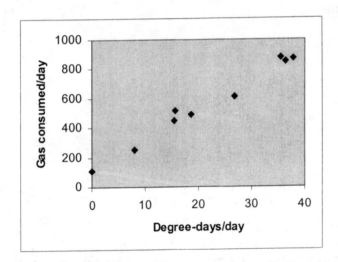

b)

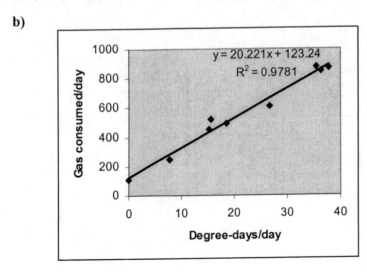

For every unit of degree-day increase, gas consumption goes up approximately 20 cubic feet.
c) Last winter Joan would have used 932 ft³ of natural gas during the month of February rather than the 870 ft³ she actually used. Yes, the insulation reduced gas consumption.

2.107 $r = 0.988966$, $\bar{x} = 21.54$, $\bar{y} = 558.9$, $s_x = 13.42$, $s_y = 274.4$. Slope has units cubic feet per degree-day.

2.108 a) The mean and median for the selling price data are $138,595 and $127125, respectively. This distribution is skewed right, as shown below, and therefore the mean is greater than the median. The standard deviation is $54,517.

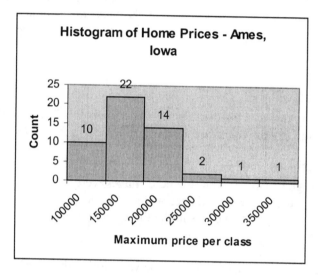

b) The relationship between square footage and selling price is positive linear.

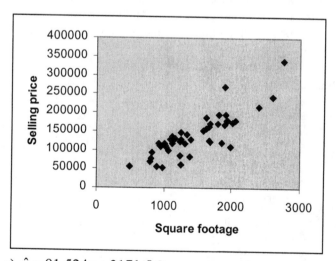

c) $\hat{y} = 91.524x + 3171.5$ On average, each square foot adds $91 to the selling price of the home.
d) I would expect the selling price of a 1600-square-foot home to sell for $149,610. **e)** 72% of the variability in the selling price of homes can be attributed to differences in square footage.

2.109 a). $\hat{y} = -1334.5x + 189,226$ **b)** $189,226, $187,892, $186,557, $185,223. Each year that the house ages drops the average selling price by approximately $1300. **c)** This regression line should not be used to predict the selling price of a home built before 1900. The regression line explains only 50% of the variability in selling prices so the model itself is not the best. In addition, extrapolation outside the range of x produces results that are unreliable.

2.110 a) Using a correlation on 0.3481 we find that only about 12% of the variation in Apple stock can be explained by the S&P index. The overall market is not a good predictor of Apple stock movement.
b) The most likely explanation is that each calculation used a slightly different data set. Perhaps the NASDAQ data set was smaller than the one used at the Yahoo Website, which was also different than the 60 months of data used by the author.

2.111 This data show that 2.3% of the physicians taking aspirin suffered a heart attack or stroke and 3.1% of the physicians that took a placebo suffered a heart attack or stroke. Because the sample size is so large it seems logical that this difference in percentages is large enough to conclude that aspirin reduces heart attacks.

2.112 a)

	Smoker	Not
Dead	139	230
Alive	438	502

The percentage of smokers that were alive after 20 years is 76% and the percentage of nonsmokers that were still alive after 20 years is 69%.

b) Within the age group 18 to 44, 93% of the smokers were alive after 20 years and 96% of the nonsmokers were still alive. Within the age group 45 to 64, the percentages were 68% and 74%, respectively. Within the age group 65 and older, the percentages were 14% and 15%, respectively.
c) This explanation makes sense. The percentage of smokers in the three age groups, starting youngest to oldest, are 46%, 55%, and 20%.

Case Study 2.1 A) A state's population explains approximately 50% of the variation in the number of Wal-Mart stores in each state. This is a good starting point for predicting Wal-Mart stores but there are likely other variables that contribute such as: tax benefits for locating in a particular state and existing buildings or suitable land for putting in a large store. A scatterplot below shows the relationship. If a state increased by 1 million people this regression line predicts another 5.27 stores will be added.

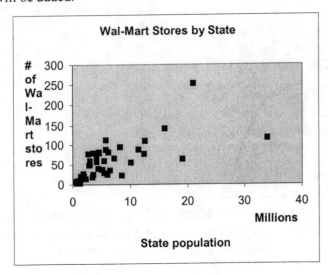

B) By removing California from the data set, the value of r^2 increases to 0.60, an improvement from the previous value of 0.50. California could be considered an influential data point.

	Correlation with GPA
HSM	0.436499
HSS	0.329425
HSE	0.289001
SATM	0.251714
SATV	0.11449

Case Study 2.2:

A)

The correlation values for the explanatory variables tell us the strength of the linear relationship between each variable and GPA. HSM and HSS are the two best predictor variables. This makes sense for computer science majors.

B)

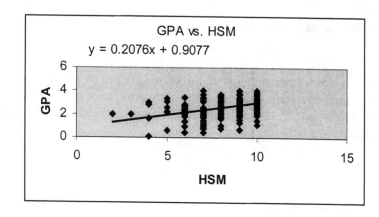

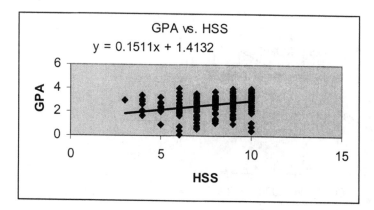

The scatterplots show that while there is a relationship between HSS and GPA and HSM and GPA, there are other variables that would probably help the prediction. There is one unusual observation seen on the plot of GPA vs. HSS. This point shows a fairly high GPA but the student had a low HSS score.

Case Study 2.3:
  A)

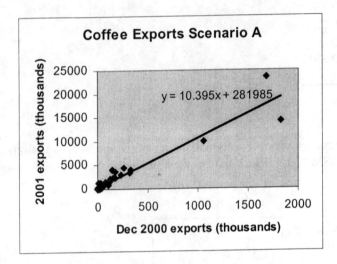

Brazil, Vietnam, and Columbia all have extremely high exports compared to the rest of the countries in the data set. This can be seen on the scatterplot above. The correlation between Dec 2000 exports and 2001 exports is strong with an $r = 0.9516$. Approximately 91% of the variation in 2001 exports can be explained by the December 2000 exports.

B)

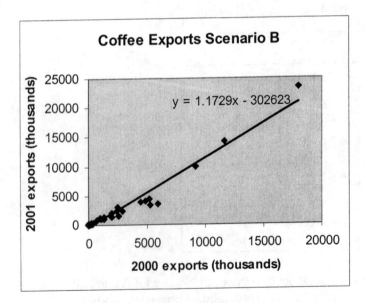

The correlation between 2000 exports and 2001 exports is 0.9788. Approximately 96% of the variation in 2001 exports can be explained by 2000 exports. The three countries mentioned in part A still have very high export values but they fit in to the linear pattern better in this prediction scenario. (Brazil, Vietnam, and Columbia are the three values to the right on the scatteplot above.) This regression is a better predictive tool than the one from part A.

C)

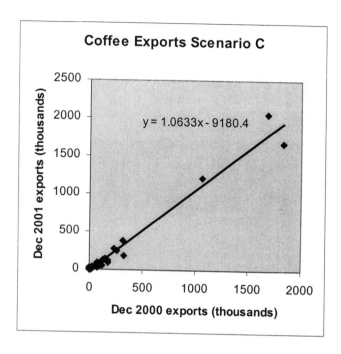

The correlation between December 2000 and December 2001 exports is 0.9864. Approximately 97% of the variation in December 2001 exports can be explained by December 2000 exports. One would expect this r^2 to be higher than the others because there will be less variation in a month than in a year.

Chapter 3
Producing Data
Solutions

3.1 This is not an experiment. The researcher is merely asking a question, not imposing a treatment.

3.2 This is an experiment. The company is imposing a treatment by controlling which study method a group is given. The explanatory variable is type of study method and the response variable is increase in test scores.

3.3 Certainly the state of the economy will affect the unemployment rate. The change in population over time with respect to demographics and size will also affect the unemployment rate.

3.4 The population is all employed women. The sample is the 48 women who returned the questionnaire. The nonresponse rate is 52%.

3.5 a) US population of adults. **b)** US households. **c)** All voltage regulators produced at this plant.

3.6 I would not be convinced that the movie is bad based on the Internet rating. My friends would be a biased sample. The Internet raters are also biased. Neither group is a random sample.

3.7 Starting at line 139 will result in the sample 04, 10, 17, 19, 12, and 13. The sample of minority managers will vary depending on how the student numbers the names. One possible result is: Bowman, Fleming, Liao, Naber, Gates, and Goel.

3.8 Starting at line 145 will result in the sample 19, 26, 06, and 09. The individuals will vary depending on how the student numbers the names. One possible result is Liu, Sanchez, Collins, and Gonzalez.

3.9 The retail outlets could be labeled 001–440. Starting at line 105 the sample would be 400, 077, 172, 417, 350, 131, 211, 273, 208, and 074.

3.10 Starting at line 121, the sample of four would include 07, 22, 10, and 25. The sample of two is 05 and 09. The names will vary depending on how the student numbers the lists. One possible result is: Fisher, Hein, O'Brien, Reinmann, Kim, and West.

3.11 The first strata, midsize accounts, could be numbered 001–500. The second strata, small accounts, could be numbered 0001–4400. The first five numbers for the first strata are 417, 494, 322, 247, and 097. The first five from the second strata are: 3698, 1452, 2605, 2480, and 3716.

3.12 a) Households not listed in the phone directory will be left out of the sample. These people either don't own telephones or have unlisted numbers. **b)** Those people with unlisted numbers will be included in this sampling frame.

3.13 The period from July 1 to August 31 most likely gave the highest nonresponse rate. Many people vacation during those months and may be away from home. High nonresponse rates can bias results because the group that chooses to respond may have different views from the group that chooses not to respond.

3.14 Question A most likely drew 80% favoring banning contributions. Question A used the phrases "special interest" and "huge sums of money." Question B appealed to our sense of fairness by using the phrases "right to contribute" and "candidates they support."

3.15 a) Population–all small businesses, Sample–150 eating and drinking establishments. **b)** Population–all constituents, Sample–228 letters received. **c)** Population–all loss claims from automobile policy holders, Sample–the SRS from that month

3.16 a) The sample size is 29777. **b)** This is a voluntary response sample, not an SRS. It is likely the results are biased. **c)** Since women may be underrepresented the percentage of "yes" responses may be too low.

3.17 These results may not reflect the views of the entire population of constituents. The letters were not part of an SRS and may be biased toward those with strong negative opinions.

3.18 a) One might put a question in the campus newspaper and ask students to respond via email. **b)** One might choose a sample from only those students who purchased a parking permit. This could result in biased results.

3.19 Starting at line 111, the sample numbers are: 12, 04, and 11. The bottle numbers will vary depending on how the student numbers the bottles. A possible result is: A1117, B1102, and A1098.

3.20 Starting at line 117, the sample numbers are: 16, 32, and 18. The apartment complexes will vary depending on how the student numbers the complexes. A possible results is: Fairington, Waterford Court, and Fowler.

3.21 Start by numbering the blocks from 01 to 44 where 01 corresponds to block 1000 and 44 corresponds to block 3025. Starting at line 125 in Table B, the sample numbers are 21 (block 3002), 18 (block 2011), 23 (block 3004), 19 (block 3000) and 10 (block 2003).

3.22 a) False–Over many, many rows of 40 digits, the proportion of zeroes in each row should be 0.10 (4 out of 40) but this will not be true for every single row. **b)** True–there are 100 pairs of digits and each is equally likely. **c)** False–this is a random pattern. Even though a string of four zeroes is not as likely as a string of different digits it can still occur.

3.23 a) Because we need to choose five clusters out of 200 we can think of the list as five lists of 40 clusters. Using Table B, starting at line 120, the first cluster is 35. The other four would be 75, 115, 155, and 195. **b)** Before the first item is selected, all individuals have an equal chance of being selected. Once the first item is selected, the sample is determined. With an SRS, the sample is not determined based on the first item selected.

3.24 This is not an SRS because there are some samples that have no chance of being chosen. A sample with all men cannot be selected.

3.25 Use a systematic random sampling technique. With the male engineers, once the first engineer is chosen, the next engineers will be every 10th in the alphabetized list of 2000. The labels might go from 0001–2000. The female engineers could be labeled from 001–500. Once the first female is selected you can choose every third engineer in the list. Starting with line 122 the first five male engineers would be 1387, 1397, 1407, and 1427. The first five female engineers would be 138, 141, 144, 147, and 150.

3.26 a) This is a poorly worded question because it suggests a link between cell phones and brain cancer. **b)** This question is worded in order to elicit a response in favor of economic incentives for recycling by using the phrases "escalating environmental degradation" and "incipient resource depletion."

3.27 Answers will vary.

3.28 The first question most likely drew 60% favoring a tax cut. The question gave "fund new government programs" as an alternative to a tax cut. This phrase was vague and drew on most people's desire to reduce new government spending. The second question gave popular areas of concern as alternative recipients of excess funds, which are less controversial.

3.29 The subjects are the 300 sickle-cell sufferers. This experiment has one factor: type of medication given to the subjects. This factor had two levels: Hydroxyurea and a Placebo. With one factor and two levels this experiment has two treatments. The response variable is the number of episodes of pain each subject reported.

3.30 a) The individuals are the 20 pairs of package liners. **b)** The factor is jaw temperature. It has four levels: 250° F, 275° F, 300° F, and 325° F. **c)** The response variable is the force needed to peel each seal.

3.31 a) The individuals are the production batches. The response variable is the yield. **b)** There are two factors and six treatments.

Factor A
Stirring Rate

		60 rpm	90 rpm	120 rpm
Factor B Temperature	50°C	1	2	3
	60°C	4	5	6

c) She will need twelve batches.

3.32 a)

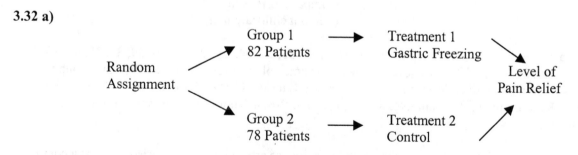

b) The subjects can be labeled 01-82. Starting at line 131, the first five members of the gastric freezing group would be: 05, 71, 66, 32, and 81.

3.33

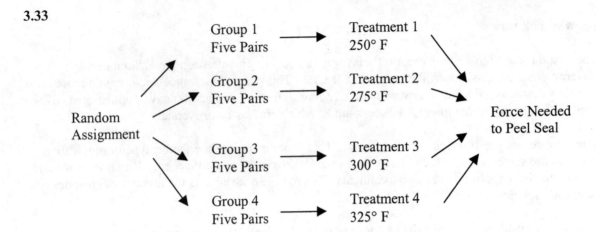

Using Table B at line 120, the 20 pairs could be assigned as follows:

16, 04, 19, 07, 10   Group 1
13, 15, 05, 09, 08   Group 2
18, 03, 01, 06, 11   Group 3
02, 20, 12, 14, 17   Group 4

3.34 a)

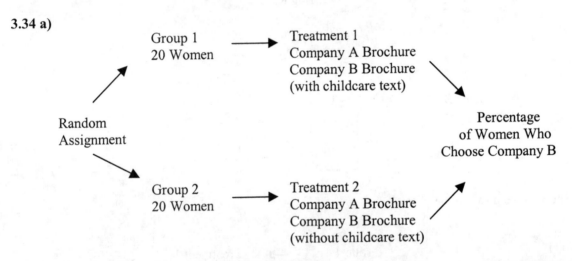

b) Starting at line 131, the random numbers are: 05, 32, 19, 04, 25, 29, 20, 16, 39, 31, 18, 07, 13, 33, 02, 36, 23, 27, 37, and 35. Numbering down the name columns results in the following group that reads the version with childcare: Adamson, Brown, Cansico, Cortez, Garcia, Gupta, Howard, Hwang, Iselin, Kim, Lippman, McNeill, Ng, Rivera, Roberts, Rosen, Thompson, Travers, Turing, and Williams.

3.35 In order to ensure that factors influencing electricity use are equal for comparison groups a control group is needed. Comparing electricity use last year to this year (with the indicator) does not control the factors that may be different between the two years.

3.36 The second design includes the element of randomization to reduce the chance variation. Also, in the second design the treatment is imposed (exercise regimen) rather than using an observational study as in the first design.

3.37 "Significant difference" means the salary differences were so large they could not have been due to chance alone. "No significant difference" means the differences could be due to change only.

3.38 The experimenter rated their anxiety level both before and after treatment and the experimenter knew which subjects had received meditation instruction and which had not. Bias could have been introduced if the experimenter had an expectation that meditation would reduce anxiety. It is likely the experimenter unknowingly communicated this expectation to the subjects also.

3.39 This experiment is not conducted in a real-world setting. There are other reward factors that contribute to a team member's frustration level (or lack of frustration) in a real-world setting that cannot be replicated over the course of a single evening of game playing. (One evening is a much shorter time than three months.)

3.40 Design 1: Randomized Design

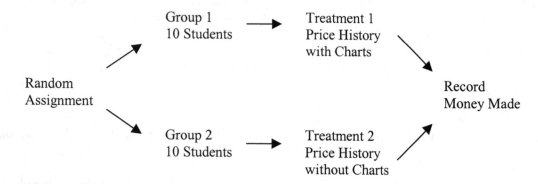

Design 2: Matched Pairs Design
   Each student is randomly assigned treatment 1 first or treatment 2 first. The money each student makes using each set of information is compared. The random groups and assignments will vary.

3.41 a) Block 1: Williams, Deng, Hernandez, and Moses. Block 2: Santiago, Kendall, Mann, and Smith. Block 3: Brunk, Orbach, Rodriguez, and Loren. Block 4: Jackson, Stall, Brown, and Cruz. Block 5: Birnbaum, Tran, Nevesky, and Wilansky. **b)** One way to randomly assign the 20 individuals after separating into five blocks is as follows: Starting with block 1, give each individual a two-digit number. (Williams will be 01, Deng 02, Hernandez 03 and Moses 04.) Continue with the remaining four blocks in this fashion. As an example, starting at line 113 on Table B the first acceptable two-digit random number is 02. Deng is assigned to weight loss treatment A. We could then assign numbers 06, 10, 14, and 18 to weight-loss treatment A. Continue using Table B to find suitable random numbers for assignments to the next three weight loss treatments. The assignments are given below.
Treatment A: 02, 06, 10, 14, and 18.
Treatment B: 08, 12, 16, 20, and 04.
Treatment C: 11, 15, 19, 03, and 07.
Treatment D: 01, 05, 09, 13, and 17.

3.42 This is an observational study because no treatment is imposed. The explanatory variable is acceptance of public housing (yes or no) and the response variable is income (along with other variables that were not specified.) There are certainly lurking variables that affect income levels that will confound the results of this study.

3.43 This is an experiment because the students see a treatment (steady price versus price cuts). The explanatory variable is which price history is shown and the response variable is what price the student expects to pay.

3.44 If, in addition to the usage variables of the new system, the experimenter would like to compare how many phone calls are made with the current phone system and how many are made with the computer system, then a control group should be used. There would then be three treatments: low flat rate for group 1, two-rate structure for group 2, and no new service for group 3.

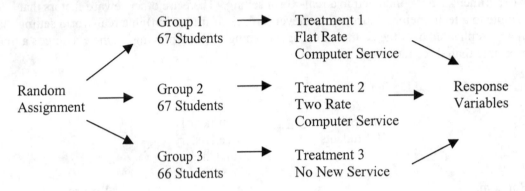

If no control group is wanted, then randomly assign 50 students to group 1 and 50 students to group 2.

3.45 a) The subjects are the 210 children. **b)** The factor is the beverage set and there are three levels. The response variable is which type of drink is selected.

c)

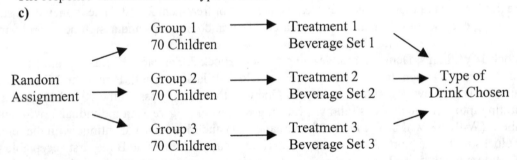

d) Assign the numbers 001–210 to the list of children. Starting at line 125 in Table B, the first five subjects for treatment 1 would be: 119, 033, 199, 192, and 148.

3.46 a) It is important to have a control group that receives a placebo but is handled the same way as the group that receives the new medication. The placebo effect needs to be considered in any testing of new medications.

b)

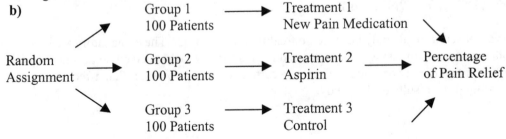

c) No, patients should not be told which drug they are receiving. This information might affect how they perceive their pain relief. **d)** Yes, the experiment should be double-blind as well. Double-blind will ensure that the medical personnel handle the three groups the same way.

3.47 a) Two possible lurking variables could be age of the patient and severity of the cancer.

b)

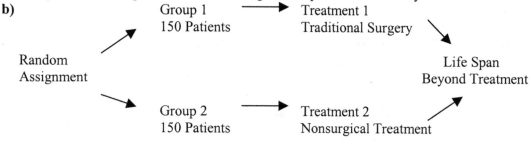

Random Assignment

Group 1
150 Patients → Treatment 1
Traditional Surgery

Group 2
150 Patients → Treatment 2
Nonsurgical Treatment

Life Span
Beyond Treatment

3.48 a) The subjects were the 22,000 physicians. The factor was the pill the subject took every other day. There were two levels: aspirin and placebo. The response variable was number of heart attacks each group experiences.

b)

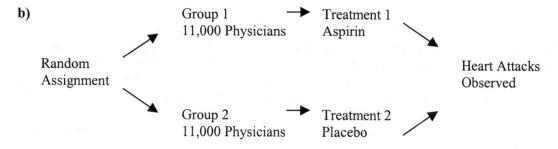

Random Assignment

Group 1
11,000 Physicians → Treatment 1
Aspirin

Group 2
11,000 Physicians → Treatment 2
Placebo

Heart Attacks
Observed

c) This phrase means that the difference in the number of heart attacks observed in each group was so large that it was not due to chance alone.

3.49 A controlled study is a study that has been conducted by looking at recovery rates while accounting for differences in individuals. Some differences to be considered would be age, gender, type of ailment, and severity of ailment.

3.50 a)

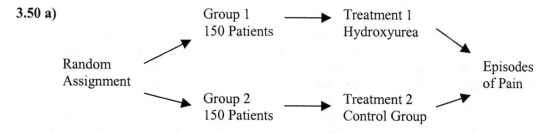

Random Assignment

Group 1
150 Patients → Treatment 1
Hydroxyurea

Group 2
150 Patients → Treatment 2
Control Group

Episodes
of Pain

b) The placebo effect is the phrase used to describe the phenomenon of an individual showing a positive response (in this case a reduction in pain episodes) to a treatment even when the treatment is a placebo (inert). Without comparing the hydroxyurea treatment to a control group the experimenters would not know if the positive results were due to the medication or due to the placebo effect.

3.51 a)

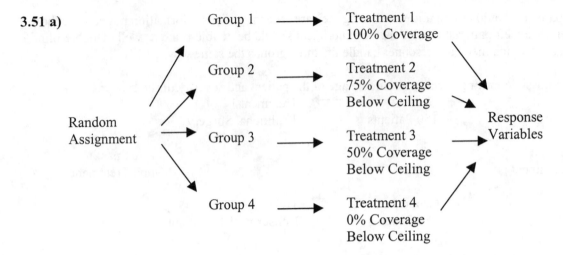

b) Randomly assigning individuals to this type of insurance plan is not an easy task. An individual may not be willing to take part in this experiment if they are assigned to treatments 2, 3, or 4 if these treatments are less than their current coverage. From an ethical perspective, it would be difficult for a company to justify providing less coverage to some individuals than to others.

3.52 Random assignment will assign six students to each of the six treatments. The treatments are as shown in figure 3.3. The students' responses toward recall of the commercial, their attitude toward the camera, and their intention to purchase the camera will be compared between the six treatment groups. The random assignments are shown here. Group 1: James, Chao, Vaughn, Liang, Bikalis, and Padilla. Group 2: Trujillo, Maldonado, Imrani, Kaplan, Denman, and Wei. Group 3: Asihiro, Zhang, O'Brian, Han, Rosen, and Willis. Group 4: Marsden, Valasco, Plochman, Durr, Farouk, and Fleming. Group 5: Hruska, George, Howard, Solomon, Montoya, and Clemente. Group 6: Alomar, Bennett, Edwards, Ogle, Tullock, and Wilder.

3.53 a)

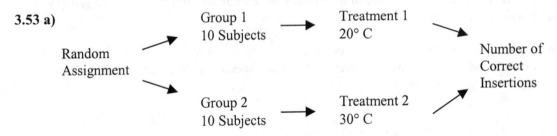

b) A matched pairs experiment would have each subject perform the dexterity test at both temperatures. The order of the treatments would be randomly selected for each subject so that order does not play a role. After each subject performs the dexterity test twice, the difference in the number of correct insertions for each subject would be used to determine if the temperature of the work place has an effect.

3.54 a) A matched pairs design involves administering the two tests (BI and ARSMA) to each individual in the experiment. The randomization in the design will come into play when choosing which test the individual will receive first. **b)** Depending on whether the student uses Table B or whether they use a software package will determine the random sample. Answers will vary.

3.55

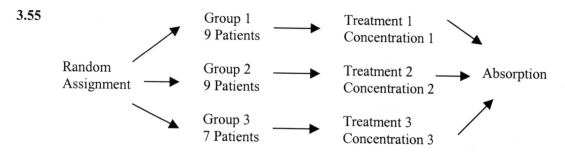

3.56 There are two factors with three levels each so there will be nine treatments for this comparative experiment. The students' diagram should show that they have a different combination of concentration and method for each treatment level.

3.57 Using Table B, starting at line 145, to randomly select the 10 plots that will be planted with method A, the randomized experiment looks like the following:

Plot 01 Method A	Plot 02 Method A	Plot 03 Method B	Plot 04 Method B
Plot 05 Method B	Plot 06 Method A	Plot 07 Method A	Plot 08 Method A
Plot 09 Method A	Plot 10 Method A	Plot 11 Method B	Plot 12 Method B
Plot 13 Method B	Plot 14 Method B	Plot 15 Method B	Plot 16 Method A
Plot 17 Method B	Plot 18 Method B	Plot 19 Method A	Plot 20 Method A

3.58 52% is a parameter and 43% is a statistic.

3.59 68% is a parameter and 73% is a statistic.

3.60 a) 60% of the digits in the random number table will be a 0, 1, 2, 3, 4, or 5. 40% of the digits will be a 6, 7, 8, or 9. This simulates a population where 60% of the people find shopping frustrating and 40% do not. **b)** If drawing one digit simulates drawing one person at random then drawing 100 digits will simulate drawing 100 people at random. A table of random digits is generated with each digit independently selected from a distribution where each digit has a 10% chance of being selected. **c)** Starting at line 104, 56 of the digits are between 0 and 5, so $\hat{p} = 56 / 100 = 0.56$.

3.61 a) $\bar{x} = 25.324$ million dollars. This value is less than the mean from the first two samples. **b)** s = 30.788 million dollars. This value is also less than the standard deviation from the first two samples. **c)** The median is 13.1 million dollars, which is also less than the median from the first two samples. Note, however, that the medians are much closer in value than either the means or standard deviations.

3.62 a) This histogram shows a slightly skewed shape to the right with a center at approximately 25 million dollars and a spread of 60 million dollars. **b)** It is reasonable to say that the sample mean from a sample of 25 could be as much as 30 million dollars greater or 20 million dollars less than the true mean.

3.63 a) The approximate range is 60 (70 – 10) million dollars. **b)** The approximate range is 75 (80 – 5) million dollars. The spread is greater with the smaller sample size. **c)** The approximate range is 26 (42 – 16) million dollars. This range is smaller than the range in parts (a) and (b). **d)** These three sampling distributions illustrate that as the sample size increases, the spread of the distribution (or variability) decreases.

3.64 The firm increases its sample size to decreases sampling variability (decrease margin of error).

3.65 a) The population for this survey is all the people in Ontario. **b)** Yes, these sample statistics are likely to be very close to the true population parameters because the sample size is very large and the sample was a probability sample.

3.66 6.2% is a statistic because it is a number that describes the sample.

3.67 The value 2.503 is a parameter because it is the true mean of the carload. 2.515 is a statistic because it describes the sample from the carload.

3.68 a) high variability, high bias. **b)** low variability, low bias. **c)** high variability, low bias. **d)** low variability, high bias.

3.69 The larger sample size will reduce sampling variability and the sample statistics will likely be closer to the population parameters than with a sample of only 25 students.

3.70 a) The sampling variability will be the same for each state as long as the sample size is the same for each state. Sampling variability depends on sample size, not population size. **b)** Sampling variability *will* be different for each state if the sample size is a percentage of the population rather than a fixed amount. Because each state has a different population the sample sizes will also be different.

3.71 The margin of error for men is larger because the sample of men was smaller than the sample of all adults.

3.72 a) Answers will vary. **b)** Be sure the student properly constructs the stemplot or histogram. The center should be close to 0.50.

3.73 a) Using Table B starting at line 119, the first random sample would be invoice numbers 9, 5, 8, and 7. The days late for this sample are 6, 3, 7, and 9 which gives an $\bar{x} = 6.25$. **b)** Be sure the student properly constructs the stemplot or histogram. The center should be near 8.2.

3.74 Applet

3.75 a) The sample is 19, 22, 39, 50, and 34. Of these only 39, 50, and 34 are white. The proportion in this sample that thinks shopping is frustrating is 0.60. **b)** The next nine samples are:

73, 67, 64, 71, and 50	$\hat{p} = 0.4$
45, 46, 71, 17, and 09	$\hat{p} = 0.6$
52, 71, 13, 88, and 89	$\hat{p} = 0.4$
95, 59, 29, 40, and 07	$\hat{p} = 0$
68, 41, 73, 50, and 13	$\hat{p} = 0.6$
82, 73, 95, 78, and 90	$\hat{p} = 0.2$
60, 94, 07, 20, and 24	$\hat{p} = 0.8$

36, 00, 91, 93, and 65 $\hat{p} = 0.6$

38, 44, 84, 87, and 89 $\hat{p} = 0.6$

c)

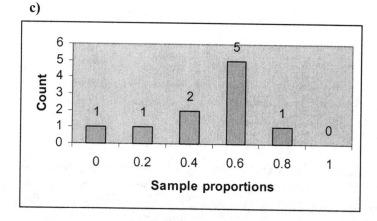

d) There were five samples that had a proportion equal to 0.6. This is the highest column, although the distribution is slightly skewed to the left. If we took many samples of a larger size we should see 0.6 in the center of the distribution because that is the true population proportion. The sample proportion will approximate the true proportion, as the sample sizes get larger.

3.76 This is an observational study because there are no treatments imposed on the subjects.

3.77 This is an experiment because there is a treatment imposed: the subjects are asked to taste two muffins and compare the tastes.

3.78 There are many variables that will affect a fund's performance. The fund manager does not have total control over the performance of a mutual fund.

3.79 Opinion polls can often produce conflicting results when the wording of the statements or questions is subjective. As an example, the phrase "Employees with higher performance must get higher pay" received a 72% agreement in a recent survey on the attitudes Spaniards have toward private business and state intervention. This conflicts with a 71% agreement with the phrase "Everything a society produces should be distributed among its members as equally as possible and there should be no major differences." The first phrase focused on the individual, which appeals to our desire to be rewarded for individual efforts. The second phrase focused on a group–society–and appealed to our desire to have a fair and equitable treatment of society as a whole.

3.80 a) An experiment to help answer this question would need to compare the number of accidents in an area where most cars have daytime running lights and the number of accidents in an area where most cars do not have daytime running lights. The response variable would be the number of accidents over a specified period of time. **b)** One should be cautious when conducting this type of experiment because over time, daytime running lights will become less noticeable. It is possible that the number of accidents will drop initially but then increase as the lights become less noticeable.

3.81 a) There may be variability due to the lecture time, which might hide any true difference in performance using the on-line game. Letting only those students attending the 8:30 lecture use the on-line game does not address this potential variability. **b)** Ten recitations should be randomly assigned to Treatment 1 (using the on-line game), and ten recitations should be randomly assigned to

Treatment 2 (discussion only). At the end of the section on markets, the professor can compare performance between the two groups. Random assignments will vary.

3.82 The students can be labeled 0001–3478. Starting at line 105, the first five students would be: 2940, 0769, 1481, 2975, and 1315.

3.83 It can be difficult to gather data from a population that changes over short periods of time. As an example, consider the population of new businesses. A survey of new business owners showed only a 37% response rate. Follow up surveys had better results with a response rate of 42% from those businesses still in existence after two years. This population is likely to change over time as companies cease to exist either due to being sold or simply going out of business.

3.84 The three groups discussed in the problem would provide criteria for stratifying the population of interest. An SRS of current standard cable subscribers, an SRS of current satellite owners, and an SRS of households that do not subscribe to a pay TV service could be used. The response variable would be whether or not the subject would actually subscribe to the new service.

3.85 The four groups provide stratification of the population of faculty in this state. An SRS from each of the four groups could be used to study attitudes towards collective bargaining. Each stratum could provide 50 faculty members for the sample.

3.86 a) The population for this study could be all students enrolled at your school, including part-time students. It makes sense to include part-time students because they purchase college-brand apparel. **b)** A stratified sample makes sense here because there are distinct groups of students enrolled. Gender may be a way to stratify. Full-time or part-time status may be another way to stratify. It might make sense to stratify by whether or not a student is involved in a Greek organization or a member of an athletic team with the reasoning that those students are likely to identify with the school more than others and therefore purchase more college apparel. **c)** Mailing surveys to college students does not ensure a high response rate. Many students move frequently while in college and tend to use their parents' address for mailings. Asking for feedback on this question using the campus newspaper is not a way to collect a random sample. Perhaps a good way to contact a random sample is through the use of email. This may result in a higher response rate.

3.87 It is possible that some people who did not vote said they did when asked on the survey. Adults are told over and over to vote, that their vote does count. Many people are embarrassed to admit they did not vote.

3.88 Answers will vary.

3.89 a) The explanatory variable is risk of colon cancer. The response variable is incidence of colon cancer after four years. **b)** The experiment has one factor with four levels. The levels are: daily beta-carotene, daily vitamins C and E, all three vitamins every day, and daily placebo. Each group will have 216 subjects. **c)** The first five subjects for treatment 1 are 731, 253, 304, 470, and 296. **d)** A double-blind experiment means that neither the subjects nor the medical technicians know which subjects are receiving which treatments. **e)** The phrase "no significant difference" means that any difference between the four groups is most likely due to chance alone. **f)** People who eat lots of fruits and vegetables also tend to exercise frequently, do not smoke, and in general, lead a healthy lifestyle.

3.90 "Not significantly different from zero" means that the average returns do not appear to decrease over the first three Mondays in a month. If we compare the average return for the first three Mondays to the average return for the last two Mondays, a "significantly higher average return" means that the last two Mondays combined show a decrease that is not due to chance alone.

3.91 a) There are two factors: (1) time between harvest and processing and (2) whether the potatoes are allowed to sit an hour at room temperature or not. The first factor has three levels and the second factor has two levels. This results in an experiment with six treatments. The response variables are taste and appearance after preparation. **b)** This experiment starts with a group of potatoes of the same variety. An equal number of potatoes should be subjected to each treatment. The tasters will need to taste the French fries once the potatoes are prepared and assign their ratings. This should be a single-blind experiment, meaning the tasters should not know which treatment the potatoes received before being turned into French fries. **c)** Randomization can be used to randomly order each treatment group for each taster.

3.92 The two factors in this experiment would be time of day and zip code (yes or no). One main post office should be selected, not a drop box. (Drop boxes tend to have only one pick up time each day.) The time of day factor could have several levels such as 9:00 am, 12:00 pm, and 3:00 pm. There would then be six treatments (3 × 2). The first treatment would be mailed at 9:00 am with a zip code. There may be variability based on the day of the week the letter is mailed. To ensure equal exposure to this variability, an equal number of letters for each treatment could be mailed on each day of the week.

3.93 The consumer should not be told which two fast food restaurants are being compared and randomization should be used in determining which cheeseburger the subject is given first.

3.94 Answers will vary.

3.95 Using Table B at line 125 the first group of fifteen would be 21, 18, 23, 19, 10, 03, 25, 06, 08, 25, 11, 15, 27, 06, and 13. Out of this group five are from the group with the genetic defects. 5/15 = 1/3. This is the same proportion of rats with genetic defects in the original group of rats. 10/30 = 1/3.

3.96 The simulations will obviously give various results. Look for the students' understanding of how to use the software to simulate and their understanding of the difference between the numbers of *yes* results (a discrete value) and the $\hat{p}$ values. Shown below are three histograms for samples generated with $p = 0.1$, $p = 0.3$, and $p = 0.5$. Note that for $p = 0.1$, the average should be close to 0.1 and the standard deviation should be close to 0.0424. For $p = 0.3$, the average should be close to 0.3 and the standard deviation should be close to 0.0648. For $p = 0.5$, the average should be close to 0.5 and the standard deviation should be close to 0.0707.

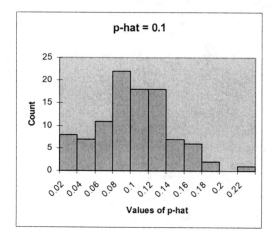

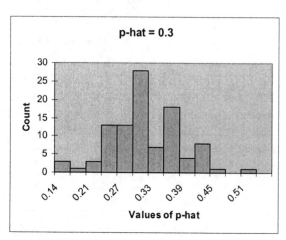

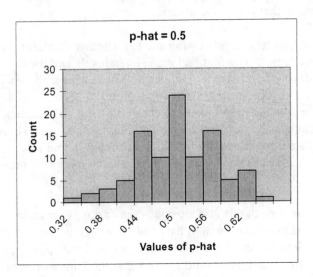

3.97 The sampling distributions will vary by standard deviation. As the sample size increases, the standard deviation will decrease. The mean for each set of simulations should be close to 0.6. For the sample size of 50, the standard deviation should be close to 0.0693, for $n = 200$, $\sigma = 0.0346$, and for $n = 800$, $\sigma = 0.0173$.

Case Study 3.2
   a)

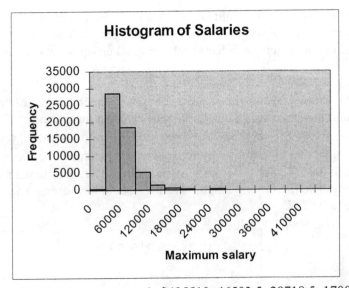

The five-number summary is $425510, 46503.5, 29718.5, 17000, -24998. The distribution is heavily skewed to the right. Removing the top 1% of the earnings data still shows a right skew.
b) To take a random sample of earnings data from such a large data set you may use the sampling function in Excel under the Tools>Data Analysis toolpak option. Note that Minitab cannot handle a data set this large. The histogram and numerical summaries will be similar to the ones found in part (a).

Chapter 4
Probability and Sampling Distributions

4.1 Previous experiments estimate the probability of a head is closer to 0.40 than 0.50. What constitutes a true spin? Do you count spins if the penny falls off the table? These decisions will affect how you determine this probability.

4.2 Students will be challenged in balancing the penny to begin with. Then the way the penny falls will be affected by how level the surface is. In one experiment the penny fell with heads up 48 out of 50 times.

4.3 0.105.

4.4 a) 0.5. **b)** 0.67.

4.5 The probability should be close to 0.5.

4.6 You would see 3 of a kind every 50 hands over the long run.

4.7 a) 0. **b)** 1. **c)** 0.01. **d)** 0.6.

4.8 Applet

4.9 Applet

4.10 Applet

4.11 a) Answers will vary but most should be between 0.31 and 0.61. The $P(X \geq 14) = 0.4166$.

   b)

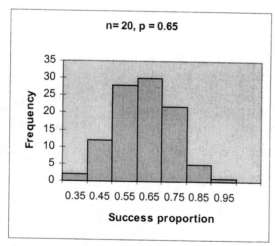

The shape is fairly symmetric with a center at 0.65 and a spread of 0.60.

c)

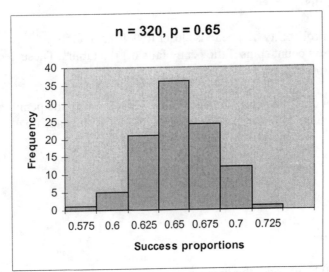

The shape is fairly symmetric with a center at 0.65 and a spread of 0.15. **d)** The histograms look very much alike except for the spread. The shape and center are the same but the variation in the sample size of 320 is much smaller, as was expected.

4.12 a) S = {open, closed}. **b)** S = $(0, \infty)$. **c)** S = {A, B, C, D, F}. **d)** S = {AAAA, AAAU, AAUA, AUAA, UAAA, AAUU, AUUA, UUAA, UAUA, AUAU, UAAU, UUUA, UUAU, UAUU, AUUU, UUUU}. **e)** S = {0, 1, 2, 3, 4}.

4.13 a) There is some variation here depending on the unit of measure. If we measure in hours S = {0, 1, ... , 24}. **b)** S = {0, 1, 2, ... , 11,000}. **c)** S = {0, 1, 2, ... , 12}. **d)** S = $(0, \infty)$. **e)** S = $(-\infty, \infty)$.

4.14 0.54.

4.15 0.253, 0.747.

4.16 a) 0.45 because the probabilities must add to one. **b)** 0.42.

4.17 Model 1 is illegitimate because the probabilities do not add to one. Model 2 is legitimate. Model 3 is illegitimate because the probabilities add up to more than one. Model 4 is illegitimate because the probabilities are all greater than or equal to one.

4.18 a) The values add to one. **b)** 0.87. **c)** 0.191.

4.19 a) 0.39 because the probabilities must add to one. **b)** 0.14.

4.20 a) 0.4. **b)** 0.6. **c)** 0.2. **d)** 0.2.

4.21 a) Area $= \dfrac{1}{2}bh = \dfrac{1}{2}(2)(1) = 1$. **b)** $P(Y < 1) = 0.5$

c) $P(Y < 0.5) = 0.125$

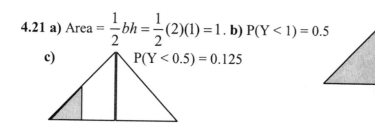

4.22 a) $P(X \geq 32)$. **b)** 0.025.

4.23 a) $P(Y > 300) = 0.50$. **b)** $P(Y > 370) = 0.025$.

4.24 a) S = {UUUU, UUUD, UUDU, UDUU, DUUU, UUDD, DDUU, UDUD, DUDU, UDDU, DUUD, DDDU, DDUD, DUDD, UDDD, DDDD}. **b)** S = {0,1,2,3,4}.

4.25 a) 0.08. **b)** 0.93. **c)** 0.07.

4.26 0.295, 0.348.

4.27 a) 0.10. **b)** 0.20. **c)** 0.50, 0.50.

4.28 1/6.

4.29 a) legitimate. **b)** not legitimate, sum > 1. **c)** not legitimate, sum < 1.

4.30 a) S = {Abby Deborah, Abby Sam, Abby Tonya, Abby Roberto, Deborah Sam, Deborah Tonya, Deborah Roberto, Sam Tonya, Sam Roberto, Tonya Roberto}. **b)** 1/10. **c)** ¼. **d)** 3/10.

4.31 a) $P(A) = 0.29$, $P(B) = 0.18$. **b)** "the farm is at least 50 acres," $P(A^c) = 1 - P(A) = 0.71$. **c)** "the farm is less than 50 acres or at least 500 acres," $P(A \text{ or } B) = 0.47$.

4.32 a) 1/38. **b)** 18/38. **c)** 12/38.

4.33 a) NNN, NNO, NON, ONN, NOO, ONO, OON, OOO. **b)** 3/8. **c)** X = {0,1,2,3}, $P(0) = 1/8$, $P(1) = 3/8$, $P(2) = 3/8$, $P(3) = 1/8$.

4.34 b) 0.86. **c)** 0.78. **d)** $P(X \geq 4) = 0.06$.

4.35 b) 0.11. **c)** 0.04. **d)** 0.32. **e)** 0.75. **f)** $P(X > 2) = 0.43$.

4.36 a) height = ½. **b)** ½. **c)** 0.4. **d)** 0.6.

4.37 a) continuous. **b)** discrete. **c)** continuous. **d)** discrete.

4.38 a) This could be either. If you count number of hours it is discrete. If you measure time it would be continuous. **b)** discrete. **c)** continuous.

4.39 a)

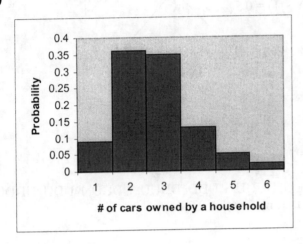

b) P(X ≥ 1) means "what is the probability that a household owns at least one car?" This equals 0.91. **c)** 0.20.

4.40 a) 0.40. **b)** 0.6. **c)** 0.2. **d)** 0.2. **d)** 0.2. **e)** 0.487.

4.41 a) 0.50. **b)** 0.0344. **c)** 0.0344.

4.42

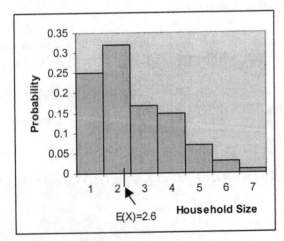

The expected value, the mean, equals 2.6. The census value is greater perhaps because they are including the few households that have more than 7 people.

4.43 The mean, μ, of hard-drive size for laptop computers is 18.5 GB. This is the expected size of hard drives for purchases over a long period of time. This is not useful because hard drives don't actually come in this size.

4.44 a and b)

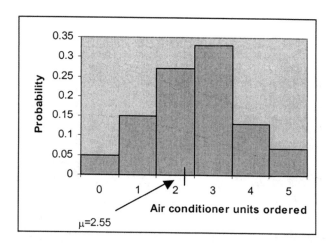

c) $P(X > 2.55) = 0.53$.

4.45 a) $\mu_X = 280$, $\mu_Y = 195$. **b)** $\mu_{\$25X} = \$7000$, $\mu_{\$35Y} = \$6825$. **c)** $\mu_{\$25X+\$35Y} = \$13,825$.

4.46 $\mu_r = 0.936\%$.

4.47 $\sigma^2_Y = 19225$, $\sigma_Y = 138.65$.

4.48 $\sigma = 10.14$.

4.49 a) $\sigma^2_X = 5600$, $\sigma_X = 74.83$. **b)** $\sigma^2_Y = 6475$, $\sigma_Y = 80.47$.

4.50 $\mu_{X-Y} = \$100$, $\sigma_{X-Y} = \$128.06$. The fact that Tamara has a higher mean sales value does not necessarily mean she sells more each day. She has a higher standard deviation and therefore may not be as consistent as Derek.

4.51 $\sigma_{X-Y} = \$100$. When two variables have a positive correlation, if one variable increases, the other will also. If one variable decreases, then the other will also decrease. This will result in their average differences being smaller than if they were independent. With independence, if one variable increases, the other could increase or decrease.

4.52 a) $\sigma_{\$25X} = \$1871$, $\sigma_{\$35Y} = \$2816$. **b)** $\sigma_{\$25X+\$35Y} = \$3381$. **c)** $\sigma_{\$25X+\$35Y} = \$4457$. **d)** same as (b). **e)** $\$1732$.

4.53 a)

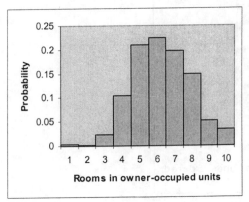 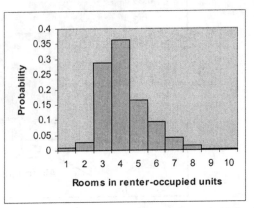

The distribution on number of rooms in owner-occupied units has more mass toward the higher end, 6 through 10 rooms. It appears that the center of the distribution is at 6. The distribution on number of rooms in renter-occupied units is slightly skewed right with a central tendency of 4. **b)** $\mu_o = 6.3$, $\mu_r = 4.2$.

4.54

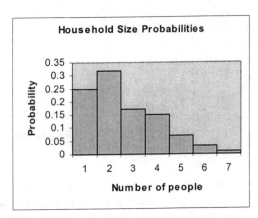 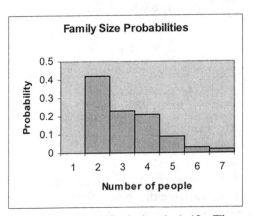

The average size of a household is 2.6 people and the standard deviation is 1.42. The average size of a family is 3.14 people and the standard deviation is 1.25. Both distributions are skewed to the right. The most obvious difference is that there are households that consist of only one person and there are no families of only one person.

4.55 The distribution on number of rooms in owner-occupied units appears to be more spread out than number of rooms in renter-occupied units. $\sigma_o = 1.64$, $\sigma_r = 1.31$.

4.56 $\mu_X = 2$. Let Y = the number of heads on a single coin toss. $\mu_Y = 0.5$. X = Y + Y + Y + Y. $\mu_X = 4\mu_Y = 4(0.5) = 2$.

4.57 Let X = expected payoff for a $1 bet on the box. X = $83.33 or $0. P($83.33) = 0.0014, P($0) = 0.9986. $\mu_X = \$0.12$.

4.58 $\sigma^2_X = 1$. $\sigma^2_Y = 0.25$. $\sigma^2_{Y+Y+Y+Y} = 4\sigma^2_Y = 4(0.25) = 1$.

4.59 a) independent. **b)** dependent. **c)** dependent.

4.60 a) dependent. **b)** independent.

4.61 a) Let X = time to bring part from bin to chassis and Y = time to attach part to chassis. $\mu_{X+Y} = 31$ seconds. **b)** No. **c)** There would be no change.

4.62 $\mu = 70$ minutes.

4.63 $\sigma_{X+Y} = 4.47$ seconds. If dependent, $\sigma_{X+Y} = 4.98$ seconds. Positive correlation means when one variable increases, the other also increases. The variation then builds to result in increased variation on their sum.

4.64 $\sigma = 2.24$ minutes.

4.65

X	p(X)
$\mu - \sigma$	0.5
$\mu + \sigma$	0.5

$\mu_X = 0.5(\mu - \sigma) + 0.5(\mu + \sigma) = \mu,\ \sigma^2_X = 0.5(\mu - \sigma)^2 + 0.5(\mu + \sigma)^2 - \mu^2 = \sigma^2$

4.66 a) $\mu_{Y-X} = 0.001$. **b)** $\mu_Z = 2.0005$, $\sigma_Z = 0.00112$. The average Z is more variable than the reading Y. Y gives a biased reading.

4.67 a) $\sigma_{X+Y} = \$2796$. **b)** $\sigma_Z = \$5,606,738$.

4.68 For $\rho = 0.01$, $\sigma_{X+Y} = \$2798$. For $\rho = 0.99$, $\sigma_{X+Y} = \$2930$.

4.69 a) The students' scores should not be influenced by each other. **b)** $\mu_{F-M} = 15$, $\sigma_{F-M} = 44.82$. **c)** No, you cannot calculate a precise probability because even though we know the mean and standard deviation, we do not know the shape of the probability distribution.

4.70 $\mu_{WY} = 1.23\%$, $\sigma_{WY} = 4.58\%$.

4.71 With $\rho = 0$, $\sigma_{WY} = 3.95\%$. There would no change in the mean.

4.72 $\mu_R = 1.034\%$. $\sigma_R = 3.82\%$.

4.73 For $\rho = 1.0$, $\sigma^2_{X+Y} = \sigma^2_X + \sigma^2_Y + 2\sigma_X\sigma_Y = (\sigma_X + \sigma_Y)^2$ and therefore $\sigma_{X+Y} = \sigma_X + \sigma_Y$.

4.74 a)

X	p(X)
\$1,690	0.25
562.50	0.25
975	0.25
975	0.25

P(X > \$1000) = 0.25.
b) $\mu_X = \$1,050.63$.

4.75 a) $\mu_X = 550°$, $\sigma_X = 5.7°$. **b)** $\mu_{X-550} = 0°$, $\sigma_{X-550} = 5.7°$. **c)** $\mu_Y = 1022°F$, $\sigma_Y = 10.26°F$.

4.76 a) $\mu = 300$ people. **b)** There is no difference in the two choices.

4.77 Parameters describe fixed populations. If we treat the set of tasks completed for this study as a sample of all tasks that could be performed on a computer, then these numbers represent statistics.

4.78

n	$\overline{x}$
1	28
2	34
3	32
4	32.25
5	29.8

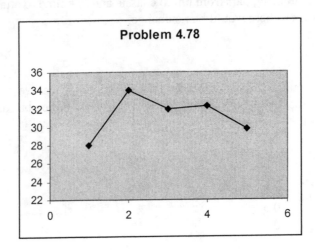

4.79 Each time Joe plays his return is either 0 or 600. If he averages his winnings over many years, he'll find an average very close to $0.60.

4.80 a) The spins of the wheel are independent of each other. This means that each time the wheel is spun, the chance of getting a red (or black) is the same as every other time the wheel is spun. **b)** No, each time a card is dealt the probability on the remaining cards changes.

4.81 The "law of averages" assumes independent trials. This means that each time Tony is at bat, his chance of getting a hit is the same. Therefore, Tony is not "due" a hit.

4.82 Applet

4.83 a) $\mu = 69.4$. **b)** Answers will vary. One sample is 7, 3, 6, 4 with an $\overline{x} = 65.25$.
   c) The histogram below is one example.

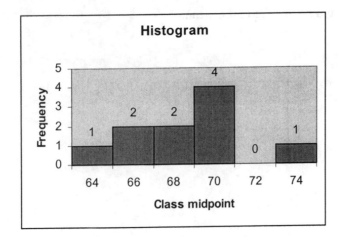

4.84 a) 5.77. **b)** $n = 4$.

4.85 a) $\bar{x}$ is an unbiased estimator of μ because if we were to take many, many samples and calculate many, many values of $\bar{x}$, the average of all the $\bar{x}$'s would be equal to μ, the mean of the population. **b)** The Law of Large Numbers tells us that when we take larger and larger samples, the value of $\bar{x}$, the sample mean, gets closer and closer to μ, the population mean.

4.86 a) 0.3409. **b)** $\mu_{\bar{x}} = 18.6$, $\sigma_{\bar{x}} = 0.834$. **c)** 0.002.

4.87 Approximately 0.0.

4.88 $P(\bar{x} > 15\%) = 0.2148$, $P(\bar{x} < 7) = 0.0089$.

4.89 The number 19 is a parameter and 14 is a statistic.

4.90 Both numbers are statistics.

4.91 Over a large number of plays, a player will win 94.7 cents for each dollar he bets.

4.92 a)

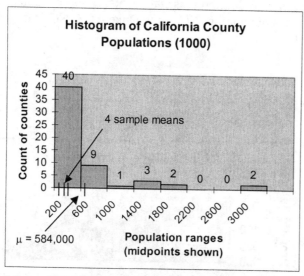

b) $\mu = 583{,}994$. **c)** $\bar{x} = 47010.5$. **d)** 97065.25, 85281, 56809, 42831.25. We would not expect all the sample means to be greater than μ. The distribution is heavily skewed to the right so most of the observations will be less than μ. **e)** Even though the distribution is skewed to the right, the center of the sampling distribution should still be close to μ.

4.93 a) $\bar{x}$ has an approximate normal distribution with a mean of 123 mg and a standard deviation of 0.0462. **b)** $P(\bar{x} > 124) \approx 0$.

4.94 $\mu_{\bar{x}} = 40.125mm$, $\sigma_{\bar{x}} = 0.001$

4.95 a) 0.1587. **b)** 0.0071.

4.96 a) 0.0668. **b)** 0.0013. **c)** In order to avoid unnecessary medical procedures, the testing method in part b would be more reliable because the method has a much smaller probability of incorrectly diagnosing Shelia as having gestational diabetes if she does not.

4.97 Between 0.1108 and 0.1892 average defects.

4.98 a) $\mu_{\bar{x}} = 2.2$ accidents, $\sigma_{\bar{x}} = 0.1941$. **b)** 0.1515. **c)** 0.0764.

4.99 a) $P(\bar{x} > 400) \approx 0$. **b)** We need the shape of the population distribution. The Central Limit Theorem allowed us to approximate the probability in part a.

4.100 a) $\mu_{\bar{x}} = 0.9$, $\sigma_{\bar{x}} = 0.0134$. **b)** L = 0.9313 NOX.

4.101 L = 133.23 mg/dl.

4.102 a) The probabilities are all between 0 and 1 and their sum is 1. **b)** 35%.

4.103 0.55.

4.104 No, Zeke has not given a legitimate assignment. Based on his statements, he has assigned the following probabilities to the teams' chances of winning: NC – 0.6, Duke – 0.3, NC State – 0.1, and UVA – 0.1. These add up to more than 1.

4.105 b) 0.43. **c)** 0.96. **d)** 0.28. **e)** 0.72.

4.106 a)

X	P(X)
2	1/36
3	2/36
4	3/36
5	4/36
6	5/36
7	6/36
8	5/36
9	4/36
10	3/36
11	2/36
12	1/36

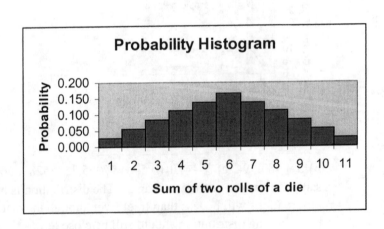

b) 8/36. **c)** 30/36.

4.107

Y	P(Y)
1	3/36
2	3/36
3	3/36
4	3/36
5	3/36
6	3/36
7	3/36
8	3/36
9	3/36
10	3/36
11	3/36
12	3/36

4.108 a) 0.3694. **b)** $\mu_{\bar{x}} = 100, \sigma_{\bar{x}} = \dfrac{15}{\sqrt{60}}$. **c)** 0.0049. **d)** The answer to (a) would be affected.

4.109 0.9535.

4.110 a) No, the distribution is not normal because the variable takes on integer values. **b)** The distribution of $\bar{x}$ is approximately normal with $\mu_{\bar{x}} = 1.5$, $\sigma_{\bar{x}} = \dfrac{0.75}{\sqrt{700}}$. **c)** 0.0793.

4.111 b) $\mu = 2.45$.

4.112 In a simulation of 100 plays of this game there were 18 outcomes that did not have a run of three heads or three tails. Using this proportion as an estimate of the probability of no runs of three, the expected amount of winnings over the long run would be $(0.18)(\$2) - (0.82)(\$1) = -\$0.46$.

4.113 If you sold only 12 policies, you would probably lose a lot of money. Even though the average loss per person is only $250, that average comes from a distribution that has some losses equal to zero and a very few losses that are greater, perhaps $200,000 or more. One loss would be much more than the profit from 11 policies. If, instead, you sold thousands of policies, the gain from the many, many policies that paid out $0 would be much more than the few losses incurred.

4.114 $P(\bar{x} > 260) = 0.0004$.

4.115 $P(\$1250) = 0.99058$, $\mu_x = \$303.35$.

4.116 For each loss of $100,000, the company would gain $1,250 many times over.

4.117 $\sigma_x = \$9707.6$.

4.118 a) $\mu_z = \$303.35$, $\sigma_z^2 = 0.5^2\sigma_x^2 + 0.5^2\sigma_y^2$, $\sigma_z = \$6864.3$. **b)** $\mu_z = \$303.35$, $\sigma_z = \$4853.8$.

4.119 a) $S = \{1,2,3, \ldots, 50\}$. **b)** Discrete because the variable takes on integer values. **c)** There are 50 possible values.

4.120 a) $S = \{0,1,2,3,\ldots\}$. **b)** Discrete because the variable takes on integer values. **c)** infinite.

4.121 a) (0, 35]. **b)** Continuous because the variable is described on intervals. **c)** infinite.

Chapter 5
Probability Theory

5.1 a) It is reasonable to assume high school ranks are independent because a student's performance is not influenced by another student's high school performance. **b)** $(0.41)(0.41) = 0.1681$. **c)** $(0.41)(0.01) = 0.0041$.

5.2 No, these events are probably not independent of each other. A college education has an influence on the type of job you take.

5.3 a) P(5 calls fail to reach an individual) $= (0.80)^5 = 0.3277$. **b)** $(0.92)^5 = 0.6591$.

5.4 $P(A) = 0.9$, $P(A^c) = 0.1$, $P(B) = 0.8$, $P(B^c) = 0.2$, $P(A^c \text{ and } B^c) = (0.1)(0.2) = 0.02$.

5.5 P(lights work for 3 years) = P(no lights fail in 3 years) $= (1-0.02)^{20} = 0.6676$.

5.6 a)

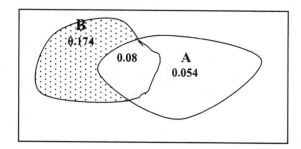

$P(A \text{ or } B) = 0.308$

b) $P(A^c \text{ or } B) = 0.174$.

5.7

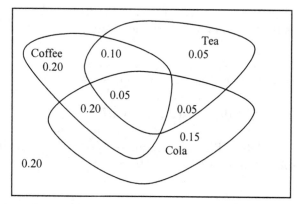

a) 15%. **b)** 20%.

5.8 P(hiring vice president) $= 0.6$, P(hiring all three managers) $= (0.8)^3 = 0.512$. Offer the job to the vice president candidate.

5.9 P(win at least once) $= 1 - $ P(lose all five times) $= 1-(0.98)^5 = 0.0961$.

5.10 P(all 12 chips work properly) $= (1-0.05)^{12} = 0.5404$.

5.11 a) $(0.65)^3 = 0.2746$. **b)** Since we assume the years are independent, the third year has probability of 0.65 of going up. **c)** P(up two years in a row or down two years in a row) = $(0.65)(0.65) + (0.35)(0.35) = 0.545$.

5.12 a)

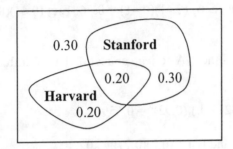

b) P(neither university admits Ramon) = 0.30. **c)** 0.30.

5.13 P(A or B) = 0.6 + 0.5 + -0.3 = 0.8.

5.14 a)

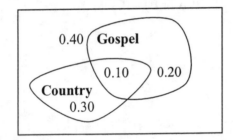

b) $P(C \text{ and } G^c) = 0.30$. **c)** $P(C^c \text{ and } G^c) = 0.4$.

5.15 If P(A)P(B) = P(A and B) then A and B are independent. We were given P(A), P(B), and P(A and B). P(A)P(B) = (0.6)(0.5) = 0.3. This is equal to P(A and B); therefore, A and B are independent of each other.

5.16 P(husband is a suitable donor for a wife with type B) = P(Type B or Type O) = 0.45 + 0.11 = 0.56.

5.17 P(husband and wife are same type) = $(0.45)^2 + (0.40)^2 + (0.11)^2 + (0.04)^2 = 0.3762$.

5.18 P(wife has A and husband has B) = (0.40)(0.11) = 0.044. P(one has A and one has B) = P(wife has A and husband has B) + P(wife has B and husband has A) = 2(0.044) = 0.088.

5.19

Blood Type/RH Factor	O Rh+	O Rh-	A Rh+	A Rh-	B Rh+	B Rh-	AB Rh+	AB Rh-
US Probability	0.378	0.072	0.336	0.064	0.0924	0.0176	0.0336	0.0064

5.20 a) P(under 65) = 0.321 + 0.124 = 0.445, P(65 or older) = 0.365 + 0.190 = 0.555.
   b) P(tests were done) = 0.321 + 0.365 = 0.686, P(tests not done) = 0.124 + 0.190 = 0.314.

c) No, the events A and B are not independent. P(A and B) = 0.190 *(from table)* P(A)P(B) = (0.445)(0.314) = 0.1397. Since P(A and B) does not equal P(A)P(B), then they are not independent. The tests were omitted more frequently on older patients.

5.21 a) P(throwing an 11) = 2/36 = 0.05556, P(throwing three 11s in a row) = $(0.05556)^3$ = 0.000172.
b) Using the probability values from part (a) and the formula given, the odds against throwing an 11 are 17 to 1. The odds against throwing three 11s in a row are 5812 to 1. The writer is correct about his first statement but not about his second statement. (He should have multiplied 18 × 18 × 18. Note that if we use (1/18) as the probability of rolling an 11, then the odds of throwing three 11s are calculated exactly to be $18^3 - 1$ or 5831 to 1. In only one out of 5832 tries will we throw three 11s in a row.)

5.22 Yes, X has a Binomial distribution. There are a fixed number of trials, 20, there are only two possible outcomes for each trial, girl or boy, the trials are independent, and we assume the probability of each child being a girl is the same.

5.23 X does not have a Binomial distribution. There is not a fixed number of trials.

5.24 X does not have a Binomial distribution. The probability of answering the question right changes since the student receives help in between the exercises.

5.25 a) 0, 1, 2, 3, 4, or 5.
b)

X	p(X)
0	0.2373
1	0.3955
2	0.2637
3	0.0879
4	0.0146
5	0.0010

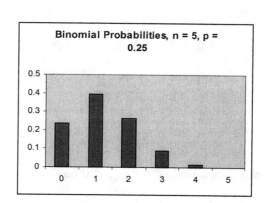

5.26 a) 0.1700. **b)** 0.2969.

5.27 0.0074.

5.28 a) The number of trials is fixed. It is reasonable to assume that the responses from the 20 different households will be independent of each other. The question asked during the survey has a yes or no answer so there are only two possible outcomes for each trial. By making the assumption that the national result is true in this local area, the probability of success should be constant from trial to trial. **b)** P(X ≥ 10) = 1− P(X ≤ 9) = 0.2466. This probability is not so small that we would believe the true proportion of people who say they are concerned about nutrition is higher than the national proportion. I would conclude that this local area is similar to the national result.

5.29 μ = 8, σ = 2.19.

5.30 a) $\mu = 4.5$. **b)** $\sigma = 1.775$. **c)** $\sigma = 1.162$, $\sigma = 0.385$. As p gets closer to zero, the standard deviation gets smaller.

5.31 a) $\mu = 16$. **b)** $\sigma = 1.79$. **c)** $\sigma = 1.34$, $\sigma = 0.445$. As p gets closer to one, the standard deviation gets smaller.

5.32 a) $\mu = 80$, $\sigma = 6.93$. **b)** $P(75 \le X \le 85) = P(-0.72 \le Z \le 0.72) = 0.7642 - 0.2358 = 0.5284$.

5.33 a) Using the Normal approximation to the Binomial, $P(X \ge 100) = P(Z \ge 2.89) = .0019$. **b)** Sample size can greatly influence the probabilities which in turn can influence your conclusions. The larger the sample size the more noticeable the differences between two populations.

5.34 a) X does not have a Binomial distribution because there are not a fixed number of trials. **b)** X does have a Binomial distribution. There are a fixed number of trials: 52. The trials are independent of each other. There are two possible outcomes for each trial: wins a prize or does not win a prize. The probability of winning a prize should be the same as long as he plays the same game each time.

5.35 a) X does not have a Binomial distribution. The probability of performing satisfactorily on the exam will be different for each machinist. **b)** X does have a Binomial distribution. There are a fixed number of trials: 100. Each trial is independent of the others. There are only two possible outcomes for each trial: yes or no. If we assume there is a fixed proportion of people in the population who choose to take part in studies, then the probability the individual will say yes is the same for each person.

5.36 a) 0.4095. **b)** $\mu = 4$.

5.37 a) $n = 10$, $p = 0.25$ **b)** $P(X = 2) = 0.2816$. **c)** $P(X \le 2) = 0.5256$. **d)** $\mu = 2.5$, $\sigma = 1.37$.

5.38 a) $n = 20$, $p = 0.25$. **b)** $\mu = 5$. **c)** $P(X = 5) = 0.2023$.

5.39 a) $n=5$, $p = 0.65$ **b)** 0, 1, 2, 3, 4, or 5. **c)**

X	p(X)
0	0.0053
1	0.0488
2	0.1811
3	0.3364
4	0.3124
5	0.1160

Binomial probabilities, n = 5, p = 0.65

$\mu = 3.25$

d) $\mu = 3.25$, $\sigma = 1.07$.

5.40 a) $P(X = 12) = 4.1 \times 10^{-9}$, $P(X \ge 1) = 0.7251$. **b)** $\mu = 2.4$, $\sigma = 1.39$. **c)** $P(X < 2.4) = P(X \le 2) = 0.5583$.

5.41 a) $\mu = 75$, $\sigma = 4.33$, $P(X \le 70) = 0.1251$. **b)** A score of 70% on a 250 question test is 175 correct answers. $\mu = 187.5$, $\sigma = 6.85$, $P(X \le 175) = .0344$.

5.42 a) $\mu = 59$. **b)** Using the Normal approximation to the Binomial, $P(X \ge 70) = .0643$.

5.43 a) It is reasonable to use the Binomial distribution to the number who respond because you have a fixed number of trials, they can be assumed to be independent, there are only two possible outcomes (either they respond or they do not) and the probability of a response stays the same for each trial. **b)** $\mu = 75$. **c)** $P(X \le 70) = 0.2061$. **d)** $n = 200$.

5.44 a) Using a software program to calculate the probability, $P(X \le 86) = 0.1239$. (Note that if you use the Normal approximation with $\mu = 90$ and $\sigma = 3$, $P(X \le 86) = 0.0918$. Some authors recommend using a continuity correction factor when approximating Binomial probabilities with the Normal distribution. In that case, $P(X \le 86) \approx P(X \le 86.5) = P(Z \le -1.17) = 0.1210$. This value is a better approximation. You will find that as the values of np and n(1-p) become much greater than 10, the approximations get closer to actual probabilities.) **b)** From our calculations we see that in more than 12 out of 100 samples, we will have a sample on-time percentage that is 86% or less **even** when the overall on-time percentage is actually 90%. This sample result is not unreasonable based on the population assumptions.

5.45 a) $\mu = 180$, $\sigma = 12.6$. **b)** $P(X \le 170) = 0.2148$.

5.46 a) $P(X = 7) = 0.0149$. **b)** $P(X \le 7) = 0.5987$.

5.47 a) Poisson with $\mu = 84$. **b)** $P(X \le 66) = 0.0248$.

5.48 a) $P(X = 110) = 0.038$. **b)** $P(X \le 100) = 0.1832$. **c)** $P(X > 125) = 1 - P(X \le 125) = 0.9866$. **d)** $P(X \ge 125) = 1 - P(X \le 124) = 0.9848$.

5.49 a) $P(X \ge 50) = 1 - P(X \le 49) = 0.445$. **b)** $\sigma = 6.98$, $\sigma = 9.87$. **c)** Using $\mu = 97.4$, $P(X \ge 100) = 1 - P(X \le 99) = 0.4095$.

5.50 a) Poisson with $\mu = 220$. **b)** Using the Normal approximation with $\mu = 220$ and $\sigma = 14.83$, $P(X \le 200) = 0.0885$.

5.51 a) $\sigma = 4.12$. **b)** $P(X \le 10) = 0.0491$. **c)** $P(X > 30) = 1 - P(X \le 30) = 0.0014$.

5.52 a) $\mu = 160$. **b)** $P(100\bar{x} > 110) = 1 - P(100\bar{x} \le 110) = 0.9999$. **c)** Using $\mu_{\bar{x}} = 1.6$ and $\sigma_{\bar{x}} = 0.126$, $P(\bar{x} > 1.1) = 1.0$. **d)** The results are very close. The question of accuracy depends on if the random variable of interest is the total number of flaws in the 100 square yards, or the average number of flaws in a square yard from a sample of 100.

5.53 a) $P(X \ge 5) = 0.9982$. **b)** $P(X \ge 5) = 0.827$. **c)** 0.2746.

5.54 a) Excel responds with the message #NUM! This means the parameters are too big for the software package to calculate a value. **b)** $P(\bar{x} \ge 106.7) = 0.8888$.

5.55 a) $\sigma = 1.52$. **b)** $P(X > 5) = 1 - P(X \le 5) = 0.03$. **c)** $P(X > 3) = 0.20$ and $P(X > 4) = 0.0838$ so k = 3.

5.56 a) $P(X < 3) = P(X \leq 2) = 3.95 \times 10^{-5}$. **b)** $P(X < 15) = P(X \leq 14) = 0.4656$. **c)** 0.4757. **d)** 0.4052.

5.57 $P(A \text{ and } B) = 0.1472$.

5.58 P(dollar falls and contract renegotiation) = 0.32.

5.59 a) 0.4335. **b)** 0.4766. **c)** 0.4617. **d)** 0.0489.

5.60 a) 0.5574. **b)** 0.4444. **c)** No, P(female) ≠ P(female | professional degree recipient).

5.61 a) $P(B \mid A) = 0.597$. **b)** $P(A \mid B) = 0.315$. **c)** No, $P(A)P(B) \neq P(A \text{ and } B)$.

5.62

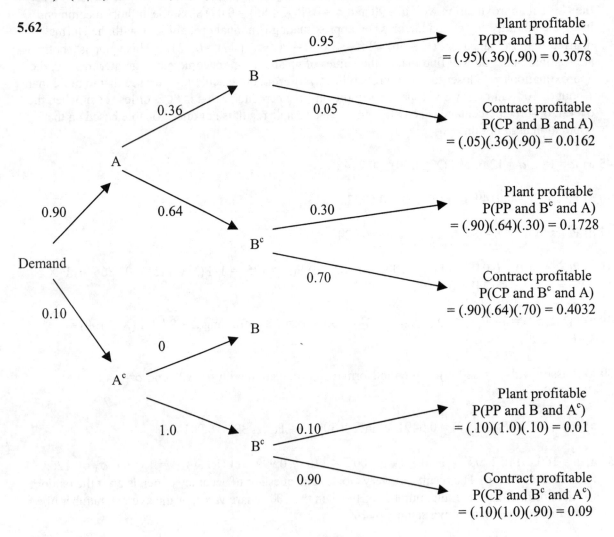

P(Plant profitable) = 0.3078 + 0.1728 + 0.01 = 0.4906.
P(Contract profitable) = 0.0162 + 0.4032 + 0.09 = 0.5094.
Because the probability of the new plant being profitable is less than the probability of the contracting decision being profitable, Zipdrive should contract with Hong Kong for the production.

5.63 $P(B \text{ and } A) = (0.04)(0.45) = 0.018$. $P(B \text{ and } A^c) = (0.01)(0.55) = 0.0055$. $P(B) = 0.018 + 0.0055$.
$P(A \mid B) = 0.766$.

5.64 a) 0.075, 0.0016. **b)** P(income $\geq$ \$100,000 and income $\geq$ \$1 MM) = P(income $\geq$ \$1 MM), P(income $\geq$ \$1MM | income $\geq$ \$100,000) = 0.0213.

5.65 a) P(G | C) = 0.25. **b)** P(G | C^c) = 0.3333.

5.66 a) P(M) = 0.4426. **b)** P(B | M) = 0.6899. **c)** P(B and M) = 0.3053.

5.67

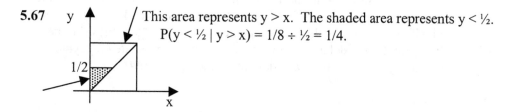

This area represents y > x. The shaded area represents y < ½.
P(y < ½ | y > x) = 1/8 ÷ ½ = 1/4.

5.68 a) P(F | A) = 0.36. **b)** P(F | D or E) = 0.1786. **c)** P(F) = 0.43, P(F) $\neq$ P(F | A) therefore gender is not independent of job type.

5.69

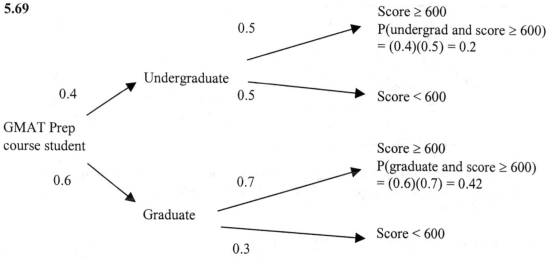

a) P(undergrad and score $\geq$ 600) = 0.2, P(graduate and score $\geq$ 600) = 0.42. **b)** P(score $\geq$ 600) = 0.62.

5.70

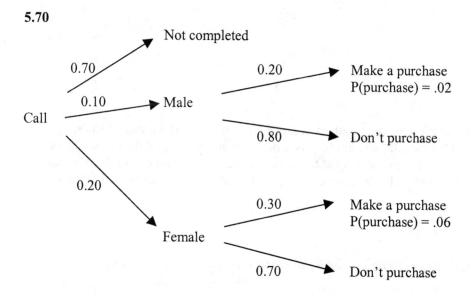

P(call ends in a purchase) = 0.08.

5.71 P(undergraduate | score ≥ 600) = 0.3226.

5.72 P(female | purchase was made) = 0.75.

5.73 Let D = event that a credit card customer defaults and L = event that a credit card customer is late for two or more monthly payments. **a)** P(D | L) = 0.0637. **b)** Between 93% and 94% of customers who have their credit denied will *not* default on their payments. **c)** No. Only 3% of the customers default. Of those who are late, only 6.37% default. Knowing that a customer is late on payments does not dramatically increase the chance that they will default on their payments.

5.74 P(A or B) = 0.6 + 0.5 – 0.3 = 0.8.

5.75 Yes, P(A)P(B) = P(A and B).

5.76 a) P(A and B) = 0.3. **b)** P(A and B^c) = 0.3. **c)** P(A^c and B) = 0.2. **d)** P(A^c and B^c) = 0.2.

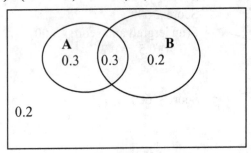

5.77 Let NC = event that an item is nonconforming and C = event that an item is conforming. Let I = event that an item was completely inspected. P(NC) = 0.08, P(C) = 0.92)P(I | NC) = 0.55, P(I | C) = 0.20. P(NC | I) = 0.1930.

5.78 a) 0.001125. **b)** 0.044125.

5.79 a) μ = 3.75. **b)** 0.000795. **c)** 0.034.

5.80 0.0123.

5.81 μ = 1250. **b)** 0.5596.

5.82 0.0934.

5.83 a) It is reasonable to use the Binomial distribution because there are a fixed number of trials, n, the trials can be considered independent, there are only two possible outcomes, and the probability stays the same for each trial (since we are observing at the same location on the same day). **b)** It is more likely that the male will be driving after a dance on campus than after church on Sunday. **c)** 0.4557. **d)** 0.1065.

5.84 a) P(A and C). **b)** P(C|A) or P(A|C).

5.85 Use the relationships P(I) = P(I and F) + P(I and S) and P(S) = P(I and S) + P(I^c and S).
P(I^c and S) = 0.84.

5.86 For those who did not finish high school the unemployment rate is 0.0774, for those who finished high school but did not attend college the unemployment rate is 0.0466. For those who have less than a bachelor's degree the unemployment rate is 0.0407 and for those with a college degree the unemployment rate is 0.0274. The unemployment rate is not independent of education because the rate goes down with increasing education levels.

5.87 a) P(L) = 0.6739. **b)** P(L|C) = 0.7870. **c)** No, P(L) ≠ P(L|C).

5.88 P(C|E) = 0.3166, P(E|C) = 0.7654.

5.89 a)

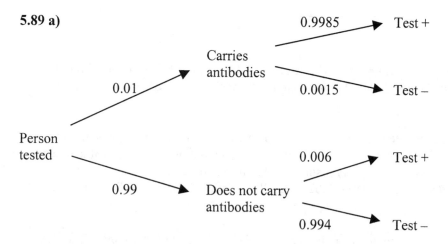

b) P(Test +) = 0.01(0.9985) + 0.99(0.006) = 0.0159. **c)** P(carry antibodies | test +) = 0.628.

5.90 a) 0.1428. **b)** 0.936. **c)** The lesson illustrated is that as the percentage of the population that has the AIDS virus increases, the chance of observing a false positive increases dramatically.

5.91 a) 0.1389. **b)** 0.1157. **c)** 0.0965, 0.0804. P(first 1 occurs on *k*th toss) = $p(1-p)^{k-1}$

5.92 a) P(A) = 0.10, P(C) = 0.20, P(A|C) = 0.05. **b)** P(A and C) = (0.05)(0.20) = 0.01.

5.93 a) 0.751. **b)** 0.48.

5.94 P(C|A) = P(A and C) / P(A) = 0.1.

5.95 a) 0.125. **b)** P(H|B) = 0.0242.

5.96

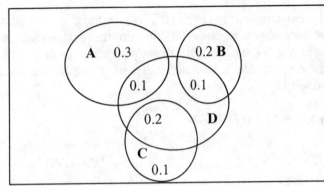

P(D) = 0.1 + 0.1 + 0.2

5.97 P(iMac) = .05, P(did not buy an iMac) = .95, P(First Time | iMac) = .32, P(First Time | did not buy iMac) = .40, P(iMac | First Time) = 0.04. Approximately 4% of first time computer buyers bought an iMac.

5.98 Let SI be the event that an employee has illegally installed software at home and knows it. Let S be the event that the individual has illegally installed software at home but does not know it is illegal. Let D be the event that a person with illegally installed software at home denies knowing it was illegal when confronted. P(SI) = 0.05, P(S) = 0.02, P(D| SI) = 0.80, P(D|S) = 1.0. P(SI | D) = 0.67.

Case Study 5.1

Verify the calculations. **a)** P(one or more errors in 365 days) = $1 - (1 - (1/9000000000))^{(365 \times 1000)} =$ 0.000041. **b)** P(one or more errors in 365 days) = $1 - (1 - (1/100000000))^{(365 \times 4200000)} = 0.9999998$.

Case Study 5.2

a) P(one or more errors in 24 days) = $1 - (1 - (1/100000000))^{(24 \times 4200000)} = 0.6351$. Based on this probability it is likely that an individual will see an error in 24 days. There is a better than 50% chance of seeing an error. **b)** P(one or more errors in one day) = 0.04113. For 100,000 users the expectation is over 4000 mistakes.

Chapter 6
Introduction to Inference

6.1 $\sigma_{\bar{x}} = \$20$.

6.2 $40.

6.3 $40.

6.4 Applet.

6.5 (180.46, 259.54).

6.6 The margin of error would be smaller. $m = 25.25$.

6.7 n = 984.

6.8 The sample size would be smaller. $n = 246$.

6.9 a) 11.3%. **b)** No, the response rate is too small to believe the results.

6.10 (490.42, 589.58).

6.11 a) (94.32, 125.68). **b)** No, this is an interval that describes the average, not a single value.

6.12 a) 0.90. **b)** (60.04, 63.56). **c)** No, this interval describes the average weights, not the weights of individual runners.

6.13 a) 135.96 pounds. **b)** 2.02. **c)** (132.0, 139.92).

6.14 (59.48, 64.12). This interval is wider than the 95% confidence interval. If we want to be more confident that our interval captures the true mean, the interval must be wider (provided the sample size and standard deviation are the same.)

6.15 (11.0, 12.6).

6.16 (28.6, 40.8).

6.17 (16567, 18491).

6.18 $n = 68$.

6.19 $n = 117$.

6.20 $n = 56$.

6.21 a) No. **b)** We are confident that 95% of all samples will provide an interval this wide that contains μ. **c)** $\sigma_e = 1.53\%$. **d)** No.

6.22 (40442, 41190).

6.23 The margin of error will probably be smaller because there is less variation once we narrow down the population of interest. This will result in less variation in the sample; therefore, a smaller margin of error.

6.24 a) 0.8574. **b)** $P(X \geq 2) = 0.9928$.

6.25 a) 95 out of 100 of the samples will produce an interval this wide that contains the true percentage. **b)** If the margin of error is 3%, we are 95% confident that the true percentage is between 49% and 55%. Because 50% lies in this interval we conclude that the election is too close to call.

6.26 If a sample of earnings for the trainee positions were used to compute this range, then it is appropriate to call this a confidence interval. The confidence level should also be reported. However, it is likely that this represents a range of salaries for all trainees. If this is the case, then this is not a confidence interval.

6.27 No, this result is not trustworthy because the results are biased. A voluntary response sample was used.

6.28 a) (61.26, 64.78). **b)** Because the mean is not resistant and can be influenced by outliers, the confidence interval calculated in 6.12 would be a better choice.

6.29 $H_o: \mu = 0$ $H_a: \mu < 0$.

6.30 $H_o: \mu = 1.4$ $H_a: \mu \neq 1.4$.

6.31 $z = -1.58$.

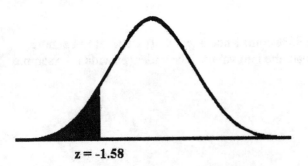

z = -1.58

b) P-value $= 2 \times 0.0571 = 0.1142$. No, this is not strong evidence that Cleveland is different than the national average.

6.32 $H_o: \mu = 31$ $H_a: \mu < 31$. The P-value is 0.0571. This P-value indicates there is strong evidence that Cleveland is less than the national average. The two results differ because the evidence is used for different alternative hypotheses. Remember that the sample evidence is used against the null hypothesis and in favor of an alternative hypothesis. The same sample may provide different evidence for different hypotheses.

6.33 You must state what you want the evidence to support *before* you take the sample, not after sampling.

6.34 "Significantly different at the 0.01 level" means that there is only a 1% chance that these sample results were observed, if in fact there is no difference in burial artifacts. The conclusion, therefore, is that the assumption of no difference is not true.

6.35 $|z| \geq 2.81$.

6.36 $z \geq 2.575$.

6.37 $\alpha = 0.0456$ (using Table A) or $\alpha = 0.05$ using the 68-95-99.7 rule, $\alpha = .0026$ (using Table A) or $\alpha = .003$ using the 68-95-99.7 rule.

6.38 No, P-value = 0.3124.

6.39 a) 0.0359. **b)** 0.9641. **c)** 0.0718.

6.40 No, we didn't set out to prove they were of the same purity. We assumed they were the same and looked for evidence to show they were different. The results of this hypothesis test tell us that we don't have strong evidence to say the purities are different but the results do not prove that they are the same.

6.41 a) Yes, a 95% confidence interval is the same as conducting a two-sided test using an $\alpha = 0.05$. Since the P-value is greater than 0.05, the results of the test are not significant and we can conclude that 10 would be in the confidence interval. **b)** No, using the same reasoning as above. A 90% confidence interval is the same as conducting a two-sided test using an $\alpha = 0.10$. Since the P-value is less than 0.10, the results of this test are significant and we can conclude that 10 would not be in the confidence interval.

6.42 a) No, the interval contains 34. **b)** Yes, 36 lies outside the interval.

6.43 a) No. **b)** No. **c)** The P-value is greater than both 0.05 and 0.01, which means the results are not significant at either of these levels. The lowest level at which this result is significant is 0.078.

6.44 a) Yes. **b)** No. **c)** Because the P-value is 0.03, the lowest level of significance would be 0.03. The results are significant for $\alpha = 0.05$ but not significant for $\alpha = 0.01$.

6.45 a) H_o: $\mu = 1250$ H_a: $\mu < 1250$. **b)** H_o: $\mu = 32$ H_a: $\mu > 32$. **c)** H_o: $\mu = 5$ H_a: $\mu \neq 5$.

6.46 a) H_o: $\mu = 18$ H_a: $\mu < 18$. **b)** H_o: $\mu = 50$ H_a: $\mu > 50$. **c)** H_o: $\mu = 24$ H_a: $\mu \neq 24$.

6.47 a) H_o: $\rho = 0$ H_a: $\rho > 0$ where ρ is the population correlation. **b)** H_o: $p_F = p_M$ H_a: $p_F < p_M$ where p is a population proportion. **c)** H_o: $\mu_A = \mu_B$ Ha: $\mu_A > \mu_B$.

6.48 a) H_o: $\mu = 62500$ H_a: $\mu > 62500$. **b)** H_o: $\mu = 2.6$ H_a: $\mu \neq 2.6$.

6.49 If there were no difference in blood pressure between those who take a calcium supplement and those who do not, then the chance of seeing this large a difference in the sample results is very small (less than 1 in 100 times). Therefore, the appropriate conclusion is that there actually is a difference in blood pressure between the two groups.

6.50 r^{2+} tells how much variation in fires can be explained by the decade variable. 61% of the change in the number of fires over the past 9 decades can be explained by the decade. A low level of significance means that the chance of observing an r^2 greater than zero from a sample if in fact there is no relationship between the two variables is so low we can conclude there is a relationship.

6.51 a) H_o: $\mu_A = \mu_B$ Ha: $\mu_A \neq \mu_B$ where group A are students who exercise regularly and group B are students who do not exercise regularly. **b)** No, the P-value is large; therefore, this sample result does not give evidence in favor of the alternative hypothesis. **c)** It would be good to know how the sample was collected and if this was an observational study or a designed experiment.

6.52 The differences seen between average earnings of men and women are large enough to be caused by true population effects rather than sampling variation. However, the differences in average earnings between black and white students are most likely due to sampling variation rather than true effects due to race.

6.53 $z = 3.56$. P-value ≈ 0. The sensible conclusion is that the poems were written by a different author.

6.54 a) The P-value = 0.0013. Yes, older students have better study attitudes. **b)** The assumptions were that the data come from a SRS and that the population has a normal distribution. The assumption of a SRS is most important.

6.55 P-value = 0.0164. Yes, since the P-value is so small, this sample provides very strong evidence against H_o. Since n = 40, this sample size is large enough to overcome a slightly non-Normal population.

6.56 a) H_o: $\mu = 1.4$ mg Ha: $\mu > 1.4$ mg. **b)** Yes, the P-value is 0.0078 which is less than 0.05. **c)** Yes.

6.57 a) No, P-value = 0.1706, which is greater than 0.05. **b)** No.

6.58 If a sample result is significant at 1%, then the P-value must be less than 0.01. This means the P-value must also be less than 0.05.

6.59 P-value < 0.001.

6.60 P-value > 0.25.

6.61 a) $z \geq 1.645$. **b)** $|z| \geq 1.96$. **c)** Part (a) is a one-sided test and part (b) is a two-sided test.

6.62 $-1.645 < z < -1.282$, $0.10 < 0.1706 < 0.20$.

6.63 a) (99.038, 109.222). **b)** H_o: $\mu = 105$ Ha: $\mu \neq 105$. Since we are 95% confident that μ is between 99.038 and 109.222 we cannot conclude that the null hypothesis is false.

6.64 a) (60.04, 63.56). **b)** No, 61.3 is in the interval. **c)** No, 63 is in the interval.

6.65 a) H_o: $\mu = 7$ H_a: $\mu \neq 7$. Yes, the interval does not contain 7 therefore it is reasonable to conclude that the null hypothesis is false. **b)** No, 5 is in the interval.

6.66 P-value = 0.1292. "Not statistically significant" means the sample results could be due to sampling variability alone. Even though the sample showed that patents and trade secrets contributed 2% to market share, this increase could be due to variation in the sample only and not a true advantage.

6.67 a) No, the z statistic is 1.64, which is less than the critical value of 1.645. **b)** Yes, the z statistic is 1.65, which is greater than the critical value of 1.645.

6.68 a) The sample data did not differ greatly from our assumption about the population. **b)** If the effects are small, then we know that our results make sense and are not due to a small sample being unable to detect a large effect.

6.69 Answers will vary. Suppose we are testing a new soft drink in a supermarket. People will be influenced by comments from other shoppers tasting the soda. Results from this type of sample are probably biased.

6.70 Looking for significant differences among many variables is likely to produce results, even though the results are not indicative of true effects. Also, consider that these variables may not be independent of each other if we have many variables on the same trainees. A better study would be to design a test for each variable of interest and collect a random sample of independent trainees.

6.71 a) No. **b)** Yes. **c)** No.

6.72 Yes, this was a designed experiment that used a control group to compare effects. The results show that the probability of observing this large of a difference is very small if in fact there is no difference in the populations. Therefore, the conclusion is that vitamin C can help prevent colds.

6.73 a) P-value = 0.3821. **b)** P-value = 0.1711. **c)** P-value = 0.0013.

6.74 a) (492.224, 543.76). **b)** (509.85, 526.15). **c)** (515.424, 520.576).

6.75 No, the sample was a voluntary response sample, which can lead to biased results.

6.76 a) No, with a significance level of 0.01, we expect five to do better than guessing. **b)** Retest the four individuals to see if they are consistently better.

6.77 The P-values 0.008 and 0.001 are statistically significant.

6.78 The P-values 0.001, 0.004, and 0.002 are statistically significant.

6.79 a) The distribution on X is binomial. **b)** $P(X \geq 2) = 0.9027$

6.80 Power = 0.2776.

6.81 a) Power = 0.496. **b)** The power will be higher with a lower value of μ because as the alternative value of the mean moves away from the null hypothesis, it is easier to distinguish between the two populations.

6.82 a) P(Type I error) = 0.2743. **b)** P(Type II error) = 0.1151. **c)** P(Type II error) = 0.0082. **d)** When n is large we can overlook slight deviations from normality in the population.

6.83 Power = 0.9099.

6.84 P(Type I error) = 0.01. P(Type II error) = 0.7224.

6.85 P(Type I error) = 0.05. P(Type II error) = 0.504.

6.86 a) P(Type I error) = 0.50. **b)** P(Type II error) = 0.30.

6.87 a) H_o: The patient is ill (or "the patient should see a doctor"); H_a: The patient is healthy (or "the patient should not see a doctor"). A Type I error means a false negative: clearing a patient who should be referred to a doctor. A Type II error is a false positive: sending a healthy patient to the doctor. Note that some students may switch the null and alternative hypotheses. They may assume the patient is healthy and let the results of the test provide evidence that the patient should see a doctor. **b)** One might wish to lower the probability of a false negative so that most ill patients are treated. On the other hand, if money is an issue, or there is concern about sending too many patients to see the doctor, lowering the probability of false positives might be desirable.

6.88 a and b)

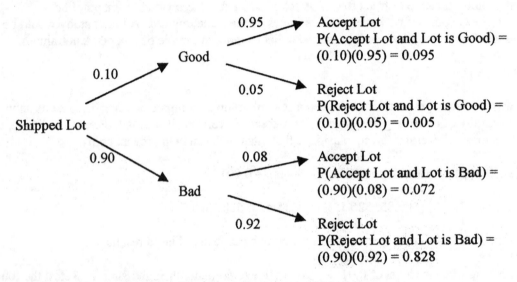

P(Accept a Lot) = 0.167. **c)** P(Lot is Bad | Accept Lot) = 0.431.

6.89 There is less than a 5% chance that this result would be observed if in fact there were no difference in companies with high SHRUSED values and companies with low SHRUSED values.

6.90 a) The sample results do not show a relationship between the level of exchange rate and foreign investment relative to domestic investment. This is consistent with our assumption that this relationship does not exist in the population as a whole. **b)** Because we have a large sample size we trust the results of this study.

6.91 a) 2 0 3 4   **b)** (26.06, 34.74). **c)** Yes, because 25 is not in the interval we can conclude that
         2   the average odor threshold of beginning students is higher.
         3 0 1 1 2 4
         3 6
         4 3

6.92 a) The 95% confidence interval would be wider. Greater confidence results in a wider interval. **b)** Yes, a two-sided hypothesis test with an $\alpha = 0.10$ can be decided using a 90% confidence interval. This interval does not contain $40,000; therefore, we can reject H_o.

6.93 ($777, $789).

6.94 a) (141.6, 148.4). **b)** H_o: $\mu = 140$ H_a: $\mu > 140$. P-value = 0.0078 therefore reject H_o. **c)** The assumptions are that the data are a SRS from a normal population.

6.95 a) The population of interest would be all nonprescription medication consumers. The conclusions can be drawn for certain about the population of Indianapolis that has their phone number listed. **b)** Food stores: (15.22, 22.12) Mass merchandisers (27.77, 36.99) Pharmacies (43.68, 53.52). **c)** Yes, the confidence intervals do not overlap, which means the averages are different from each other.

6.96 a)

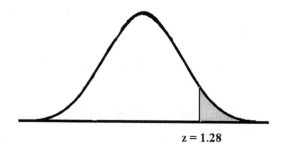

$$z = 1.28$$

b) P-value = 0.10. **c)** No, the results are not significant at the 0.05 level. This study does not give strong evidence that CEO pay went up.

6.97 a) With an increased sample size, the margin of error will decrease and the width of the interval decreases. **b)** As n increases, the sampling variability gets smaller and therefore the P-value decreases. **c)** As in part (b), as n increases the sampling variability gets smaller and the power increases.

6.98 H_o: $p = 18/38$ H_a: $p \neq 18/38$.

6.99 No, 0.05 is a probability about the sample mean, not about μ.

6.100 Yes, significant results have low P-values, which tell us the probability of making an observation due to chance alone.

6.101 a) The probability of seeing this large of a difference in the samples, if in fact the populations were not different, is very small. Therefore, the results of this study are considered to be significant. **b)** 95% confidence means that 95 out of 100 samples will provide an interval that is greater than zero. **c)** No, since the mothers voluntarily chose to participate, we cannot attribute a woman's being off welfare simply to training. There may be lurking variables involved.

6.102 A 95% confidence means that approximately 95 out of 100 samples will produce an interval that contains μ. In this simulation one would expect to see 95 that contain μ. It is possible that students will see 3, 4, 5, 6, or even 7.

6.103 As in the previous problem, one would expect to reject H_o approximately 5 times out of 100.

6.104 The Power of this test to reject when $\mu = 22.5$ is 0.2005. One would expect to reject H_o approximately 20 times out of 100.

6.105 b) With n = 100 this is a reasonable assumption. **c)** $m = 10.11$. **e)** One would expect approximately half of the intervals to contain 240. Repeated simulations will not give the exact same results (unless the same seed was used for the random number generator). In a very large number of simulations, one would expect 50% to contain μ.

6.106 Students may find that none of their tests reject H_o or perhaps one or two tests. 5% of 25 is 1.25. In a very large number of samples, 5% would falsely reject H_o.

Case Study 6.1

For the 50 - 64 year age group: When looking at the category "ambience," the response "Tables are too close together" has the highest mean. This is followed by the restaurants being too noisy and the background music being too loud. The category "menu design" showed that the complaint with the highest mean was that the menu print was not large enough. "Service" showed that most people in this age group would rather be served than serve themselves.

The rank of the responses for the 65 - 79 year age group was the same as described for the 50 - 64 year age group.

The table below contains the averages for each response. The responses with an * indicate those that showed significant differences in means between the two age groups.

Question	50-64	65-79	z	P-value
Ambience				
Tables too close	3.79	3.81	−0.25	0.8026
Restaurants too loud*	3.27	3.55	−3.50	0.0005
Background music too noisy	3.33	3.43	−1.25	0.2113
Tables too small*	3.00	3.19	−2.38	0.0176
Too smoky	3.17	3.12	0.63	0.5320
Most restaurants are too dark*	2.75	2.93	−2.25	0.0244
Menu design				
Print size not large	3.68	3.77	−1.13	0.2606
Glare*	2.81	3.01	−2.50	0.0124
Colors*	2.53	2.72	−2.38	0.0175
Service				
Want service rather than self-serve*	4.23	4.14	1.13	0.2606
Rather pay server than cashier*	3.88	3.48	5.00	5.74E-07
Service too slow	3.13	3.10	0.38	0.7077
Hard to hear*	2.65	3.00	−4.38	1.22E-05

Cases Study 6.2

The responses with an * are those that had a significant difference in means between the two age groups.

	50–64	65–79	z	P-value
Accessibility and comfort inside				
Salad bars/buffets difficult to reach	3.04	3.09	–0.63	0.5320
Aisles too narrow*	3.04	3.20	–2.00	0.0455
Bench seats are too narrow*	3.03	3.25	–2.75	0.0060
Floors around bars/buffets often slippery*	2.84	3.01	–2.13	0.0336
Bathroom stalls too narrow*	2.82	3.10	–3.50	0.0005
Serving myself is difficult*	2.58	2.75	–2.13	0.0336
Most chairs are too small	2.49	2.56	–0.88	0.3816
Outside accessibility				
Parking lots too dark at night*	2.84	3.26	–5.25	1.52E-07
Parking spaces too narrow*	2.83	3.16	–4.13	3.71E-05
Curbs near entrance difficult*	2.54	3.07	–6.63	3.49E-11
Doors too heavy*	2.51	3.01	–6.25	4.12E-10
Distance from parking lot too far*	2.33	2.64	–3.88	0.0001

Chapter 7
Inference for Distributions

7.1 a) 25.3. **b)** 9.

7.2 2.086, 2.66.

7.3 (471.77, 590.23).

7.4 The margin of error would be larger. In order to have larger confidence you need a wider interval. The new interval is: 531 ± 85.10.

7.5 H_o: $\mu = \$500$ H_a: $\mu > \$500$, t = 1.184, 0.10 < P-value < 0.15. Based on this P-value there is not strong evidence to believe that average apartment rents are greater than $500.

7.6 a) 0.01 < P-value < 0.02. The result is significant at the 0.05 level. **b)** 0.05 < P-value < 0.10. The result is not significant at the 0.05 level.

7.7 a) H_o: $\mu = 0$ H_a: $\mu \neq 0$. **b)** t = 2.26, 0.02 < P-value < 0.03. **c)** No, this result tells us about the average, not the sales in every store.

7.8 $37864 \pm \$394.

7.9 a) The t statistic must be at least 2.581. **b)** df = 1000. This shows that as the sample size increases, the t statistic gets closer to the z statistic.

7.10 H_o: $\mu = 0$ H_a: $\mu > 0$, t = -31.214, P-value < 0.0005. Based on the P-value, there is strong evidence that cooking WSB reduces the level of vitamin C.

7.11 -55 ± 4.89.

7.12

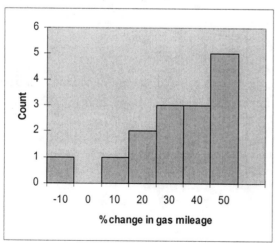

A t confidence interval for estimating the average fuel savings does not make sense with this data set. The number of observations is small, it is heavily skewed to the left, and there is one outlier.

135

7.13 a)

```
1  01233344
1  5566667778999999
2  00124444
2  5555566667
3  244
3  5
4  1
4  8
5
5
6  3
6
7
7  9
```

b) 23.56 ± 3.58.

7.14 You would expect the power to be higher. As you move further away from $\mu = 0$, the test becomes better at distinguishing between different populations.

7.15 Power = 0.9554.

7.16 H_o: $p = 0.5$ H_a: $p < 0.5$, P-value = $P(X \geq 5) = 0.0313$. Since the P-value is so low, the conclusion is that the median amount of vitamin C in WSB after cooking is less than before cooking.

7.17 a) 1.796. **b)** 2.045. **c)** 1.333.

7.18 a) 2.67. **b)** 1.691. **c)** 1.987.

7.19 a) 14. **b)** 1.761 and 2.145. **c)** 0.05 and 0.025. **d)** 0.05 and 0.025. **e)** Yes, significant at 0.05 but not significant at 0.01. **f)** 0.0345.

7.20 a) 29. **b)** 0.15 and 0.10. **c)** between 0.30 and 0.20. **d)** It is not significant at either the 0.10 or 0.05 levels. **e)** 0.2719.

7.21 a) 11. **b)** $0.01 < $ P-value < 0.02. **c)** 0.0161.

7.22 $\overline{x} = 544.75, s = 79.70, se = 39.85$. It is not appropriate to calculate a confidence interval based on these data because they do not represent a random sample. They are roommates in school and it is likely their performances are influenced by each other.

7.23 a) Rounding off to the nearest 1000 produces the following stem plot:

```
1  45
1  777
1  88999
2  01
2  2
2  445
2  66
2  8
```

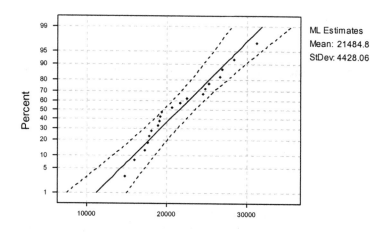

b) 21485 ± 2126.5.

7.24 a)

```
0  89
1  00234
1  55558899
2  00000000000000111112222222223
2  59
3  0
3  5
4  00
4
5  0
```

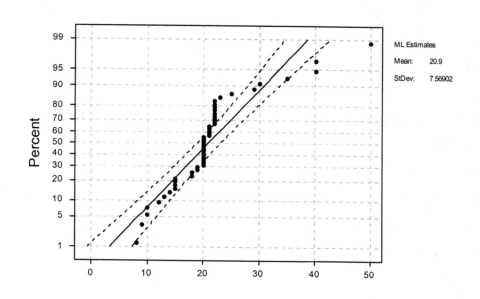

b) 20.9 ± 2.183.

7.25 No, the sample does not give good evidence that the average earnings of white female hourly workers is greater than $20,000.

7.26 No, this sample does not give evidence that the mean cost for all Internet users differs from $20 per month.

7.27 a)
```
0 389
1 023557788999
2 0023445667888
3 24689
4 1244568
5 0249
6 1
7 0
8 256
9 3
```

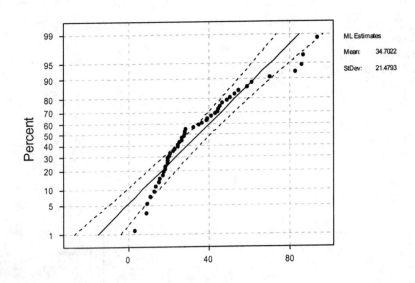

The data show a distribution heavily skewed to the right. **b)** $\bar{x} = 34.70, s = 21.70, se = 3.07$.
c) 34.70 ± 6.20.

7.28 a)
```
0  3
0  89
1  023
1  557788999
2  002344
2  5667888
3  24
3  689
4  1244
4  568
5  024
5  9
6  1
6
7  0
```

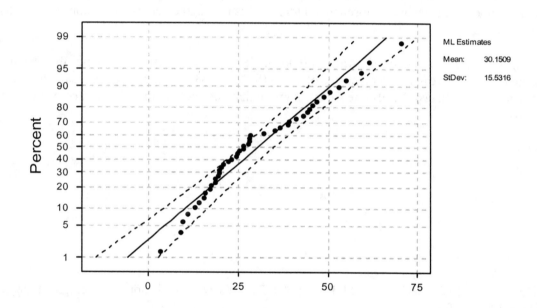

ML Estimates

Mean: 30.1509

StDev: 15.5316

b) $\bar{x} = 31.15, s = 15.70, se = 2.32$. **c)** 30.15 ± 4.69. Yes, these four high values do influence the analysis. The distribution now appears more normal and the standard deviation is smaller. The confidence interval is quite different also.

7.29 The 95% confidence interval for the total amount of access fees paid by US households is $823.5 million to $1015.7 million.

7.30 (16.76, 35.88).

7.31 (1.714, 2.446).

7.32 (87.61, 104.39).

7.33 (3.833, 3.967).

7.34 a)
```
         -3  0
         -2  00
         -1  0
         -0  0
          0  0
          1  0
          2  000
          3  00000
          4  0000000
          5  00
          6  000
          7  00000
          8
          9  00
```
b) $\bar{x} = 3.618, s = 3.055, se = 0.524$.   **c)** 3.618 ± 1.07.

7.35 H_o: $\mu = 0$ H_a: $\mu > 0$, t = 6.905, P-value < 0.0005. Conclude that piano lessons do improve the spatial–temporal reasoning of pre-school children. This is in agreement with the confidence interval found in 7.34.

7.36 a) H_o: $\mu = 0$ H_a: $\mu > 0$, t = 50.07, P-value < 0.0005. Yes, there is significant evidence that the mean amount charged increases under a no-fee offer. **b)** ($328.45, $355.44). **c)** The large sample size makes the result trustworthy. **d)** Use a control group that does not get the offer and compare the two groups.

7.37 (18.69, 70.19).

7.38 a)
```
          9  1
          9  5679
         10  134
         10  5
         11  1
         11  9
         12  2
```
b) H_o: $\mu = 105$ H_a: $\mu \neq 105$, t = -0.32, P-value > 0.50. This evidence is not convincing that the true value is different from 105 pCi/l.

7.39 a) H_o: $\mu = 0$ H_a: $\mu < 0$, where μ is the mean difference in Vitamin C level from factory to Haiti. **b)** t = -4.94, P-value < 0.0005. There is strong evidence to conclude that the Vitamin C level decreases over time. **c)** 95% confidence intervals for the factory level of Vitamin C, for the level in Haiti and for the difference are given in the following Minitab output:

T Confidence Intervals

Variable	N	Mean	StDev	SE Mean	95.0 % CI	
Factory	27	42.852	4.793	0.923	(40.956,	44.748)
Haiti	27	37.519	2.440	0.469	(36.553,	38.484)
difference	27	-5.330	5.590	1.080	(-7.540,	-3.120)

7.40 a) Each person involved in the experiment should be randomly assigned either the right-hand thread first or the left-hand thread first. **b)** H_o: $\mu = 0$ H_a: $\mu > 0$ where μ is the mean difference of left-hand thread time minus right-hand thread time. **c)** t = 2.90, P-value = .0039 (from Minitab). Conclusion is that right-handed people can turn the right-hand thread knob faster.

7.41 The 90% confidence interval for the mean difference between left-hand and right-hand thread times is (5.47 seconds, 21.17 seconds). The mean time for right-hand threads is 89% of the mean time for left-hand threads. This could be a significant difference in an assembly line. A 10% reduction in time will accumulate if the task is performed repeatedly throughout a day.

7.42 a) H_o: $\mu = 0$ H_a: $\mu > 0$, where μ is the mean of the Post test scores minus the Pretest scores.

b)

```
     Pretest
     1  5
     2  000
     2  56688999
     3  00011144

     Posttest
     1  68
     2
     2  5578899
     3  00122222234
```

The pretest and post test scores are slightly skewed to the left but the sample size is greater than 15 so the t procedures should be trustworthy.

c) t = 2.02, P-value = 0.029. The results of this test are significant at the 0.05 level but not at the 0.01 level. **d)** The 90% confidence interval for the mean increase in listening score is (0.211, 2.689).

7.43 H_o: $\mu = 0$ H_a: $\mu > 0$, t = 1.30, 0.10 < P-value < 0.15. No, the sample data do not give overwhelming evidence in support of Variety A having a higher mean yield than Variety B.

7.44 a) two sample design. **b)** matched pairs design.

7.45 a) one sample design. **b)** two sample design.

7.46 It does not make sense to estimate because this data does not represent a sample. It describes the population of the states.

7.47 a) t* = 2.423 from table. **b)** Reject H_o when t > 2.423 or Reject H_o when $\bar{x} > 37$. **c)** P($\bar{x} > 37 | \mu = 100$) = P(z > −4.12) ≈ 1. There is no need to include more customers in the study.

7.48 a) Power = P($\bar{x} > 0.48 | \mu = 0.5$) = P(z > −0.08) = 0.5319 **b)** P($\bar{x} > 0.30$) = P(z > −1.2) = 0.8849.

7.49 a) H_o: median = 0 H_a: median > 0 or H_o: $p = 0.5$ H_a: $p > 0.5$. **b)** Taking the left-hand time minus the right-hand time we count up the number of positives values (these correspond to right-hand times being faster than left-hand times.) Using the Normal approximation to the binomial, P(X ≥ 19) = P(z ≥ 2.86) = 0.0021. From software we can find that P(X ≥ 19) = 0.0033. This data shows evidence against the null hypothesis in favor of the median difference being greater than 0.

7.50 Taking the post test scores minus the pretest scores results in 14 positive values. The $P(X \geq 14)$ when $p = 0.5$ is 0.0577. The results of this experiment are significant at the 0.10 level but not at 0.05 level.

7.51 a) A two-sided test makes more sense. We don't have information to tell us if one design should be better than another. **b)** 29. **c)** $0.002 < $ P-value < 0.005.

7.52 $t > 2.045$.

7.53 The individual observations are no longer independent of each other, by design. You must compare individual sales for each day of the week.

7.54 a) Assignments will vary **b)** 1.4 ± 1.381. **c)** Yes, based on the confidence interval, we are 95% confident that the mean satisfaction index is greater than zero. There is no need to do a formal hypothesis test because a 95% confidence interval can be used in place of a two-sided test with level of significance of 0.05.

7.55 By assigning the next ten employees to a flat screen and the following ten to a standard monitor there may be influences due to time differences. At the end of the test period the flat screen users will all have greater usage times. There may also be influences simply from employees talking to each other about their impressions.

7.56 Confirm calculation.

7.57

Software	Means	Variability	Test statistic	DF	P value	Confidence interval?
Excel	Variable 1 = 2.9325 Variable 2 = 3.591	Variance = 0.000415625 and 0.000251875	t = –56.99216386	8	1 tail = 4.98679E-12 2 tail = 9.97357E-12	No
SPSS	JULY = 2.9325 SEPT = 3.591	Std. deviation = 2.03869E-02 and 1.58706E-02	t = –56.99	8	2 tail = 0.000	Yes
Minitab	JULY = 2.9325 SEPT = 3.591	StDev = 0.0204 and 0.0159	T = –56.99	7	P = 0.0000	Yes
SAS	july = 2.9072 sept = 3.5713	Std Err = 0.0091 and 0.0071	t value = –56.99	8	Pr > |t| < 0.0001	Yes

7.58 Answers will vary.

7.59 $t = 17.133$, df $= 133$, P-value < 0.001. The test shows significant results for the difference in wheat prices between September and July.

7.60 SPSS and SAS give pooled results. The pooled results give a t score $= -56.99$ with a P-value ≈ 0.

7.61 Assume $n_1 = n_2 = n$.

Show that $s_p^2\left(\dfrac{1}{n}+\dfrac{1}{n}\right)=\dfrac{s_1^2}{n}+\dfrac{s_2^2}{n}$.

$$s_p^2=\frac{(n-1)s_1^2+(n-1)s_2^2}{n+n-2}=\frac{(n-1)(s_1^2+s_2^2)}{2(n-1)}=\frac{1}{2}(s_1^2+s_2^2)$$

$$\frac{1}{2}(s_1^2+s_2^2)\left(\frac{1}{n}+\frac{1}{n}\right)=\frac{1}{n}(s_1^2+s_2^2)=\frac{s_1^2}{n}+\frac{s_2^2}{n}.$$

7.62 Yes, the data give good evidence that healthy firms have a higher ratio of assets to liabilities on the average. (t = 7.17, P-value < 0.0005.) The 99% confidence interval is 0.902 ± 0.346.

7.63 The 95% confidence interval for the difference in rent for one and two bedroom apartments is $78 \pm $87.11.

7.64 a) H_o: $\mu_1 - \mu_2 = 0$ H_a: $\mu_1 - \mu_2 > 0$. **b)** t = 2.025 with 9 degrees of freedom, 0.025 < P-value < 0.05. There is some evidence that there is a difference between one and two-bedroom apartment average rents. The results are significant at the 0.05 level. **c)** No, this is a test of means, not single observations. **d)** The confidence interval is more useful because it shows the range of averages. The 95% confidence interval actually shows that the difference of the averages could be negative.

7.65 a) H_o: $\mu_1 - \mu_2 = 0$ H_a: $\mu_1 - \mu_2 > 0$, t = 22.18, degrees of freedom are 1, 0.01 < P-value < 0.02. Based on this small P-value the conclusion is that the bread loses vitamin C after several days after baking. **b)** 26.93 ± 7.665 mg.

7.66 a) The individual observations are no longer independent. The observations are dependent on the loaf of bread. **b)** t = 49.81, 0.005 < P-value < 0.01.

7.67 a) H_o: $\mu_1 - \mu_2 = 0$ H_a: $\mu_1 - \mu_2 > 0$, t = -0.32, degrees of freedom are 1, P-value > 0.25. There is no evidence that bread loses vitamin E several days after baking. **b)** -0.55 ± 10.73.

7.68 The confidence intervals show that the test results make sense.

7.69 a) The P-value for this test is 0.03 and the conclusion would be to reject the null hypothesis. **b)** The P-value for this test is 0.97 and the conclusion would be to fail to reject the null hypothesis.

7.70 a)

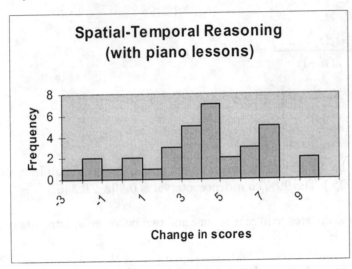

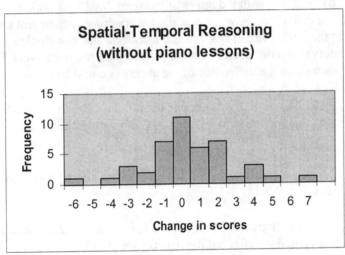

There is a wider range in score changes for the children who did not take piano lessons. It appears that the average change is close to 3 or 4 for those children with piano lessons and close to 0 for those children without piano lessons.

b)

	Piano lessons	No Piano Lessons
n	34	44
$\overline{x}$	3.617647	0.386364
s	3.055196	2.422913
se	0.523962	0.365268

c) H_o: $\mu_1 - \mu_2 = 0$ H_a: $\mu_1 - \mu_2 > 0$ t = 5.059 P-value < 0.0005. The sample data provides evidence that the children with piano lessons show an improvement in their scores of spatial-temporal reasoning.

7.71 3.232 ± 1.277.

7.72 Exercises 7.70 and 7.71 actually design an experiment with a control group to take out lurking variables due to time lapse between testing. This approach is preferable to the approach taken in exercises 7.34 and 7.35.

7.73 a) H_o: $\mu_1 - \mu_2 = 0$ H_a: $\mu_1 - \mu_2 \neq 0$, t = −8.238, P-value < 0.0005. The conclusion is that there is a significant difference in mean ego strength between the low fitness and high fitness groups. **b)** This is an observational study, not a designed experiment. There may be several lurking variables. **c)** Again, the lurking variables may be the cause of ego strength. Middle-aged men who think highly of themselves may be more disciplined and have a strong physical regimen than men who do not think highly of themselves.

7.74 a) H_o: $\mu_1 - \mu_2 = 0$ H_a: $\mu_1 - \mu_2 > 0$, t = 5.987, P-value < 0.0005. Yes, this result is significant at the 1% level. **b)** The data is integer valued. The t procedure is robust because we assume that sample averages are close to a normal distribution with samples close to 15.

7.75 In this case the observations would no longer be independent of each other. A matched pairs procedure would be used to compare individual differences in ego strength scores.

7.76 a) H_o: $\mu_1 - \mu_2 = 0$ H_a: $\mu_1 - \mu_2 < 0$, t = -7.34, P-value < 0.0005. There is significant evidence to indicate that the birth weights of babies whose mothers tested positive for cocaine use were lower than the group called "other." **b)** −385 grams ± 102.95 grams. **c)** The group "other" may have included babies whose mothers were also cocaine users. The confidence interval does not tell us much about the actual mean difference in birth weights.

7.77 a) (−1.28, 7.28). **b)** It is possible that there was actually a drop in average sales between the last year and this year. The data describes a sample of stores, not all stores in the chain.

7.78 H_o: $\mu_A = \mu_B$ H_a: $\mu_A \neq \mu_B$, t = −1.48, 0.10 < P-value < 0.20. The results do not show a significant difference in the plans. **b)** Large samples make the t procedure trustworthy.

7.79 Women

```
10  139
11  5
12  669
13  77
14  08
15  244
16  55
17  8
18
19
20  0
```

```
Men
 7 05
 8 8
 9 12
10 489
11 3455
12 6
13 2
14 06
15 1
16 9
17
18 07
```

Each distribution appears slightly skewed to the right but the sample sizes are large enough to make up for this. **b)** H_o: $\mu_W = \mu_M$ H_a: $\mu_W > \mu_M$, t = 2.06, 0.025 < P-value < 0.05. The data support the belief that men have a lower mean SSHA score than women. **c)** (-36.57, -3.05) for $\mu_M - \mu_W$.

7.80 a) 917.23 ± 195.03. **b)** The sample sizes are large enough to make the procedure trustworthy. **c)** Yes, there is no reason to think there is bias based on an alphabetized list of names. **d)** It would be nice to know the response rate for this survey.

7.81 Verify.

7.82 The confidence interval is 1.4 ± 1.2831. The margin of error is smaller because the degrees of freedom are larger. The conclusions may be different depending on your choice of method.

7.83 a) t = 12.71. **b)** t = 4.303. **c)** With the pooled procedure, it is easier to see a significant result in sample data.

7.84 For part (a) the width is 30.86 and for part (b) the width is 10.448. The unpooled interval has a larger width than the pooled interval.

7.85 a) F* = 2.39. **b)** This value is significant at the 10% level but not at the 5% level.

7.86 a) F* = 2.30. Yes, this is significant at the 5% level. **b)** 0.002 < P-value < 0.02.

7.87 H_o: $\sigma_1 = \sigma_2$ H_a: $\sigma_1 \neq \sigma_2$, F = 1.59, 1.46 < $F^*_{(33,43)}$ < 1.63, 0.1 < P-value < 0.20. The results indicate that the standard deviations are not equal.

7.88 F = 1.162, P-value > 0.20. If the populations are normally distributed, the results of this sample give no indication that the standard deviations are not equal.

7.89 a) F* = 647.79. The power is extremely low for unequal variances. **b)** F = 3.96. Fail to reject the null hypothesis.

7.90 a) F* = 647.79. The power is extremely low for unequal variances. **b)** F = 4.90. Fail to reject the null hypothesis.

7.91 a) H_o: $\sigma_1 = \sigma_2$ H_a: $\sigma_1 > \sigma_2$. **b)** F = 1.54. **c)** $F^*_{(19,17)}$ >1.54 for $\alpha = 0.10$. This means that the P-value is greater than 0.10. The results of this sample are not significant.

7.92 Using the normal approximation to the noncentral t distribution gives the power of this test for a sample size of 100 to be 0.9452.

7.93 For n = 25, Power = 0.4801. For n = 50, Power = 0.7422. For n = 75, Power = 0.879.

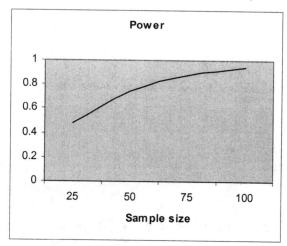

7.94 For n = 25, m = 369.4. For n = 50, m = 257.9. For n = 75, m = 210.6. For n = 100, m = 182.38.

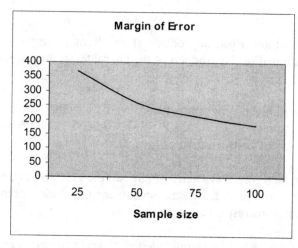

7.95 a) Power = 0.5948. **b)** Power = 0.7794.

7.96 2.555 ± 0.139.

7.97 **Female Earnings**

```
1 2
1 455
1 6667777777
1 8888999999
2 001
2 2
2 445
2 66
2 8
3 1
```

Male Earnings

```
1 5
1 6666777
1 88889999
2 01
2 2223
2 4
2 6
2 89
3 0
```

Two sample T for Female vs Male

	N	Mean	St Dev	SE Mean
Female	35	19789	4121	697
Male	27	20626	4196	808

95% CI for mu Female - mu Male: (-2974, 1300)
T-Test mu Female = mu Male (vs not =): T = -0.78 P = 0.44 DF = 55

These results do not indicate that there is a significant difference between the average male salary and the average female salary. Even if the findings were significant, it would not mean the difference is due to discrimination.

7.98 The 95% confidence interval on percentage of lower priced products at the alternate supplier is (64.55, 92.09). This suggests that more than half of the products at the alternate supplier are priced lower than the original supplier.

7.99 Testing the two-sided test that there is no difference between owners who did evacuate some pets and owners who did not evacuate pets results in a t = 3.65 and a P-value < 0.0005. This indicates there is a significant difference in average scores between the two groups.

7.100 a) This study used a matched pairs design therefore they used a single sample t test. **b)** The average weight loss in this program was significantly different from zero and we can conclude that the program is effective. **c)** The P-value is approximately equal to zero.

7.101 $H_o: \mu_1 = \mu_2$ $H_a: \mu_1 < \mu_2$, t = -0.76, 0.20 < P-value < 0.25. Conclude that there is no strong evidence to indicate that nitrites decrease amino acid uptake.

7.102 a) $H_o: \mu_1 = \mu_2$ $H_a: \mu_1 < \mu_2$, t = −8.954, P-value ≈ 0. Conclude that the workers were faster than the students. **b)** The t procedures are robust for large sample sizes even when the distributions are slightly skewed. **c)** The middle 95% of scores would be from 29.66 to 44.98. **d)** The scores for the first minute are clearly much lower than the scores for the 15th minute.

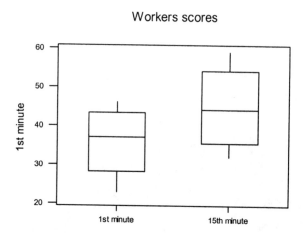

7.103 a) "se" stands for standard error.

$\overline{x}$	Drivers	Conductors
Total calories	2821	2844
Alcohol	0.24	0.39

s	Drivers	Conductors
Total calories	435.6	437.3
Alcohol	0.594	1.002

b) t = −0.35, P-value = 0.3636. There is no evidence that conductors consume more calories than drivers. **c)** t = −1.197, P-value = 0.1174. This is not strong evidence that conductors use more alcohol than drivers.

7.104 a) (0.207, 0.573). **b)** (-0.312, 0.012).

7.105 Since the sample standard deviations are close in value, using the pooled two-sample t test is justified. The t value is 0.35, which is the same as the value in 7.103.

7.106 a) No, the t test is robust to skewness. **b)** Yes, the F test is not robust to skewness.

7.107 It is not proper to apply the one-sample t method to this data set. The data describe a population, not a sample.

7.108 a)

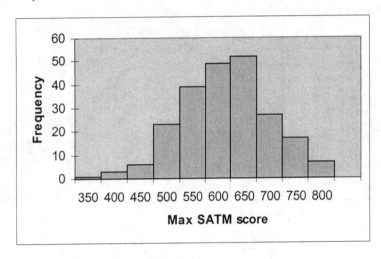

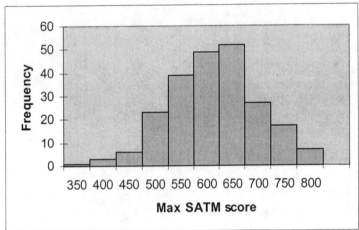

The tables below give the Excel output for the F test used to compare variances, the two-sample t test assuming equal variances and assuming unequal variances. The F test result shows that there is no reason to believe the variances of the two sexes are unequal. Results of the t tests show that there is a significant difference in the average SATM scores between the two sexes. The P-values were both approximately zero.

Sex2 avg SATM	Sex1 avg SATM
565.0253165	611.7724
82.92937599	84.02056

F-Test Two-Sample for Variances

	Sex 2	Sex 1
Mean	565.0253	611.7724
Variance	6877.281	7059.455
Observations	79	145
df	78	144
F	0.974194	
P(F<=f) one-tail	0.455695	
F Critical one-tail	0.713212	

t-Test: Two-Sample Assuming Equal Variances

	Sex 2	Sex 1
Mean	565.0253	611.7724
Variance	6877.281	7059.455
Observations	79	145
Pooled Variance	6995.448	
Hypothesized Mean Difference	0	
df	222	
t Stat	-3.99687	
P(T<=t) one-tail	4.37E-05	
t Critical one-tail	1.651747	
P(T<=t) two-tail	8.74E-05	
t Critical two-tail	1.970707	

t-Test: Two-Sample Assuming Unequal Variances

	Sex 2	Sex 1
Mean	565.0253	611.7724
Variance	6877.281	7059.455
Observations	79	145
Hypothesized Mean Difference	0	
df	162	
t Stat	-4.01237	
P(T<=t) one-tail	4.58E-05	
t Critical one-tail	1.654314	
P(T<=t) two-tail	9.16E-05	
t Critical two-tail	1.974718	

7.109

Difference in means	Power
0.5	0.339
0.75	0.746
1	0.959
1.25	0.997

Note that as the difference in means increases, the power increases.

7.110 As the degrees of freedom increase for small values of n, the value of t rapidly approaches the z score. As sample sizes get larger the t values are close to $z = 1.96$ but never become greater than 1.96.

7.111 The margin of error is a function of the sample size. Graphing the margin of error as a function of n, shows the margin of error decreases quite rapidly for smaller values of n, and then the decrease becomes less pronounced.

Case Study 7.2

```
Stem-and-leaf of 4 BR       N = 9
Leaf Unit = 10000


        1 23
        1 55
        1 7
        1
        2
        2 23
        2 4
        2
        2 9

Stem-and-leaf of 3 BR       N = 28
Leaf Unit = 10000


        0 6777
        0 8899
        1 01111
        1 22222223
        1 445
        1
        1 9
        2 0
        2
        2 5
        2 6
```

Both distributions appear skewed heavily to the right. It is more difficult to see this with the four-bedroom homes because the data set is very small. The Minitab output for the two-sample t test assuming unequal variances is given below. It appears that there is strong evidence to indicate there is a difference in mean selling prices of four bedroom and three bedroom homes. A one-sided alternative would make sense because it is logical to expect that four bedroom homes would sell for more than three bedroom homes. While these are not SRSs, one might justify using the t test if we treated these as samples of homes from all future homes that will be sold in West Lafayette, Indiana.

```
Two sample T for 4 BR vs 3 BR

         N       Mean     St Dev    SE Mean
4 BR     9      194944     57204     19068
3 BR    28      129546     49336      9324

95% CI for mu 4 BR - mu 3 BR: (19152, 111644)
T-Test mu 4 BR = mu 3 BR (vs not =): T = 3.08   P = 0.0095   DF = 12
```

Chapter 8
Inference for Proportions

Note: The calculations in this chapter were done on Minitab. You may see small differences in numerical values if you use a different software package. The conclusions should all be consistent however. All confidence intervals were calculated based on the Wilson estimate.

8.1 (0.16, 0.43).

8.2 (0.556, 0.644).

8.3 a) $\tilde{p} = 0.778$. **b)** $m = 0.272$. **c)** No, this result applies only to this salesperson and her customer base.

8.4 a) H_o: $p = 0.2$ H_a: $p > 0.2$. Use a one-sided alternative because we will decide to go with the upgrade only if more than 20% agree to the additional cost. **b)** $z = 1.186$. P-value = 0.117. **c)** No, the sample does not give strong enough evidence to conclude that more than 20% are willing to pay for the upgrade.

8.5 a) (0.2369, 0.4169). This interval could be found from the interval on proportion of employees who would answer "yes" by subtracting the interval endpoints from 1. This is because P (an employee says "yes") = 1 – P (an employee says "No"). Also, the standard errors are the same for each proportion, which results in the same interval widths. **b)** H_o: $p = 0.25$ H_a: $p \neq 0.25$. $z = 1.62$. Fail to reject H_o. The reasoning is the same as in part (a).

8.6 n = 93.

8.7 n = 381.

8.8 a) $\tilde{p} = 0.1932$. **b)** (0.124, 0.2624).

8.9 No, it is possible an applicant attended college but did not graduate. Therefore it may be possible that some applicants lied about which major they studied in college and having graduated.

8.10 a) $\tilde{p} = 0.8393$. **b)** (0.8072, 0.8714).

8.11 (0.7769, 0.9155).

8.12 (0.1266, 0.2644).

8.13 (0.5918, 0.722).

8.14 (0.186, 0.2016).

8.15 a) $\tilde{p} = 0.3172, SE_{\tilde{p}} = 0.01124$. **b)** (0.2952, 0.3392). **c)** No, this data does not explain cause and effect relationships.

8.16 (0.2064, 0.246).

8.17 a) No, the sample size is too small. **b)** Yes. **c)** No, we do not have 10 or more observations of successes and failures. **d)** Yes.

8.18 H_o: $p = 0.36$ H_a: $p \neq 0.36$. $z = 0.9317$. P-value = 0.3524. There is no evidence to believe the sample does not represent the population with respect to rural versus urban residence.

8.19 a) H_o: $p = 0.64$ H_a: $p \neq 0.64$. **b)** $z = -0.9317$. P-value = 0.3524. **c)** The results are the same as in problem 8.18. Fail to reject H_o.

8.20 n = 1048.

8.21 (0.1034, 0.2764).

8.22 H_o: $p = 0.48$ H_a: $p \neq 0.48$. $z = -1.79$. P-value = 0.0734. The results are significant at the 10% level but not at the 5% level.

8.23 a) H_o: $p = 0.5$ H_a: $p \neq 0.5$. $z = 1.34$. P-value = 0.1802. There is no significant evidence that Kerrich's coin does not have probability 0.5 of coming up heads. **b)** (0.4969, 0.5165).

8.24 a) H_o: $p = 0.5$, H_a: $p > 0.5$. $z = 1.7$. P-value = 0.0446. Yes, it appears that the majority of people prefer fresh-brewed coffee. **b)** (0.502, 0.7202).

8.25 a) H_o: $p = 0.384$ H_a: $p > 0.384$. **b)** $z = 3.13$. **c)** P-value = 0.0009. Reject H_o. **d)** (0.4933, 0.7339). This is convincing evidence. **e)** These free throws need to be considered a SRS of free throw shots he will take throughout the year.

8.26 n = 381.

8.27 n = 242.

8.28 a) higher. **b)** higher. **c)** lower. **d)** no influence on sample size.

8.29 n = 352, $m = 0.0436$.

8.30 n = 4715, $m = 0.0113$.

8.31

$\hat{p}$	$\tilde{p}$	m
0.1	0.1154	0.0614
0.2	0.2115	0.0785
0.3	0.3077	0.0887
0.4	0.4038	0.0943
0.5	0.5000	0.0961
0.6	0.5962	0.0943
0.7	0.6923	0.0887
0.8	0.7885	0.0785
0.9	0.8846	0.0614

8.32 If the survey uses a sample size of 500 rather than 100, the margin of error will be reduced by almost half. This will give a much better estimate for the true proportion of students who support an increase in fees.

8.33 a) $\mu_{\hat{p}_1} = p_1, \mu_{\hat{p}_2} = p_2, \sigma_{\hat{p}_1} = \dfrac{p_1(1-p_1)}{n_1}, \sigma_{\hat{p}_2} = \dfrac{p_2(1-p_2)}{n_2}$. **b)** $\mu_D = \mu_{\hat{p}_1} - \mu_{\hat{p}_2}$. **c)**

$$\sigma_D^2 = \dfrac{p_1(1-p_1)}{n_1} + \dfrac{p_2(1-p_2)}{n_2}.$$

8.34 (−0.0082, 0.2302).

8.35 (0.0298, 0.08).

8.36 H_o: $p_1 = p_2$ H_a: $p_1 \neq p_2$. z = 1.83. P-value = .0672. The results of this study are significant at the 10% level but not at the 5% level. This study gives fairly strong evidence different types of companies offer different types of benefits.

8.37 H_o: $p_1 = p_2$ H_a: $p_1 > p_2$. z = 4.46. P-value ≈ 0. Yes, it appears that customers who complain leave the HMO.

8.38 H_o: $p_1 = p_2$ H_a: $p_1 > p_2$. z = 1.82. P-value = 0.0344. Yes, the proportion of birth defects observed during the period of time that residents drank from the contaminated well is higher than the proportion after. We need to assume that the observations are independent and represent an SRS.

8.39 a) $\hat{p}_1 = 0.5107, \hat{p}_2 = 0.4082$. **b)** $SE_D = 0.0293$. **c)** (0.0266, 0.1776).

8.40 a) H_o: $p_1 = p_2$ H_a: $p_1 \neq p_2$. **b)** $\hat{p} = 0.454$. **c)** $SE_D = 0.0295$. **d)** z = 3.47, P-value = 0.0006. Yes, it appears that Tippecanoe County has a higher proportion of producers in favor of the checkoff program than Benton County.

8.41 a) H_o: $p_1 = p_2$ H_a: $p_1 \neq p_2$. **b)** z = 1.22, P-value = 0.2224. There is no evidence to suggest that there is a difference in tree preference between rural and urban populations. **c)** (-0.0205, 0.1386).

8.42 a) H_o: $p_1 = p_2$ H_a: $p_1 \neq p_2$, z = 5.07, P-value ≈ 0. This data provides strong evidence that the proportion of men college students employed during the summer is greater than women college students employed during the summer. **b)** (0.0443, 0.1369). Yes, this difference has practical importance. A difference of 4% can translate into hundreds of unemployed women from a large campus.

8.43 a) H_o: $p_1 = p_2$ H_a: $p_1 \neq p_2$, z = 5.33, P-value ≈ 0. There is a statistically significant difference in the proportion of the two types of shields removed. **b)** (0.2087, 0.4065). I would recommend the new tractors have a flip-up shield.

8.44 a) $\tilde{p}_F = 0.7903, \tilde{p}_M = 0.3955$. **b)** (0.264, 0.526). The data show that there is gender bias in the text because women are more often referred to with a juvenile reference.

8. 45 a) $\tilde{p}_1 = 0.3390$, $\tilde{p}_2 = 0.1451$, where population 1 represents the males and population 2 represents the females. (0.1477, 0.2402). **b)** The quantity that contributes the most to the standard error is $\dfrac{\tilde{p}_2(1 - \tilde{p}_2)}{n_2 + 2}$ because n_2 is a smaller sample size.

8.46 H_o: $p_1 = p_2$ H_a: $p_1 \neq p_2$, z = 5.22, P-value = 0. Based on this P-value there is gender bias.

8.47 H_o: $p_1 = p_2$ H_a: $p_1 > p_2$, z = 5.53, P-value = 0. Yes, the gender bias is significant.

8.48 (–0.1116, 0.0763). It does not appear that the proportion of applicants lying is changing over time.

8.49 a) $\tilde{p}_1 = 0.5488$, $\tilde{p}_2 = 0.5301$. **b)** SE = 0.0776. **c)** (–0.109, 0.1463) No, since the interval contains zero it does not appear that the Yankees are more likely to win at home.

8.50 H_o: $p_1 = p_2$ H_a: $p_1 \neq p_2$, z = -0.34, P-value = 0.733. The results do not give strong evidence that applicants are lying in different proportion than they did 6 months ago.

8.51 a) H_o: $p_1 = p_2$ H_a: $p_1 > p_2$ **b)** 0.5404. **c)** SE = 0.0786. **d)** z = 0.24, P-value = 0.4052. The sample does not give us reason to believe the Yankees win more games at home.

8.52 A 90% confidence interval on the difference in proportion of games won at home and games won on the road is (0.0456, 0.2929). It appears that the Mets do win more games at home.

8.53 H_o: $p_1 = p_2$ H_a: $p_1 < p_2$, where p_1 represents the proportion of men without the abnormal chromosome who had criminal records. z = -3.48, P-value = 0.001. The data supports the belief that abnormality in chromosomes is associated with increased criminality.

8.54 a) $\tilde{p}_1 = 0.8$, $\tilde{p}_2 = 0.557$, where population 1 represents the patients who took aspirin. **b)** (0.1027, 0.3833). **c)** H_o: $p_1 = p_2$ H_a: $p_1 > p_2$, z = 3.34, P-value = 0. The proportion of patients with favorable outcomes out of those who took aspirin is significantly greater than the proportion of patients with favorable outcomes who did not take aspirin.

8.55 a) (–0.4495, 0.0495). **b)** H_o: $p_1 = p_2$ H_a: $p_1 < p_2$, z = –1.37, P-value = 0.086. This data does not give a significant result at the 5% level but it is significant at the 10% level.

8.56 a) z = 1.62, P-value = 0.106. Based on this P-value it does not suggest that male college students are employed at a higher rate than female college students. **b)** Sample size plays a role in the significance of data. The larger the sample size, the more significant the results can be.

8.57 a) z = 1.93, P-value = 0.027. Based on this P-value, it appears that diazinon persists longer on plasterboard. **b)** As sample size increases the significance of the results increases.

8.58 a) 32, 180, (0.1124, 0.2143). **b)** (0.854, 0.9381). **c)** (0.6665, 0.7988) (66.7%, 79.9%).

8.59 a) H_o: $p_1 = p_2$ H_a: $p_1 \neq p_2$, z = 6.98, P-value = 0. Yes, the proportion of college graduates among internet users is significantly higher than the proportion among nonusers. **b)** (0.1142, 0.2019).

8.60 H_o: $p_1 = p_2$ H_a: $p_1 \neq p_2$, z = 5.59, P-value = 0. The proportion of nonusers with income less than $50,000 is significantly greater than the proportion of users with income less than $50,000. (0.0921, 0.1871).

8.61 The total number of users and nonusers, respectively, who answered the question about education are 1,132 and 852. The total number of users and nonusers, respectively, who answered the question about income are 871 and 677. The proportion of users who chose "Rather say not" is 0.2305. The proportion of nonusers who chose "Rather say not" is 0.2054. H_o: $p_1 = p_2$ H_a: $p_1 \neq p_2$, z = 1.34, P-value = 0.18. A 95% confidence interval is (−0.0116, 0.0615). The conclusion is that there is no significant difference between proportion of nonrespondents. The nonresponse rate is approximately 20%. This could bias the results.

8.62 a) Diehard: 121, Less loyal: 161. **b)** z = 4.85, P-value = 0. The diehard fans are more likely to have watched the Cubs as children. **c)** (0.141, 0.2975).

8.63 H_o: $p_1 = p_2$ H_a: $p_1 \neq p_2$, where p_1 represents the proportion of diehard fans that attend a Cubs game at least once a month. z = 9.07, P-value = 0. 95% confidence interval on the difference is (0.3743, 0.5623). Diehard fans are more likely to attend games at least once a month than the less loyal fans.

8.64 (0.7329, 0.7851).

8.65 779 people responded that they had at least one credit card. $0.41 \times 779 = 319$. The margin of error for a 95% confidence interval on the proportion of credit card holders who do not pay off the balance each month is 0.0344.

8.66 H_o: p = 0.485 H_a: p ≠ 0.485, z = 4.03, P-value = 0. The proportion of heavy players who are men is significantly different from the proportion of men in the US population.

8.67 The 95% confidence interval is (0.5509, 0.6713).

8.68 H_o: $p_1 = p_2$ H_a: $p_1 < p_2$ where p_1 represents the proportion of 4 - 5 year olds who sort correctly. The alternative hypothesis means that we expect older children to be better at sorting. z = -3.45 P-value ≈ 0. Based on this P-value, it appears that the 6-7 year age group has a higher proportion of children who sort correctly. The 90% confidence interval to describe the difference in proportions is (−0.4709, −0.1801).

8.69 H_o: p = 0.11 H_a: p < 0.11, z = −3.14, P-value = 0.001. The results indicate there has been a significant decrease in the proportion of nonconformities. We are assuming the sample used is a SRS from the process.

8.70 95% confidence interval for the new proportion of nonconformities is (0.0327, 0.0857). The 95% confidence interval on the difference between the new proportion and the old proportion is (-0.1004, -0.0122).

8.71 $\hat{p}_M = 0.227$, $\hat{p}_F = 0.1698$, H_o: $p_M = p_F$ H_a: $p_M \neq p_F$, where the proportions represent the proportion of male and female students who engage in binge drinking. z = 9.34, P-value = 0. The sample data provides strong statistical evidence in favor of the alternative hypothesis. The difference between the proportion of men who engage in binge drinking and the proportion of women is estimated to be (0.045, 0.0694) with a 95% confidence level.

8.72 a) (0.4259, 0.5091).

8.73 a) $p_o = 0.2515$. **b)** H_o: $p = 0.2515$ H_a: $p > 0.2515$, $z = 3.34$, P-value ≈ 0. Based on this data it appears that women are more likely to be in the top of their class than their proportion enrolled would suggest.

8.74 H_o: $p_1 = p_2$ H_a: $p_1 \neq p_2$ where p_1 represents the proportion of blacks at this convention who are vegetarians and p_2 represents the proportion of whites who are vegetarian. $z = -2.15$, P-value = 0.032. Yes, it appears that there is a higher proportion of whites who are vegetarian than blacks. This was not an SRS of all Seventh-Day Adventists; therefore, the conclusions hold only for those attending this convention. We certainly cannot generalize to the populations of all blacks and whites.

8.75 a) (−0.0141, −0.003). (Example 8.8 calculated a positive interval with the same magnitudes by taking the difference between those with high blood pressure and those without.) **b)** H_o: $p_1 = p_2$ H_a: $p_1 < p_2$, $z = -2.98$, P-value = 0.001. This study leads us to believe that death rates are higher among men with high blood pressure.

8.76 The hypotheses for each set of study data would be: H_o: $p_1 = p_2$ H_a: $p_1 \neq p_2$. For each study, p_1 represents the proportion of deaths among those taking aspirin and p_2 represents the proportion of deaths among those not taking aspirin. For the British study: $z = -0.50$ and the P-value = 0.309. This does not give conclusive evidence that taking aspirin reduces deaths due to cardiovascular disease. For the American study: $z = -5.0$ and the P-value = 0. This study gives statistically significant evidence that taking aspirin reduces death due to cardiovascular disease. These conclusions differ in two important ways: The British study had the doctors taking aspirin daily and the deaths included deaths due to stroke. The American study had the doctors taking aspirin every other day and the deaths counted were only those due to heart attack. This may explain the different outcomes.

8.77

n	m
10	0.526
30	0.322
350	0.253
100	0.180
200	0.128
500	0.081

8.78 a) $n = 767$. **b)** $n + 2 = 0.5 \left[\dfrac{z*}{m} \right]^2$.

8.79 Starting with a sample size of 20 for the first sample, it is not possible to guarantee a margin of error of 0.1 or less. $m = 1.645 \sqrt{\dfrac{.5(.5)}{20} + \dfrac{.5(.5)}{n_2}}$. This leads to a negative value for n_2, which is not feasible.

8.80 This proposal would not lead to trustworthy results using the techniques we have seen in this chapter. The sample sizes are too small to guarantee at least 10 observations of success and failures.

8.81 a) $p_o = 0.791$. **b)** $\hat{p} = 0.3897$, $z = -29.11$, P-value = 0. The proportion of Mexican-Americans on juries in this county is significantly lower than their proportion in the population. **c)** $z = -28.96$, P-value = 0. The results agree with the results in part (b).

Case Study 8.1

When comparing proportions of "girl" references to proportion of "boy" references, there does not appear to be any pattern that differentiates the male authors from the female authors. Texts 2, 3, 6, and 10 showed a significant difference between the two proportions (with P-value < 0.05) with proportion of "girl" references greater than proportion of "boy" references.

Case Study 8.2

p1hat	p2hat	n	z	P-value
0.6	0.4	15	1.0954	0.2733
0.6	0.4	25	1.4142	0.1573
0.6	0.4	50	2.0000	0.0455
0.6	0.4	75	2.4495	0.0143
0.6	0.4	100	2.8284	0.0047
0.6	0.4	500	6.3246	2.55E-10

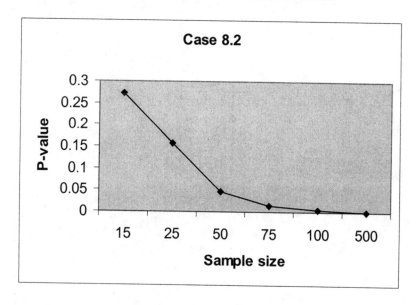

p1hat	p2hat	n	SE	Margin of Error
0.6	0.4	15	0.1789	0.3506
0.6	0.4	25	0.1386	0.2716
0.6	0.4	50	0.0980	0.1920
0.6	0.4	75	0.0800	0.1568
0.6	0.4	100	0.0693	0.1358
0.6	0.4	500	0.0310	0.0607

As the sample size increases, the significance of the hypothesis test increases and the margin of error decreases.

Chapter 9
Inference for Two-Way Tables

9.1 a)

	French Music Playing	French Music Not Playing
Purchased French Wine		
Did Not purchase French Wine		

b) Yes, having French music playing would be the explanatory variable. This is something the storeowner can control in an attempt to influence a customer's purchase, which is the response variable. This influences the outline with the explanatory variable as the columns and the response as the rows.

9.2

	40 years or less	Over 40 years	Totals
Terminated	30	80	110
Not Terminated	570	720	1290
Totals	600	800	1400

9.3 108/123 = 87.8% of successful firms and 34/47 = 72.3% of unsuccessful firms were offered exclusive territories.

9.4 123/170 = 72.3% of firms were successful and 142/170 = 83.5% of firms were offered exclusive contracts.

9.5 28 firms lacked exclusive territories and 27.6% were unsuccessful firms. The expected count is 28(47/170) = 7.74. If there is no association between success of a firm and having an exclusive contract, then we would expect the count of unsuccessful firms without exclusive contracts to be equal to the number of unsuccessful firms times the percent of all firms that did not have an exclusive contract.

9.6 123(142/170) = 102.74; the total number of successful firms is 123, the percent of firms that have exclusive territories is the total of "yes" exclusive territories, 142, the product of these numbers is divided by the overall total, 170. This gives you an expected count of 102.74.

9.7 $(5 - 1)(3 - 1) = 8$ degrees of freedom.

9.8 $.025 < P < .05$.

9.9 a) $\chi^2 = 10.95$. The value of $z^2 = (3.31)^2 = 10.95$. **b)** $(3.291)^2 = 10.83$. **c)** The statement of no relation between gender and label use is equivalent to stating that the proportion of female label users is equal to the proportion of male label users.

9.10 a)

	Not over 40	Over 40	Totals
Released	7	41	48
Not released	504	765	1269
Totals	511	806	1317

7 / 511 = 1.40% not over 40 was released. 41 / 806 = 5.1% over 40 was released. There appears to be a relationship. **b)** $\chi^2 = 12.29$, df = 1, and $P < .0005$. There is significant evidence that there is a relationship between employee's age and being released.

9.11 $\chi^2 = 50.81$, df = 2, $P < .0005$. The older employees appear to receive lower performance evaluations. They are twice as likely to fall into the lower performance category but only 1/3 as likely to fall in the highest category.

9.12 a) $\chi^2 = 10.77$, df = 3, $.01 < P < .02$. There is strong evidence that there is a relationship between majors and gender.

b)

	Female	Male
Accounting	30.22%	34.78%
Administration	40.44%	24.84%
Economics	2.22%	3.73%
Finance	27.11%	36.65%

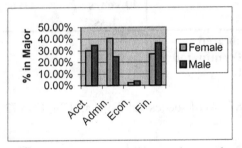

A large percentage of women have Administration for their major, while men have a larger proportion with finance. **c)** The largest terms are in Administration for both male and female genders. More females and fewer men are enrolled than expected. **d)** Even though the expected count of 4.6 is less than 5, we can still say the test is acceptable because it is such a small deviation. **e)** 386 responded; 46.5% did not respond to the questionnaire.

9.13 $\chi^2 = 3.277$, df = 4, $P > .25$. The data shows no evidence that the response rates are related to industry.

9.14 a) H$_0$: $p_1 = p_2$, where p_1 and p_2 are the proportions of women in each city. p_1: 203/241 = .842; p_2: 150/218 = .688. z = 3.92, $P < .0004$. **b)** $\chi^2 = 15.33$, which equals $(3.92)^2 = 15.33$. With a df = 1, P-value < .0005. **c)** (.0764, .2299).

9.15 With a df = 4, $P > .25$. There is not enough statistical evidence to tell if the 2 stores have different income distributions.

9.16 a)

	Black %
Household	7%
Nonhousehold	14%
Teachers	13%

b)

	Black	**Other**	**Total**
Household	172	2283	2455
Nonhousehold	167	1024	1191
Teachers	86	573	659
Total	425	3880	4305

c) Yes, because expected counts are all 5 or more.
H_o: There is no relationship between racial background and being a childcare worker.
H_a: There is a relationship between race and being a childcare worker.
d) With a df = 2 the $P < .0005$. **e)** There is statistical evidence that there is an association between being a childcare worker and racial background.

9.17 a)

	Response Rate %
Letter	43.70%
Phone Call	68.20%
None	20.60%

b) H_o: There is no relationship between intervention type and response rate. H_a: There is a relationship. **c)** $\chi^2 = 163.413$, df = 2, P is essentially 0. There is significant evidence that intervention is related to response rate with a phone call being more effective than a letter.

9.18 a) Those who received letters positively responded 51.2% of the time. Those who received no letter positively responded 52.6%. **b)** H_o: There is no relationship between a prenotification letter and physicians' responding. $\chi^2 = 1.914$, df = 1, and $.15 < P < .20$. There is no relation between prenotification letters and physicians response rate due to a lack of statistical evidence.

9.19 Based on the information from the two previous studies, recognize there will be considerable nonresponse so an initial survey must have a larger sample size so the number of respondents will be large enough to have reliable results. Also recognize that by making some contact with the survey individuals, one can increase the response rate.

9.20 $\chi^2 = 38.41$, df = 1, and a $P < .0005$. There is a relationship between doing well in one year and doing well again in the next. Conclude that the fund performance is persistent.

9.21 $z = 6.1977$, $P < .0004$. $(6.1977)^2 = \chi^2$ or 38.41.

9.22 A retrospective study will give the same difference in proportions as a prospective study and will also give the same standard error for use in calculating the z statistic. For a prospective study the two proportions are 85/120 and 37/120. For the retrospective study the proportions are 85/122 and 35/118.

9.23 $\chi^2 = 19.683$, df = 1, and $P < .0005$. There is strong evidence of a relationship between winning or losing this year and winning or losing next year. The difference between the study in exercise 9.20 and this study shows that in the current study, winning last year means there is a higher chance of losing next year. This result is opposite of the results in exercise 9.20.

9.24

	Men %	Women
Completed	81.2%	18.8%
Still enrolled	80.2%	19.8%
Dropped out	70.8%	29.2%

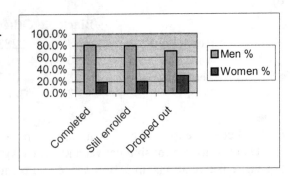

H_o: There is no relationship between gender and status in college. H_a: There is a relationship. $\chi^2 = 13.40$, df = 2, and $.001 < P < .0025$. There is strong evidence that there is a relationship between gender and status in college. Other factors that may influence drop out rates are: age of students, degree subject and job prospects (both within academia and outside academia).

9.25 a) For the data set comparing on time flights and delayed flights for Alaska Airlines and America West, the χ^2 statistic is 13.572 with a P-value ≈ 0. This is a statistically significant result showing that America West has fewer delayed flights. **b)** When running the test for the five different cities the following results are found. For LA $\chi^2 = 3.241$, P-value = 0.072. For Phoenix $\chi^2 = 2.346$, P-value = 0.126. For San Diego $\chi^2 = 4.845$, P-value = 0.028. For San Francisco $\chi^2 = 21.223$, P-value = 0. For Seattle $\chi^2 = 14.903$, P-value = 0. **c)** The effect of city where flights originate, which illustrates Simpson's Paradox, shows statistically significant results.

9.26 $\chi^2 = 6.556$, df = 6, and $P > .25$. The results of this study show no relationship between receiving a student loan and type of field studied.

9.27 Minitab calculates $\chi^2 = 43.487$, df = 12, P is essentially 0. There is strong evidence of a relationship between the PEOPLE score and field of study. Science has a much larger percentage of students scoring Low on the PEOPLE score than other fields. Liberal arts and education has a much larger percentage of students scoring high on the PEOPLE score than other fields.

9.28 $\chi^2 = 359.677$, df = 8, and the P-value is essentially 0.

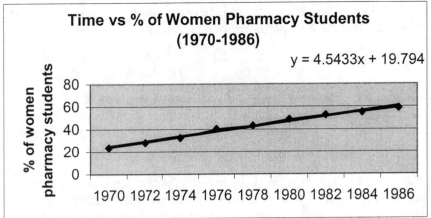

There is a statistically significant relationship between time and the percentage of women enrolled as pharmacy students. This is seen as an increasing trend over time. Yes, the plot is roughly linear. Least squares line: y = 4.5433x + 19.794. The data were coded so that x represents the data point number. For example, the first observation given was for 1970. This translates to an x = 1. The years are multiples of twos and there are nine different pairs of data.

9.29

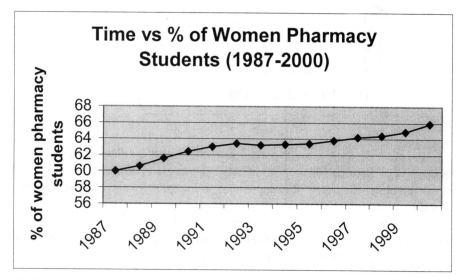

From 1970 to 2000 the percent of women pharmacy students has been increasing. However, when analyzing the data from 1987 through 2000, the statistical evidence shows a significant increase (χ^2 = 6.61, df = 2, and 0.25 < P-value < 0.05) but the percentage increase does not seem very high. From 1970 to 1986, the sample results showed an increase from approximately 24% to 59%. From 1987 to 2000 the increase rose from 60% to 66%.

9.30 χ^2 = 852.433 DF = 1, P-value = 0.000. Problem 8.81 gave a z statistic equal to 29.11. 29.11^2 = 847.4. The error is due to round off.

9.31 a) It makes sense to compare percentages by source of pet because this is the explanatory variable and the more interesting statistics. Use column percents.

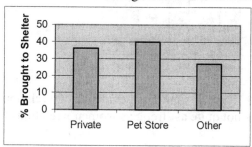

b) χ^2 = 6.61, df = 2, and .025 < P < .05. There is significant evidence that there is a relationship between the source of the cat and whether or not the cat is brought to the shelter.

9.32 χ^2 = 26.942, df = 2, and P = 0. There is significant evidence that there is a relationship between the source of the dog and whether or not the dog is brought to the shelter.

9.33 Comparing the source variable for the two control groups of cats and dogs, χ^2 = 90.624, df = 2, P-value = 0. It appears that there is a statistically significant relationship between type of pet and the source of the pet. The following column chart shows the different sample percentages for the source of the two pet types: cat or dog.

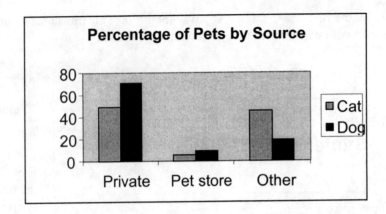

9.34 Minitab calculates $\chi^2 = 8.41$, df = 4, and a P-value = .077 for cats. Minitab calculates $\chi^2 = 33.21$, df = 4, and P < .0005 for dogs. The P-value for the test on cats has increased with more cells. The result is no longer significant at the 5% level. It is significant at the 10% level. The P-value for dogs has stayed very small.

9.35 For problem 9.12–independence using data from a single sample (model 2). 9.13–many samples (model 1) 9.14–two different samples (model 1) 9.16 – model 2

9.36 a) There is strong evidence that a higher proportion of men die in such situations with $\chi^2 = 332.205$, df = 1, and P-value essentially 0. This probably occurred because women and children are usually instructed to go first. **b)** $\chi^2 = 103.76$, df = 2, and the P-value is essentially 0. There is significant evidence of a relationship between women's deaths and social class.

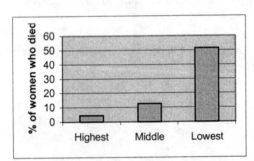 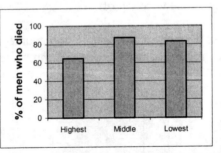

c) $\chi^2 = 34.621$, df = 2, and the P-value is essentially 0. There is significant evidence of a relationship between men's deaths and social class; however, it is not quite as strong as women's relationship.

9.37 a) $\chi^2 = 24.9$, df = 3, and P-value < .0005. There is a relationship between gender and sports goals. It appears that men have a higher percentage in both of the HSC categories while women have a higher percentage in both of the LSC categories. **b)** $\chi^2 = 23.45$, df =1, and P-value < .0005. This result shows that the percentages of females and males in the HSC and LSC categories are different. **c)** $\chi^2 = .03$, df =1, and P = .863. This shows no evidence of a relationship between the HM and LM categories and gender. **d)** In regards to sports goals, there is evidence of a relationship between gender and sports goals. The relationship appears to exist between the variable *social comparison* goal but no relationship exists between gender and *mastery* goals.

9.38 a)

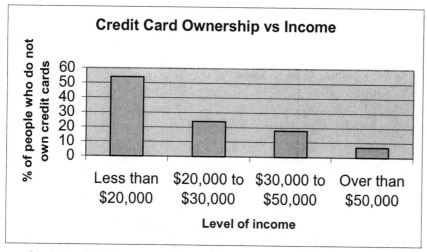

b) A much higher percentage of lower income people do not own credit cards. As income level increases, the percentage that does not own credit cards decreases. **c)** The percentages do not add up to 100%. Also, we do not know how many out of 1,025 people answered the income questions. It is expected that some people may not give out information about their income. Without sample sizes for each income category we cannot perform a significance test.

Case Study 9.1

Characteristic	Chi-square Value	P-value
Age	26.711	0.00
Gender	2.178	0.14
Education	72.929	0.00
Income	65.730	0.00
Occupation	67.835	0.00
Race	4.329	0.363

The table above shows the Chi-square values and P-values for the six different demographic characteristics in the problem. Students may choose many different ways to graphically display the data. Note that there is a significant relationship between age, education level, household income, and occupational category and whether or not the individual chooses to use the World Wide Web for their travel information source or some other source. Gender and race do not show significant results.

Chapter 10
Inference for Regression

10.1 a) $\beta_0 = 4.7$. This number means that when the US market is flat, the average overseas return will be 4.7%. **b)** $\beta_1 = 0.66$. This number means that for every 1% increase in the US market, the overseas return will increase 0.66%. **c)** $y_i = 4.7 + 0.66x_i + \varepsilon_i$. ε_i is the error term that represents variation in overseas returns.

10.2 a) Total cost = $\beta_0 + \beta_1 \times$ Number of Units + ε. β_0 represents the fixed cost for setting up the production line. **b)** $\beta_1 > 0$. **c)** ε.

10.3 a)

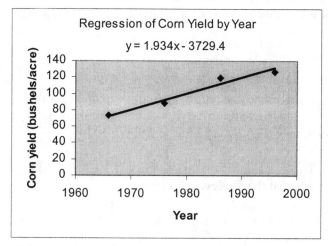

Yes, the data points show a strong linear relationship. **b)** See plot above. **c)** s = 6.8473. **d)** The estimates for β_0 and β_1 are –3729.4 and 1.93, respectively.

10.4 The scatterplot shows a fairly strong linear relationship in the positive direction.
$\hat{y} = 2.666 + 0.627x$.

10.5 $b_1 = 0.627$, $SE_{b1} = 0.0992$, H_o: $\beta_1 = 0$ H_a: $\beta_1 > 0$, t = 6.32, df = 49, P-value ≈ 0. There is significant evidence to conclude that β_1 is greater than 0.

10.6 (0.4277, 0.8263).

10.7 Chance plays a role in the performance of a fund. The group of mutual funds that performed well last year will be influenced by chance this year and will likely see a smaller return than last year.

10.8 Since chance influenced the performance of those companies that did extremely well or extremely poorly, chance will also influence their performance in coming years. This means that over time, companies that did extremely well will likely have a year or two when they are not considered the best. Likewise, companies that did very poorly will see an improvement in their performance.

10.9 a) r = 0.67, t = 6.318, df = 49, P-value < 0.0005. Based on this P-value it is reasonable to conclude that there is a positive correlation between return on treasury bills and inflation. **b)** Verify.

10.10 a) $\hat{y} = -12.24 + 0.212x$. **b)** Average wages = \$391, average length of service = 70.5 months. **c)** Use t = 2.853.

10.11 a) The vertical stacks appear because age has been truncated to the nearest year. This results in many x's with the same numerical values. **b)** Older men have more experience. Younger men may have a more current education. It does not appear that age has a strong relationship with income. **c)** $\hat{y} = 24874 + 892x$ The slope tells us that for every year a man is older his income increases by \$892.

10.12 a) The large sample size almost guarantees that there will be a statistically significant result. **b)** (771, 1013). **c)** (732, 1052).

10.13 a) The close cluster of values between 0 and 100,000 and the scattered points above 100,000 indicate a distribution skewed to the right for each value of x. **b)** Large sample sizes help make up for any skewness in the sample data.

10.14 (20536, 29212).

10.15 a) If there is no inflation in a particular year, β_0 represents the return on T-bills. In order for the government to issue treasury bills, there must be a positive return. **b)** $b_0 = 2.666$ and $SE_{b_0} = 0.5039$. **c)** Yes, there is good evidence that $\beta_0 > 0$. (P-value < 0.0001). **d)** $2.666 \pm 2.009(0.5039)$.

10.16 For n = 20, t = -2.45, 0.01 < P-value < 0.02. This is a significant result. For n = 10, t = -1.633, 0.05 < P-value < 0.10. This result is not significant at the 5% level.

10.17 a)

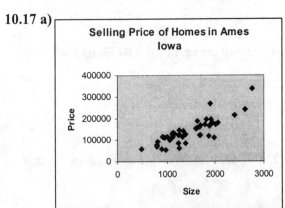

$r^2 = 0.696$. Yes, size is helpful in predicting selling price.
b) $\hat{y} = 4786 + 93x$, t = 10.5, P-value < 0.0001. The small P-value means that there is a significant linear relationship between size and selling price.

10.18 a)

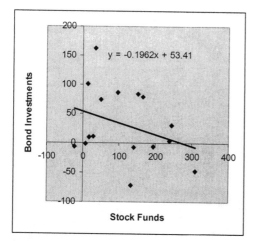

The data suggest a negative linear relationship between stock funds and bond investments. **b)** H_o: $\beta_1 = 0$ H_a: $\beta_1 < 0$, t = −1.27, P-value = 0.113. Conclude that there is not enough evidence to say that the slope is less than zero. **c)** The scatterplot does not show any kind of relationship between the two variables.

10.19 r = 0.8345, t = 10.5, P-value < 0.0001. Conclude that the population correlation is greater than zero.

10.20 r = −0.321, t = −1.27, P-value = 0.113. There is no significant evidence that the correlation is less than zero.

10.21 a) No, the value of r actually increases so our conclusion would not change. **b)** Removing these four pairs of data lowers the value of r but not enough for us to change our conclusions.

10.22 a) $r^2 = 0.7998$. The data show a strong positive linear relationship.

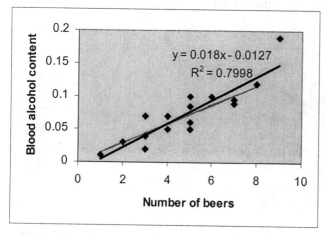

b) H_o: $\beta_1 = 0$ H_a: $\beta_1 > 0$, t = 7.48, P-value < 0.0001. Conclude that drinking more beers increases blood alcohol on the average.

10.23 a)

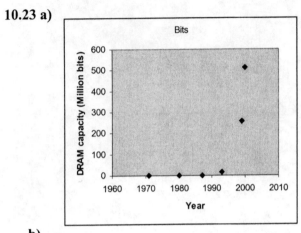

b)

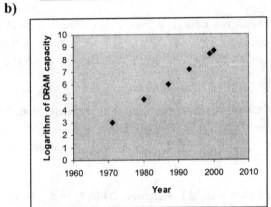

c) $\hat{y} = -379 + 0.194x$. (0.18765, 0.20035).

10.24 a) Yes, this student has the largest residual. No, it does not appear extreme in the x direction.

b)

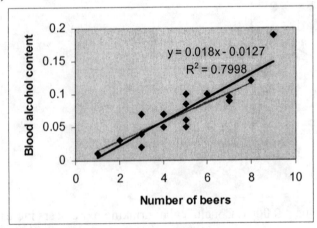

The regression line, the r^2 value and the P-value for a test on slope do not change greatly. This was not an influential observation.

10.25 a) Verify. **b)** 423.2 ± 26.1456.

10.26 a) Verify. **b)** (0.561, 9.410).

10.27 a) Verify. **b)** (49780, 53496). **c)** (–41735, 145010). This interval is not very useful.

10.28 The narrow interval describes an average. The wider interval predicts an individual's income. There is more variation in individual incomes than in average income.

10.29 (58918, 62200).

10.30 a) (4.4715, 5.5005). **b)** We need the standard error on y. We don't have that in this output.

10.31 a) (44446, 55314). **b)** More data was used to develop the confidence interval in exercise 10.27 than was used in part (a) of this problem. Since standard errors are a function of sample size, when we have large samples we have smaller standard errors.

10.32 a) $\bar{x} = 1441.58$, $\bar{y} = 138595.2$, $\hat{y} = 4786 + 92.8x$. For x = 144.58, y = 138593.5 (The difference is due to round-off error.) **b)** ($76967, $200224).

10.33 The 90% prediction interval for Steve's BAC is (.04, .11424). He should not drive.

10.34 ($211619, $243494).

10.35 $SE_{b1} = 0.00994$.

10.36 $s_x^2 = 9.6123$, (0.563, 9.409).

10.37 H_o: $\beta_1 = 0$ H_a: $\beta_1 \neq 0$, t = 6.3177, F = 39.914, t^2 = F, P-value = 7.563E-08.

10.38 a) 189.705 + 232.89 = 422.596. **b)** Total: 51 – 1 = 50, Residual: 51 – 2 = 49. **c)** MS_{Reg} = 189.705/1, MS_{Res} = (232.89/49) = 4.753. **d)** F = (189.705/4.753) = 39.913.

10.39 a) r^2 = (189.705/422.596) = 0.4489. **b)** $s = \sqrt{\dfrac{232.89}{49}} = 2.1801$.

10.40 The row reads:

DF	SS	MS
28	10152.4	362.586

10.41 r^2 = (3445.9/13598.3) = 0.2534, $s = \sqrt{\dfrac{10152.4}{24}} = 19.042$.

10.42 $SE_{b1} = 0.215$, (0.297, 1.029).

10.43 a) H_o: $\beta_1 = 0$ H_a: $\beta_1 \neq 0$, t = 6.041, P-value = 0.0001. Yes, this data gives a statistically significant result. Reputation helps explain profitability. **b)** r^2 = 0.1936. 19.36% of the variation in profit can be explained by the reputation of the company. **c)** Statistical significance does not always translate in practical significance. While there is some relationship between reputation and profitability, reputation explains a small percentage of the variation in profitability. There are likely many more variables that would help predict profitability of a company.

10.44 Slope tells how much the profitability will increase for every one point increase in a company's reputation. (0.022, 0.056).

10.45 The 95% confidence interval for mean profitability for companies with a reputation of 7 is (0.110604, 0.141804) with appropriate round-off error.

10.46 A prediction interval will be wider than the confidence interval. There is much more variation in a single company's profitability than in the average profitability for all companies with a reputation score of 7. The 95% prediction interval is (-0.01766, 0.27006).

10.47 The F statistic is equal to the t statistic squared. The P-values will be the same. $F = 36.492 = 6.041^2$.

10.48 $s^2 = (SS_{error}/df) = (.78963/153) = 0.005195$, $s = (0.005195)^{1/2} = 0.072076$.

10.49 $r^2 = (SS_{model}/SS_{total}) = 0.1936$

10.50 $r = 0.44$, $t = 6.041$, P-value = 0.0001. Yes, this data provides good evidence that the population correlation is positive.

10.51 The relationship between price and age of house has a moderately strong negative relationship. 46.5% of the variation in selling price can be explained by age of home. One would expect the price of a home to decrease as the home ages. For each year the house ages, the average price decreases by $1,334.50. New houses sell for $189,226 on average. This is the value of the intercept.

10.52 **a)** (−1749.8, −919.2). **b)** H_o: $\beta_1 = 0$ H_a: $\beta_1 < 0$, $t = −6.46$, P-value ≈ 0. Yes, there is strong evidence that there is a negative linear relationship between age and home price.

10.53 **a)** ($159,569, $192,193). **b)** ($93,236, $258,526). **c)** Individual prices of homes of the same size have much more variation than the average of many homes, all the same size.

10.54

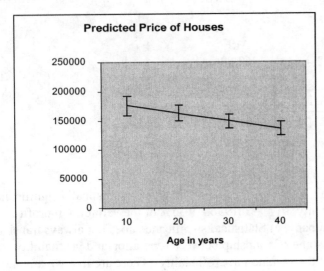

10.55 ($139252, $159130).

10.56 a)

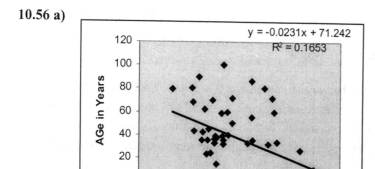

The relationship between size and age is as we expected. There is a slight negative linear relationship. As the size of the home gets larger, we see that the age of the home gets smaller. Yes, newer homes tend to be larger. **b)** Yes, it appears that age can help predict the price of a home if the size is known. R = 0.6217.

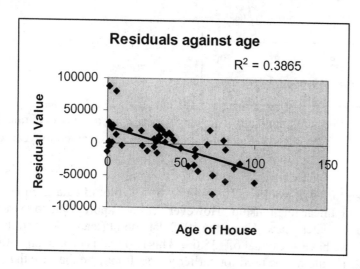

10.57

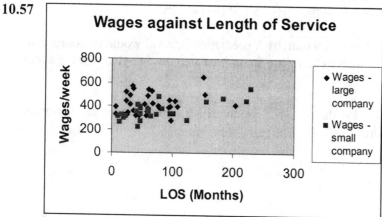

It appears that women with large companies generally have higher wages. It is probably easier to predict wages from LOS for the group of women who work for small companies.

10.58 H_o: $\mu_{wages\text{-}large}$ = $\mu_{wages\text{-}small}$ Ha: $\mu_{wages\text{-}large}$ ≠ $\mu_{wages\text{-}small}$, t = 3.02, P-value = 0.0038. There is a significant difference in wages. H_o: $\mu_{LOS\text{-}large}$ = $\mu_{LOS\text{-}small}$ Ha: $\mu_{LOS\text{-}large}$ ≠ $\mu_{LOS\text{-}small}$, t = -0.819, P-value = 0.4177. There is no significant difference in wages.

10.59 For regressing wages on length of service for large companies, $\hat{y} = 390 + 0.425x$, t = 1.27, P-value = 0.2134. There is not a significant linear relationship between LOS and wages for large companies. For regressing wages on length of service for small companies, $\hat{y} = 289 + 0.84x$, t = 4.49, P-value = 0.00017. There is a significant linear relationship between wages and length of service for small companies.

10.60 a)

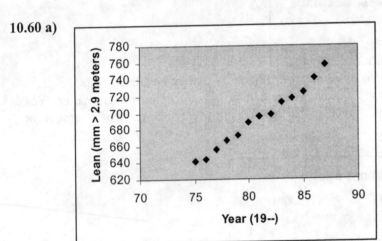

The plot shows a strong positive linear relationship. The lean is increasing at a positive rate. **b)** The regression line is: $\hat{y} = -61.12 + 9.32x$. 98.8% of the variation in lean is explained by year. **c)** (8.636, 10.0).

10.61 a) The predicted amount of lean for 1918 would be 106.64 mm. **b)** The plot of data from 1975 through 1987 shows a very strong linear relationship. However, it is not appropriate to extrapolate that relationship for earlier years or later years. Using the 1918 data point (lean = 71) and its predicted value (lean = 106.64) we have a residual of –35.64. This residual is clearly an outlier and therefore the prediction formula should not be used for earlier years. It may be the case that the lean was increasing at a much slower rate in the early part of the century.

10.62 a) The predicted lean in 2000 would be 870.9 mm. **b)** A prediction interval would be appropriate for estimating the lean in 2000. We want to know the amount of lean for that year, not the average lean over the course of the year.

10.63 H_o: $\beta_1 = 0$ H_a: $\beta_1 \neq 0$, t = 2.16, 0.02 < P-value < 0.04. Yes, there is a significant linear relationship between pretest and final exam scores.

Case Study 10.1

a)

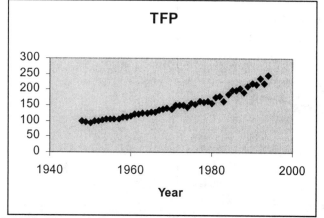

Around 1980 the rate of increase of TFP started to go up. TFP started to increase at a faster rate. The variation also appears to have increased.

b)

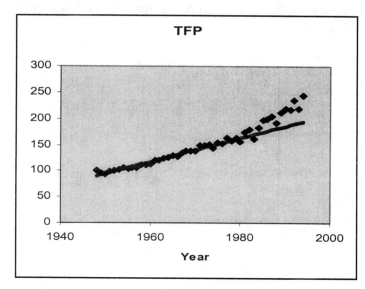

c) (2.127, 2.411).
d) (4.012, 6.911).

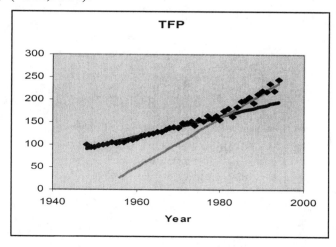

Case Study 10.2

a)

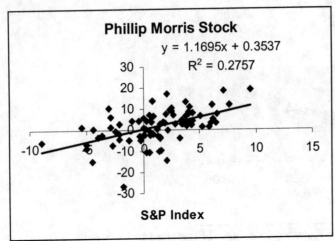

b) (0.82, 1.52). **c)** Data points 33 and 73 have large negative residuals. These are not likely to be influential because many other data points anchor them above. **d)** Aside from the two low outliers, the residuals appear fairly normal. **e)** (6.653, 11.597).

Chapter 11
Multiple Regression

11.1 a) The response variable is bank assets. **b)** The explanatory variables are the number of banks and deposits. **c)** There are two explanatory variables; therefore, p = 2. **d)** The sample size is 54; therefore, n = 54.

11.2

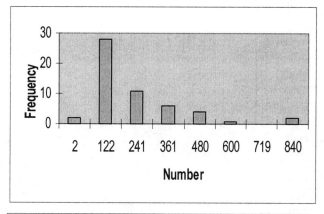

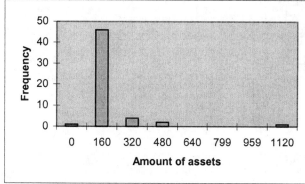

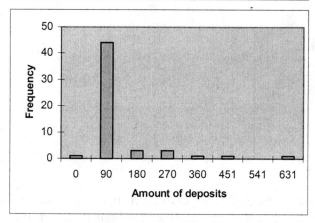

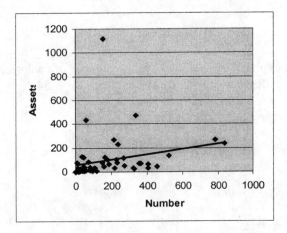

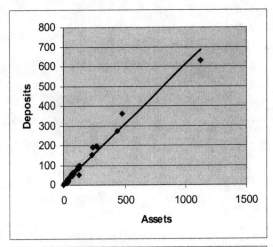

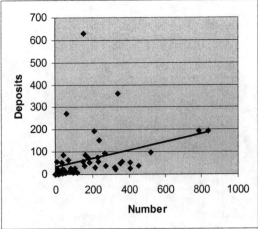

The distribution of the number of banks, the assets, and the deposits each appear to be skewed to the right with at least one outlier. Texas and Illinois each have a significantly higher number of banks than the other states or other area. The state of New York has a significantly larger amount of deposits and assets than any other state or other area. New York is by far the most significant outlier of the data set.

11.3 The distribution of the sales of DJIA companies is skewed to the right with two possible outliers when considering the sales of Wal-Mart and General Motors compared to the other DJIA companies.

No, there are no companies that are outliers in assets that are also outliers in the form of sales. We should not be surprised that Wal-Mart has high sales relative to its assets because Wal-Mart's primary business function is the distribution of products to final users. This would require less in the form of assets and increase the amount of sales.

11.4 The distribution of the profits of the DJIA companies appears to be slightly skewed to the right; however, certainly not as skewed as assets or sales. The distribution for profits also does not appear to have any outliers. One aspect of the distribution that Excel's descriptive statistics fails to capture is the large amount of companies whose profits were between 7 and 8 billion.

11.5

Correlation	Assets	Sales	Profits
Assets	1		
Sales	0.642513	1	
Profits	0.526326	0.569048	1

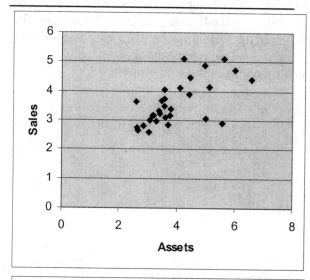

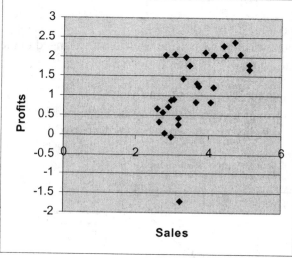

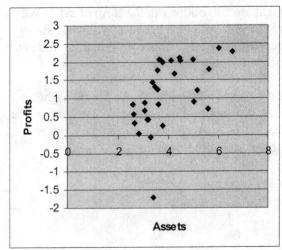

The largest difference between the analysis of the original variables and the logarithmic variables is the difference between the correlation of assets and sales. With the original analysis the correlation was r = 0.45 and once adjusted the correlation increased to r = 0.64. The correlation between profits and assets decreased slightly after the new analysis, while the correlation between sales and profits increased slightly. Using the logarithm transformation did indeed reduce the skew of the distributions while also decreasing the spread of the data points in the scatter plots.

11.6 Excel **SPSS**
$b_0 = 2.340454802$ $b_0 = 2.340$
$b_1 = 0.007406337$ $b_1 = 7.406E\text{-}03$
$b_2 = 0.026100013$ $b_2 = 2.610E\text{-}02$
Minitab **SAS**
$b_0 = 2.3405$ $b_0 = 2.34045$
$b_1 = 0.007406$ $b_1 = 0.00741$
$b_2 = 0.02610$ $b_2 = 0.02610$

11.7 Regression Equation:
log (profits) = −1.49842 + 0.238021 x log (Assets) + 0.478135 x log (Sales)

11.8 New Regression Coefficients: $b_0 = 2.345977$, $b_1 = 0.007127$, $b_2 = 0.026381$
Once Citigroup was removed from the regression analysis, the regression coefficients changed to the new values above. b_0 and b_2 both slightly increased, while b_1 was slightly decreased.

11.9 New Regression Coefficients: $b_0 = 1.554698$, $b_1 = 0.004965$, $b_2 = 0.055349$
Once General Motors and Wal-Mart were removed from the regression analysis, the regression coefficients changed to the new values above. b_0 and b_2 both increased, while b_1 decreased.

11.10

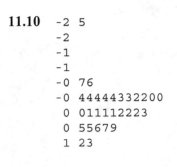

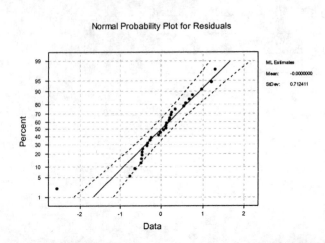

11.11

Excel
s = 2.449581635
s^2 = 6.000450185
name for s: Standard Error

SPSS
s = 2.44958
s^2 = 6.000
name for s: Standard Error of the Estimate

Minitab
s = 2.450
s^2 = 6.000
name for s: S

SAS
s = 2.44958
s^2 = 6.00045
name for s: Root Mean Square Error (MSE)

11.12 s_y = 3.036641161. We expect s to be smaller than s_y because we expect assets and sales to have some effect upon profits. Although there are many variables that affect the response variable profits, a smaller value for s when considering the effects of sales and assets demonstrates their contribution towards explaining the response in the variability of profits.

11.13 a)

Market Share

Column1	
Mean	8.96
Standard deviation	7.74
Median	8.85
Minimum	1.3
Maximum	27.50
Q1	2.80
Q3	11.60

Accounts

Column1	
Mean	794
Standard deviation	886
Median	509
Minimum	125
Maximum	2500
Q1	134
Q3	909

Assets

Column1	
Mean	48.91
Standard deviation	76.16
Median	15.35
Minimum	1.30
Maximum	219.00
Q1	5.90
Q3	38.80

b) Market Share

```
0 | 1 2 3 4
0 | 8 9
1 | 0 2 3
1 |
2 |
2 | 8
```

Accounts

```
0 | 1 1 1 2 4
0 | 6 6 9
1 |
1 |
2 | 3
2 | 5
```

Assets

```
0 | 0 0 0 0 1 2 2 4
0 |
1 |
1 | 6
2 | 2
2 |
```

c) All three stem plots are skewed to the right. The market share data set has one outlier, and both Accounts and Assets each have two outliers within the distribution of the set.

11.14 a)

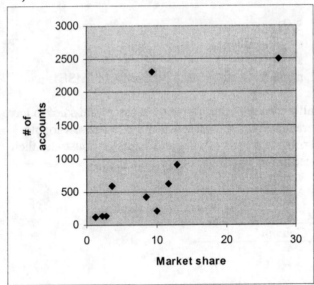

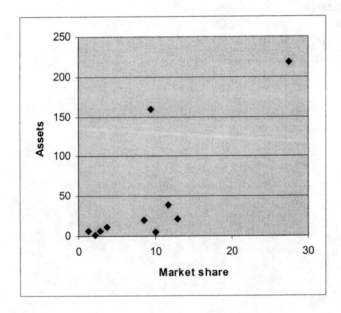

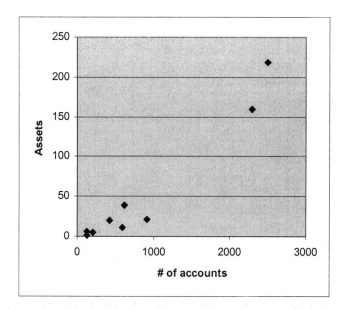

b) Each of the relationships between the market share, number of accounts and assets appears to be positively correlated, with the strongest being assets versus number of accounts. There also appears to be two outliers with each of the three scatter plots. These outliers are the online brokerage firms of Charles Schwab and Fidelity. Charles Schwab is an obvious outlier in each of the examined variables; however, Fidelity is an outlier only in the number of accounts and assets. The market share for Fidelity seems lower than it should be. This factor could be responsible for a lower correlation between market share and the other variables.

c)

	Market share	Accounts	Assets
Market share	1		
Accounts	0.75318288	1	
Assets	0.7801696	0.968272	1

11.15 a) Market Share = 5.159 + −0.000312 × Accounts + 0.08277 × Assets.
   b) Regression Standard Error (s) = 5.4876.

11.16 a)

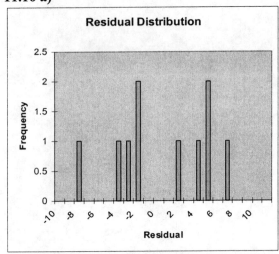

There may be one possible outlier with regard to Fidelity, or observation #5, which has a residual value of −8.

b)

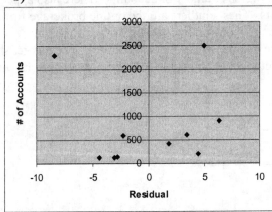

Again, the two outliers are Charles Schwab and Fidelity.

c)

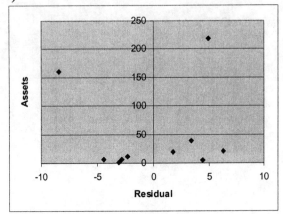

Again, the two outliers are Charles Schwab and Fidelity.

11.17

Market Share	
Mean	6.6
Standard deviation	4.6
Median	6.0
Minimum	1.3
Maximum	12.9
Q1	2.5
Q3	10.8

Accounts	
Mean	392
Standard deviation	292
Median	317
Minimum	125
Maximum	909
Q1	132
Q3	603

Assets	
Mean	13.8
Standard deviation	12.3
Median	9.0
Minimum	1.3
Maximum	38.8
Q1	5.7
Q3	19.8

b)) Market Share   Accounts   Assets

```
0 | 1  2  3  4      0 | 1  1  1  2  4      0 | 1  6  6  7
0 | 8               0 | 6  6  9            1 | 1
1 | 0  2  3         1 |                    2 | 0  1
1 |                 1 |                    3 | 9
```

c) The distribution of brokerage firms without the data for Schwab and Fidelity has a much shorter range and no outliers compared to the results of 11.13. The largest effect was on the mean and standard deviation.

11.18 a)

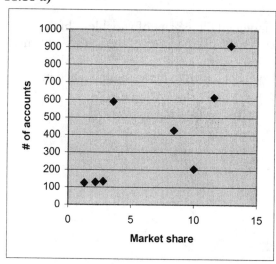

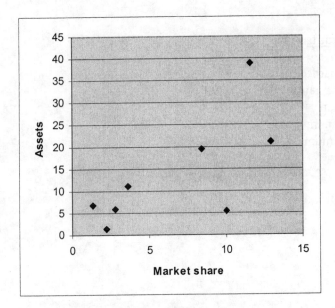

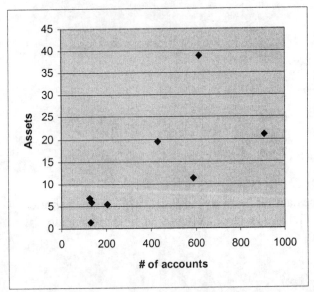

b) There appears to be moderate positive correlation among all three pairs of variables. In the absence of Schwab and Fidelity it is much easier to see the relative position of the brokerage firms to each other with respect to the different variables.

c) The correlation between the variables has been reduced compared to the values obtained in exercise 11.14, and the values are consistently around (r = 0.7).

	Market share	*Accounts*	*Assets*
Market share	1		
Accounts	0.711784	1	
Assets	0.710687	0.707353	1

11.19 a) Market Share = 1.845 + 0.00663 × Accounts + 0.1566 × Assets.
   b) Regression standard error (s) = 3.50.
   The coefficients of the regression equation have all changed when a regression analysis was done without Schwab and Fidelity. The standard error (s) was also reduced.

11.20 a)

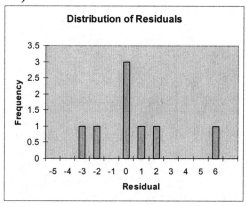

There is a possible outlier for Datek with a residual value of 6.
b)

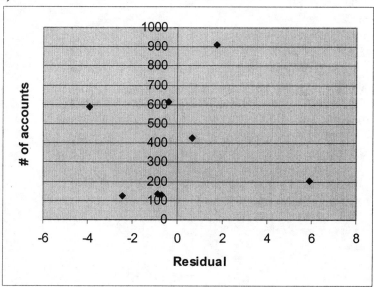

The distribution appears well spread out with no obvious trend.

c)

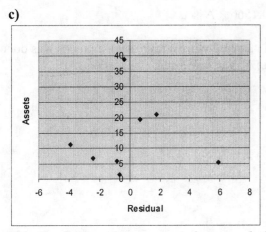

This distribution also appears to have no obvious trend, with one possible outlier, TD Waterhouse.

11.21 a)

Gross Total Sales	
Mean	320.30
Standard error	36.02
Median	263.29
Standard deviation	180.09
Skewness	1.66
Range	798.20
Minimum	92.30
Maximum	890.50

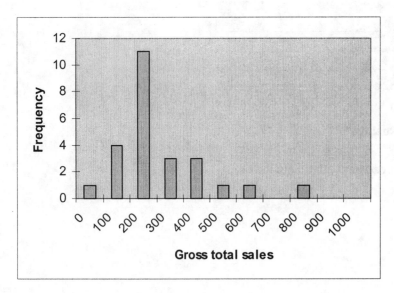

	Cash Items
Mean	20.52
Standard error	2.36
Median	19.00
Standard deviation	11.80
Skewness	1.26
Range	50.00
Minimum	5.00
Maximum	55.00

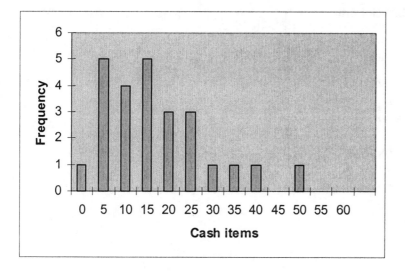

	Check Items
Mean	20.04
Standard error	2.82
Median	15.00
Standard deviation	14.07
Skewness	1.45
Range	54.00
Minimum	3.00
Maximum	57.00

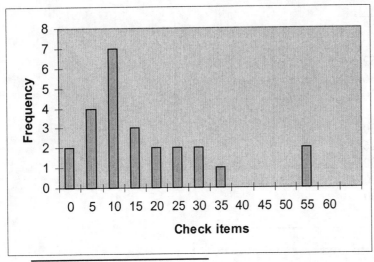

Credit Card Items	
Mean	7.68
Standard error	1.60
Median	5.00
Standard deviation	7.98
Skewness	1.33
Range	28.00
Minimum	0
Maximum	28.00

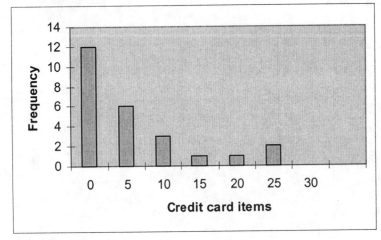

Each of the distributions of the variables is skewed to the right. Both Gross Total Sales and Cash Items appear to have potential outliers. The distribution for Check Items has two obvious outliers.

b)

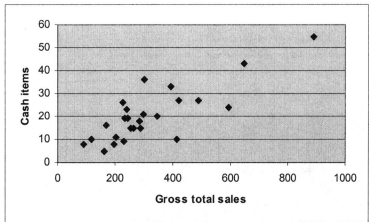

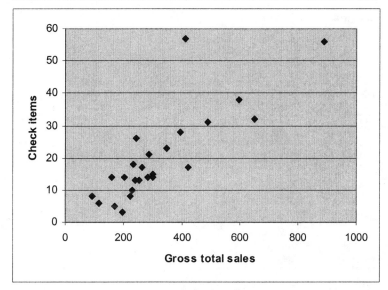

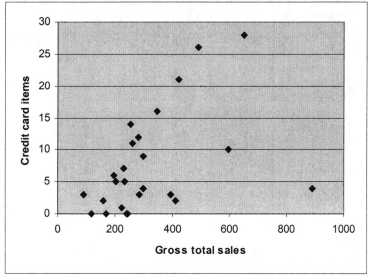

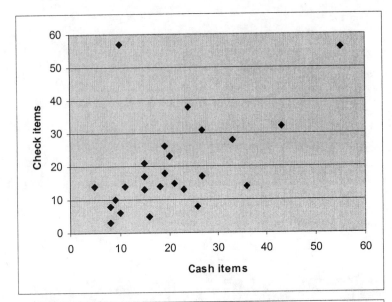

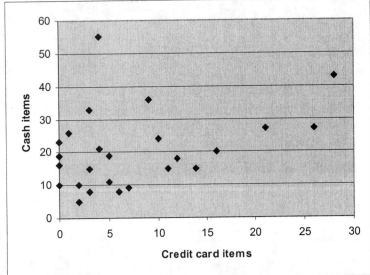

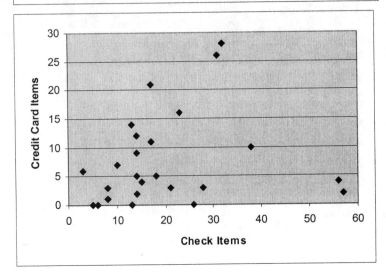

	Gross Total Sales	Cash Items	Check Items	Credit Card Items
Gross Total sales	1			
Cash items	0.816956	1		
Check items	0.821062	0.516425	1	
Credit card items	0.457943	0.352708	0.176447	1

After observing the relationship between each pair of variables and the correlation analysis, it can be concluded that both Cash Items and Check Items have a fairly strong correlation with Gross Total Sales. Credit Card Items appears to have a weak correlation with all the other variables.

11.22 a) Gross Total Sales = 0.3412 + 7.1003 × Cash Items + 6.987 × Check Items + 4.4579 × Credit Card Items. **b)** Regression Standard Error (s) = 54.8476.

11.23

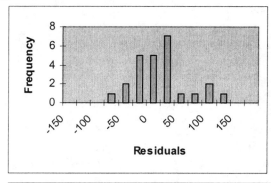

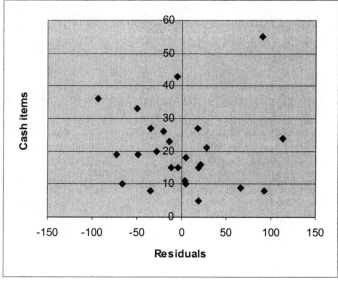

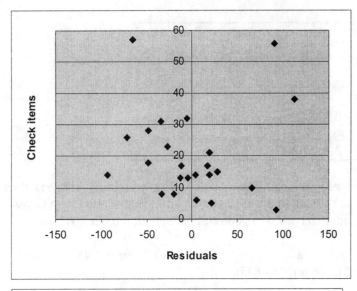

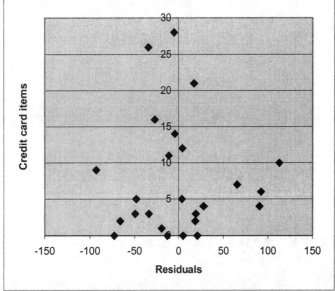

There are no obvious problems with the distribution of the residuals or the plots against the three explanatory variables.

11.24 a)

Total Billing	
Mean	6.30
Standard error	0.85
Median	6.30
Mode	2.70
Standard deviation	4.26
Skewness	0.54
Range	13.40
Minimum	1.60
Maximum	15.00

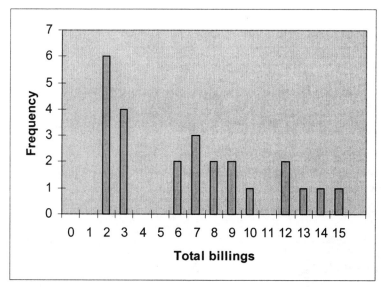

The distribution is skewed to the right and has no obvious outliers.

Architects	
Mean	10.04
Standard error	1.74
Median	5.00
Mode	5.00
Standard deviation	8.68
Skewness	1.26
Range	29.00
Minimum	2.00
Maximum	31.00

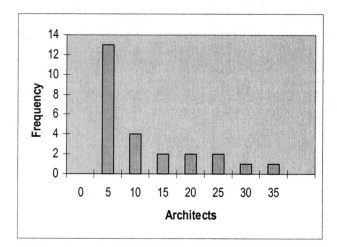

The distribution is skewed to the right and has no obvious outliers.

	Engineers
Mean	7.08
Standard error	1.92
Median	2.00
Mode	0
Standard deviation	9.62
Skewness	1.49
Range	35.00
Minimum	0
Maximum	35.00

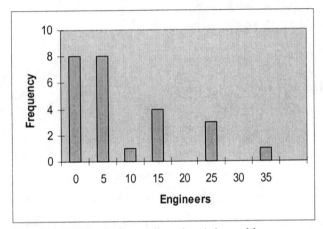

The distribution is skewed to the right and has one possible outlier.

	Staff
Mean	60.6
Standard error	8.94
Median	61.00
Mode	15.00
Standard deviation	44.71
Skewness	0.51
Range	148.00
Minimum	7.00
Maximum	155.00

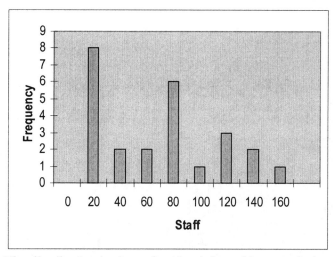

The distribution is skewed to the right and has no obvious outliers.

b)

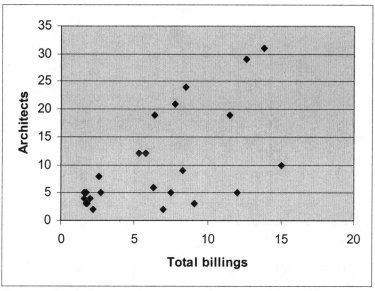

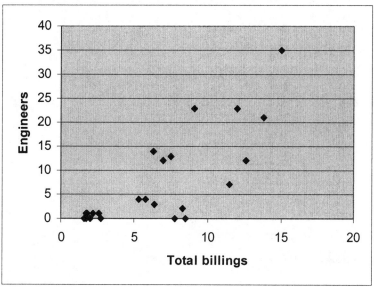

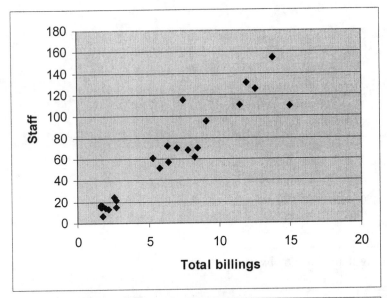

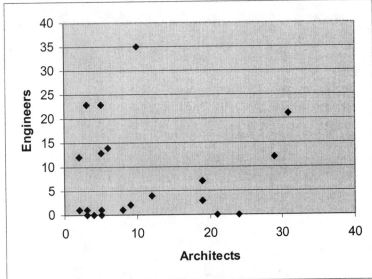

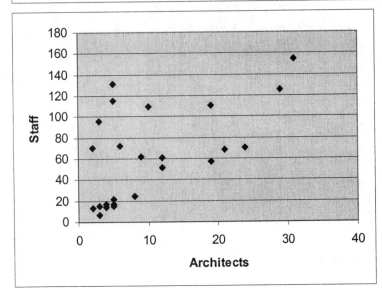

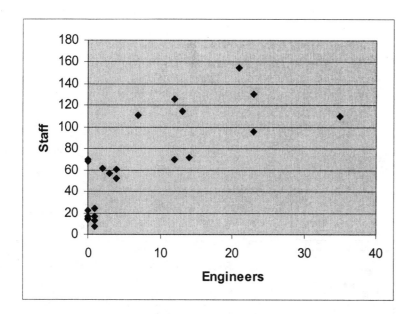

	TBill98	*Arch*	*Eng*	*Staff*
TBill98	1			
Arch	0.618034	1		
Eng	0.788269	0.125229	1	
Staff	0.947341	0.580601	0.778777	1

11.25 a) Total Billings = 0.8832 + 0.1378 × Architects + 0.16008 × Engineers + 0.04783 × Staff.
b) Regression standard error (s) = 1.1617.

11.26

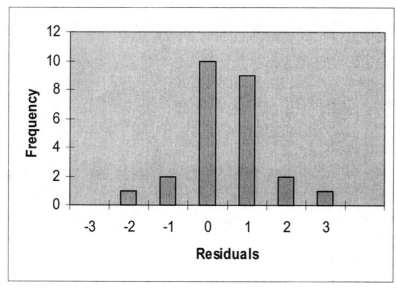

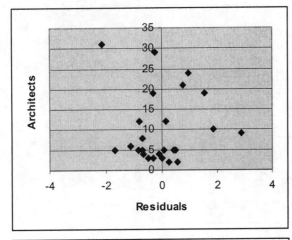

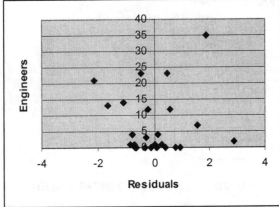

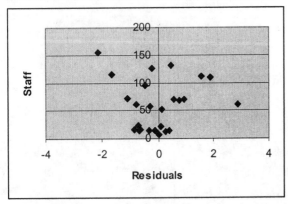

The distribution of the residuals and the plots against the explanatory variables does not appear to have any problems.

11.27   Excel
Regression Coefficient for HSS: 0.034315568
Standard Error for HSS: 0.03755888
t-stat for HSS: 0.913647251
DOF: 223
P-value: 0.361902429

SPSS
Regression Coefficient for HSS: 3.432E-02
Standard Error for HSS: 0.038
t-stat for HSS: 0.914
DOF: 223
P-value: 0.362

Minitab
Regression Coefficient for HSS: 0.03432
Standard Error for HSS: 0.03756
t-stat for HSS: 0.91
DOF: 223
P-value: 0.362

SAS
Regression Coefficient for HSS: 0.03756
Standard Error for HSS: 0.03756
t-stat for HSS: 0.91
DOF: 223
P-value: 0.3619

From this information we can conclude that HSS does not help predict GPA, given that HSM and HSE scores are also available.

11.28 P-value = 4.55E-07. Though science grades are not significant when math and English grades are also in the model, when regression analysis is performed on HSS alone it can be highly significant in predicting college GPA. This is a good demonstration of how the inference of any one explanatory variable depends upon what other explanatory variables are in the model. Alone high school science grades are helpful in predicting future performance; however, when coupled with math and English grades in the model science grades are not as helpful in predicting future performance.

11.29 GPA = 0624 + 0.183 × HSE + 0.0607. HSM is still the most important explanatory variable in predicting college GPA with a P-value = 3.51E-08, which is smaller than the model including HSS. HSE also became more helpful in predicting GPA in the absence of HSS in the model with a smaller P-value = 0.0820.

11.30 Predicted Values

```
   Fit   StDev Fit        95.0% CI              95.0% PI
 1.5818     0.1557   ( 1.2750, 1.8886)   ( 0.1689, 2.9948)
```

11.31 Predicted Values

```
   Fit   StDev Fit        95.0% CI              95.0% PI
 1.5975     0.1547   ( 1.2927, 1.9023)   ( 0.1855, 3.0095)
```
The two models give fairly close predictions.

11.32 F = 27.89, df = 223, P-value = 1.577E-11. When HSS is removed from the model, the F-statistic is increased from a previous value of 18.86 and the P-value is also significantly reduced. From this data we can conclude that there is no evidence to suggest that the remaining variables HSM and HSE are equal to zero.

11.33 a) HSM, HSS, HSE (20.5%). **b)** HSM, HSE (20.2%). **c)** HSM, HSS (20%). **d)** HSS, HSE (12.3%). **e)** HSM (19.1%). Almost all the information used to predict GPA is contained in HSM scores.

11.34 a) Yes, R^2 is equal to 21.15% according to the model.

b)

All var. in	Coefficients	Standard error	t Stat	P-value
SATM	0.000943593	0.000686	1.37618690	0.17017578
SATV	−0.000407850	0.000592	−0.68905989	0.49151830

Just SAT var.	Coefficients	Standard error	t Stat	P-value
SATM	0.002282834	0.000663	3.44363406	0.00068651
SATV	−2.45619E-05	0.000618	−0.03971405	0.96835695

When the scores from HSM, HSS, and HSE are included in the model, it becomes apparent from examining the data that the SATM scores are somewhat more helpful in predicting college GPA than SATV scores. When an analysis is performed with only the SAT data, this distinction between the two different scores becomes even greater. SATV scores are terrible at predicting future college GPA's for computer science majors, while SATM scores become a better predictor in the absence of the other explanatory variables.

11.35 $R^2_1 = 21.15\%$, $R^2_2 = 6.34\%$. F = 13.65, n = 224, p = 5, q = 3. Software provides a P-value < 0.0001. High school grades contribute significantly to explaining GPA even when SAT scores are included in the model.

11.36 a) F-statistic: df = 80 and 4. **b)** Standard Deviation is equal to the square root of the mean standard error (MSE) = 5. **c)** (8.434, 21.966). **d)** t = 4.47, df = 80, P-value < 0.0005.

11.37 a) F = 3, which has the F(3, 100) distribution. P-value = 0.0342. **b)** R^2 = SSR / SST. SST = SSR + SSE = 90 + 1000 = 1090.
R^2 = 90 / 1090 = 0.83.

11.38 a) H_0: All 13 explanatory variables have a coefficient of zero. H_a: At least one of the variables has a nonzero coefficient. df are (13,2215) P-value = 0. Conclude that at least one of the coefficients is not zero. **b)** 29.7% of the variation in interest rates is explained by the 13 explanatory variables.

11.39 a) The hypotheses for each of the explanatory variables are $H_0 : \beta = 0$ and $H_a : \beta \neq 0$. The degrees of freedom for the *t* statistics are 2,215. Values that are less than −1.96 or greater than 1.96 will lead to rejection of the null hypothesis. **b)** The significant explanatory variables are loan size, length of loan, percent down payment, cosigner, unsecured loan, total income, bad credit report, young borrower, own home and years at current address. If an explanatory variable is concluded to be insignificant, then that means the variable does not contribute significantly to the prediction of the response variable. **c)** After examining the signs of each of the 13 explanatory variables with regards to the nature of the variable, it is obvious that a favorable interest rate is awarded to variables that demonstrate some form of lower risk. The interest rate is lower for larger loans, lower for longer length loans, lower for a higher percent down payment; cosigner, lower when there is a cosigner, higher for an unsecured loan, lower for those with higher total income, higher when there is a bad credit report, higher when there is a young borrower, lower when the borrower owns a home and lower when the years at current address is higher.

11.40 a) The hypotheses about the explanatory variables are $H_0 : \beta_j = 0$ and $H_a : \beta_j \neq 0$. The degrees of freedom for the F statistic are 5650 and 13. P-value = 0. At least one of the explanatory variables has a coefficient that is not zero. **b)** 14.1% of the variation in interest rates is explained by the 13 explanatory variables.

11.41 a) The hypotheses about the *j*th explanatory variable are $H_0: \beta_j = 0$ and $H_a: \beta_j \neq 0$. The degrees of freedom for the *t* statistics are 5650. At the 5% level, values of that are less than −1.96 or greater than 1.96 will lead to rejection of the null hypothesis. **b)** The statistically significant explanatory variables are loan size, length of loan, percent down payment and unsecured loan. **c)** The interest rate is lower for larger loans, lower for longer length loans, lower for a higher percent down payment and higher for an unsecured loan. Again these results indicate banks' tendency to give lower interest rates to loans that demonstrate lower risk of default. For example, an unsecured loan is more risky than a secured loan.

11.42 Less than half of the variance in the interest rates is explained by the explanatory variables in the indirect loan analysis than the explanatory variables in the direct loan analysis. This means that the borrower's characteristics examined through the explanatory data has much more weight when determining the interest rate through a direct loan.

11.43 a) y varies normally with a mean $\mu_{\mathrm{GPA}} = \beta_0 + 9\beta_1 + 8\beta_2 + 7\beta_3$.
b) $\mu_{\mathrm{GPA}} = 0.59 + 9(0.17) + 8(0.034) + 7(0.045)$. The GPA of students with an A− in math, B+ in science and B in English have a normal distribution with an estimated mean of 2.70.

11.44 a) y varies normally with a mean $\mu_{\mathrm{GPA}} = \beta_0 + 6\beta_1 + 7\beta_2 + 8\beta_3$.
b) $\mu_{\mathrm{GPA}} = 0.59 + 6(0.17) + 7(0.034) + 8(0.045)$. The GPA of students with a B− in math, B in science and B+ in English have a normal distribution with an estimated mean of 1.29.

11.45 a) $y_i = \beta_0 + \beta_1 x_{i1} + \beta_2 x_{i2} + \varepsilon_i$. **b)** β_0, β_1, β_2. **c)** $b_0 = 7499$, $b_1 = -267.6$, $b_2 = 1.1022$ and $s = 4123$.
d) F = 111.50 with degrees of freedom 2 and 13, and P-value = 6.56E-09. We conclude years in rank and 1996 salary contain information that can be used to predict 1999 salary. **e)** $R^2 = 94.5\%$ **f)** For salary, $t = 8.69$, df = 13 and P-value = 0.000. For years in rank, t = −1.27, df = 13 and P-value = 0.227. Salary is useful for prediction with years in rank in the model, but years in rank is not useful when salary is in the model.

11.46 a)

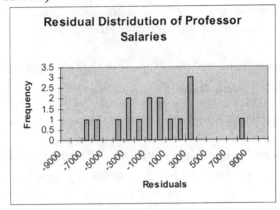

b)

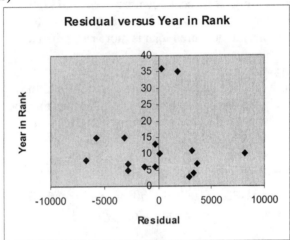

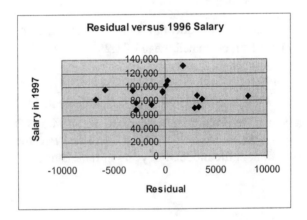

11.47 a) 1999 Predicted Salary = 86973 + 1308 (years in rank). **b)** $t = 4.83$, df = 14 and *P*-value = 0.000268. Years in rank are useful for predicting 1999 salary. **c)** Years in rank included with 1996 salary produced these results, coefficient = -267.64, $t = -1.27$, df = 13 and *P*-value = 0.227. When included with the data concerning 1996 salary, years in rank is not very useful in predicting 1999 salary; however, rank in years is useful when performing the same regression analysis without the data from 1996 salary.

11.48 $F = [(n-p-1)/q] [(R^2_1 + R^2_2)/(1-R^2_1)]$, $F = [(82-10-1)/4] [(0.77-0.06)/(1-0.77)]$
$F = 54.8$, df = 71 and 10, P-value = 0. The conclusion is that the human capital variables do provide significant prediction of bank branch manager salaries.

11.49 Price (leaf unit $1000)

```
 5  22
 6  2459
 7  2233566
 8  01124444779999
 9  234469
10  4
11  449
12  4499
13
14
15
16
17  39
18
19  9
```

Sq Ft (leaf unit 100sf)

```
0  67777
0  88899999
1  000011
1  22223333
1  455555
1  66666
1  89
2  01
2  22
```

The seven homes excluded do appear to skew the distributions to the right.

11.50

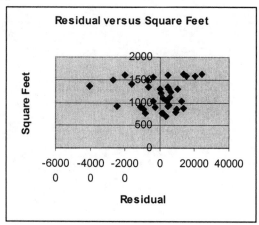

11.51 a) Price = 45,298 + 34.32 (Sq Ft), For Sq Ft = 1000, Predicted Price = $79,622. For Sq Ft = 1500, Predicted Price = $96,783.

11.52

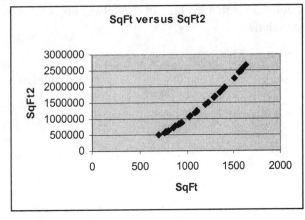

	Sq Ft	*Sq Ft2*
Sq Ft	1	
SqFt2	0.995168	1

11.53 Price = 81273.37 + −30.14 (Sq Ft) + 0.027 (Sq Ft2). For Sq Ft = 1000, Predicted Price = $78,253. For Sq Ft = 1500, Predicted Price = $97,042. Overall, the two sets of predictions are fairly similar.

11.54 a) Mean Price for houses with 3 or more bedrooms = $90,845.83. Mean Price for houses with fewer than 3 bedrooms = $75,700. **b)** $90,845.83 − $75,700 = $15,145.83. This is indeed the value of the coefficient in Ex. 11.16.

11.55 From Minitab, t = -2.88   P = 0.0068   DF = 35.   These values agree with example 11.16.

11.56 a) Homes with 1 bathroom: Price = $77,504 + 20,553(0) + 12,616(0) + 44,896(0) = 77.504. **b)** Homes with 1.5 bathrooms: Price = 77,504 + 20,533 (1) + 12,616(0) + 44,896(0). **c)** Homes with 2 bathrooms: Price = 77,504 + 20,533 (0) + 12,616(1) + 44,896(0) = 90,120. **d)** Homes with 2.5 bathrooms: Price = 77,504 + 20,533 (0) + 12,616(0) + 44,896(1) = 122400. **e)** We can say that homes with two bathrooms are sold for $12,616 more than houses with only one bathroom on average.

11.57

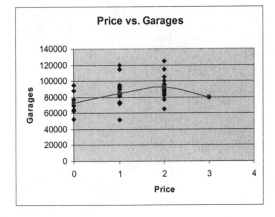

The trend is increasing and roughly linear as one examines from 0 to 2 garages and then levels off.

11.58 Though the inclusion of the price of the house with three garages will not change the results of the scatter plot significantly, it would probably be the best idea to remove it as an unusual data point and only examine the scatter plot regarding houses with two or fewer garages.

11.59 When a 1400 ft^2 home has an extra half bath the average price is $99,719. When the same size home does not have an extra half bath the average price is $84,585. The difference in price is $15,134.

11.60 For a home with a half bath, price = $113,311. For a home without a half bath, price = $87,615. The difference is $25,696. Comparing the difference in problem 11.59 and this difference we see it can be found using the difference in the square footage:

$(1600 - 1400) \times 52.81 = 10,562$. $25,696 - 15,134 = 10,562$.

11.61 No, it does not make sense to compare homes with whole and half baths less than 100 ft^2 because in this study no homes that small have a half bath.

11.62 a)

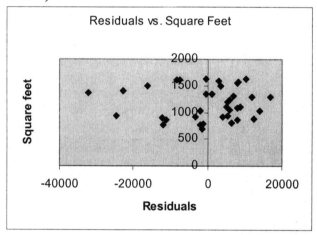

The residuals seem to be on the positive side rather than evenly distributed between positive and negative. There is a greater spread in values on the negative side than on the positive side. **b)** These low residuals correspond to homes 1, 8, and 24. These are lower priced homes with larger square footage than would be expected. **c)** The histogram shows that the residuals are not normally distributed but heavily skewed to the left.

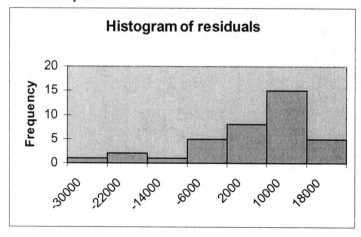

11.63 a)

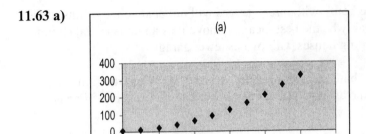

The relationship to the left is increasing and curved.

b)

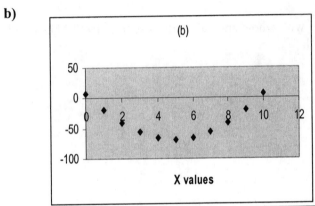

The relationship shown to the left is curved and decreases up to x = 5 and then begins to increase.

c)

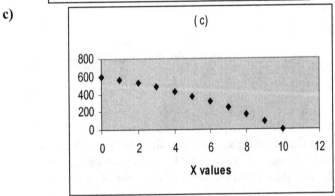

The relationship to the left is decreasing and slightly curved.

11.64 a) For Group A the mean response is 5 and for Group B the mean response is 7. **b)** For Group A the mean response is 5 and for Group B the mean response is 25. **c)** For Group A the mean response is 5 and for Group B the mean response is 205.

11.65 For each equation, the difference in means is equal to the coefficient of x. This will be true in general.

11.66 a)

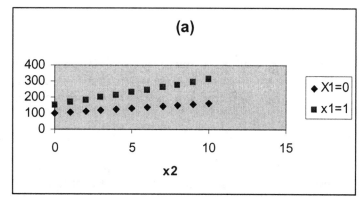

The relationships are both increasing, with the values of μ_y greater for $x_1 = 1$ than for $x_1 = 0$.

b)

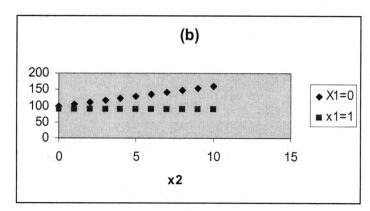

The relationship for $x_1 = 1$ is a horizontal line, while the line representing $x_1 = 0$ is increasing.

c)

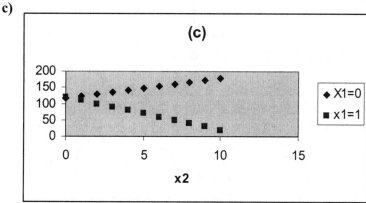

The relationships are opposite of each other. For $x_1 = 0$ the relationship is increasing, for $x_1 = 1$, the relationship is decreasing.

11.67 For part (a), the difference in slopes is $16 - 6 = 10$. This is the coefficient of $x_1 x_2$. The difference in intercepts is $150 - 100 = 50$, which is the coefficient of x_1. This is true in general.

11.68 a) $\mu_y = \beta_o + \beta_1 x + \beta_2 x^2 + \beta_3 x^3$. **b)** $\mu_y = \beta_o + \beta_1 x_1 + \beta_2 x_2 + \beta_3 x_3$, where $x_1 = 0$ or 1, $x_2 = 0$ or 1, $x_3 = 0$ or 1. $x_1 = 1$, $x_2 = 0$, and $x_3 = 0$ corresponds to the first value of the categorical variable. $x_1 = 0$, $x_2 = 1$, and $x_3 = 0$ corresponds to the second value of the categorical variable. $x_1 = 0$, $x_2 = 0$, and $x_3 = 1$ corresponds to the third value of the categorical variable. $x_1 = 0$, $x_2 = 0$, and $x_3 = 0$

corresponds to the fourth value of the categorical variable. **c)**
$\mu_y = \beta_o + \beta_1 x_1 + \beta_2 x_2 + \beta_3 x_3 + \beta_4 x_1 x_3$, where $x_1 = 0$ or 1 and $x_2 = 0$ or 1.

11.69 a) Assets $= 7.6 - 0.00457 \times$ Account $+ 3.36 \times 10^{-5} \times$ Account^2 **b)** $(1.25 \times 10^{-5}, 5.47 \times 10^{-5})$ **c)** $t = 3.76$, df $= 7$, P-value $= 0.007$. The squared term lends predictive power to the model. **d)** Since the variables account and account^2 are dependent (or correlated) the model without the squared term will give a different coefficient on the account variable.

11.70 The regression model with the squared term is:
Salary $= 78896 + 2628 \times$ Rank $- 32.8 \times$ Rank^2. The t statistic for the squared term is $t = -1.045$, df $= 13$, and the P-value $= 0.315$. The squared term does not contribute significantly to the prediction of salaries.

11.71 a) $R_1^2 = 0.654$, $R_2^2 = 0.625$. **b)** F $= 1.09$, df $= 1$ and 13, P-value $= 0.3155$. The squared term does not add significant prediction of salaries. **c)** $(-1.045)^2 = 1.09$.

11.72 Let b_0 be the constant and b_1, b_2, and b_3 represent the coefficients on acetic acid, hydrogen sulfide, and lactic acid, respectively.

b_0	b_1	b_2	b_3	R^2
−61.50	15.65*	0	0	0.3020
−9.79	0	5.78*	0	0.5712
−29.86	0	0	37.72*	0.4960
−26.94	3.80	5.15*	0	0.5822
−27.59	0	3.95*	19.89*	0.6517
−51.37	5.57	0	31.39*	0.5203
−28.88	0.33	3.91*	19.67*	0.6518

The results above show that hydrogen sulfide and lactic acid concentration positively influence the taste variable in cheese. The best model would be the one with the highest R^2 value (0.6517). The model is: $\hat{y} = -27.50 + 3.95 \times$ hydrogen sulfide $+ 19.89 \times$ lactic acid.

11.73 a) A 95% confidence interval would be (2.11, 2.16). **b)** Based on the previous confidence interval, the value 2.13 falls within the interval, so the logical conclusion is that the price is within the expected range of variability. I agree with the court ruling.

11.74 a) Vitamin C $= 46 - 6.05 \times$ days, $t = -10.62$, df $= 8$, P-value $= 0$. It appears there is a significant linear relationship between vitamin C level and the number of days after baking. **b)**

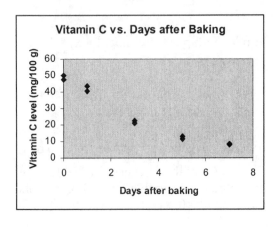

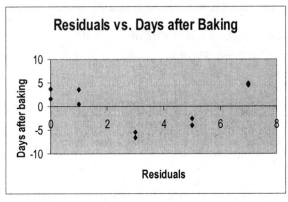

It appears that the relationship may be slightly curved. The residuals show a systematic pattern in that the values go from positive to negative to positive as the number of days increases. **c)** Vitamin C = 50.1 − 11.3 × days + 0.763 × days^2. The squared term t statistic is 6.08 and df = 7. The P-value = 0.000503. It appears that the squared term is significant in the model. **d)** R^2 without the squared term is 0.93 and with the squared term is 0.99. A look at a scatterplot of residuals vs days in the second model shows that there is no systematic pattern. Choose the model with the squared term.

11.75 As bread sits after baking it loses a significant amount of Vitamins C and A but Vitamin E does not appear to decrease over time. If one were to model the decrease in vitamins, the best model for loss of Vitamin C is a quadratic model using days after baking as the explanatory variable. See problem 11.74 for the model. The model that best describes the loss of Vitamin A would be a linear model: Vit A = 3.34 − 0.04 × days. It does not make sense to predict Vitamin E loss using a regression model.

11.76 Wages = 349 + 0.6 × LOS, t = 2.86, P-value = 0.006. R^2 = 0.12. While the t statistic shows that the coefficient on the variable LOS is significantly different from zero, it does not appear that this is a strong linear model. LOS does not explain more than 12% of the variation in wages.

11.77 a) Wages = 354.2 + 63.9 × Size, t = 2.96, P-value = 0.0046. R^2 = 0.133. While the t statistic shows that the coefficient on the variable Size is significantly different from zero, it does not appear that this is a strong linear model. Company size does not explain more than 14% of the variation in wages. **b)** t = 2.96, df = 57, P-value = 0.0045. Since size takes on only two values, 0 or 1, it makes sense that the t statistics would be the same. **c)** The plot of residuals vs. LOS shows a slight increasing trend. This is confirmed by r, the correlation, which is 0.22. Adding LOS to the model using Size may be beneficial.

11.78 Wages = 302.5 + 0.67 LOS + 71.8 Size, R^2 = 0.29, t statistics have small P-values.

11.79 a) Corn Yield = −3544 + 1.84 × Year, R^2 = 0.82, t = 13.06, P-value = 0. **b)** The residuals appear fairly normal. **c)** The residuals plotted against soybean yield do not show an increasing trend. The correlation between the two is positive. There may be some benefit to using soybean yield in addition to year to predict corn yield.

11.80 a) Corn Yield = −46.2 + 4.8 × Soybean Yield, R^2 = 0.87, t = 16.04, P-value = 0. **b)** The residuals appear fairly normal. **c)** It appears that there is an increasing and then decreasing effect when looking at the residuals plotted against year. It makes sense to include year in the regression model.

11.81 a) H$_o$: All coefficients equal zero. H$_a$: At least one coefficient is not equal to zero. F = 176, df = 2 and 37, P-value = 0. This model provides significant prediction of corn yield. **b)** R^2 = 0.90, compared to 0.82 with only year as the explanatory variable and 0.87 with only soybean yield as the explanatory variable. **c)** Corn yield = −1510 + 0.765 × Year + 3.085 x Soybean yield, Year and Soybean yield are dependent on each other, so one would expect the coefficients to be different when both variables are used in the regression model. **d)** For the coefficient on Year, t = 3.62 and the P-value = 0.0009. For the coefficient on Soybean yield, t = 5.82 and the P-value = 0. Both of these results tell us that the coefficients are significantly different from zero. **e)** For β$_1$: (0.337, 1.194). For β$_2$: (2.01, 4.16). **f)** The residual plot against soybean yield shows no pattern. The residual plot against year shows an increasing and then decreasing trend with time. This indicates it might make sense to include the year squared as an additional term in the model.

11.82 a) Corn yield = −607.5 + 0.3 × Year − 0.045 × Year2 + 3.9 × Soybean Yield **b)** H$_o$: All coefficients are equal to zero. H$_a$: At least one coefficient is not equal to zero. F = 233, df = 3 and 36, P-value =

0. This indicates that the model provides significant prediction of corn yield. **c)** $R^2 = 0.95$, compared to 0.90 from previous model. **d)** In the order they appear in the model, the t statistics for the coefficients are: $t = -5.82$ with a P-value $= 0$, $t = 1.73$, P-value $= 0.09$, $t = 9.512$, P-value $= 0$. **e)** The residuals all appear random when plotted against the explanatory variables.

10.83 a) The t statistic for the coefficient on year2 is -1.476 with a P-value $= 0.148$. This indicates the term is not significant in the model with only year and year2. **b)** Since year and year2 are highly correlated, if these are the only two explanatory variables, we can obtain just as good predictions using year only. **c)** Note that the two fits differ towards the end of the data sets, in the early and late years.

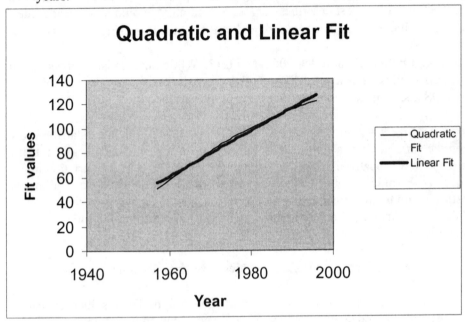

11.84 For the linear model, predicted yield for 2001 was 136.41 with a 95% prediction interval of (114, 158.61). For the quadratic model, predicted yield for 2001 was 127.14 with a 95% prediction interval of (101.82, 152.45). The linear model gave a closer prediction to actual.

11.85 The 2002 predicted value using the linear model is 138.24 with a 95% prediction interval of (115.95, 160.54). For the quadratic model, predicted yield is 127.98 with a 95% prediction interval of (101.88, 154.09).

11.86

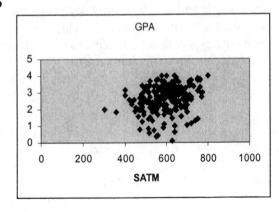

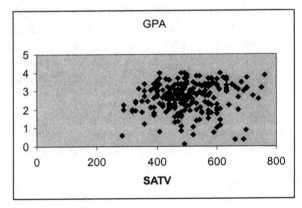

The scatterplots do not show strong relationships. The plot of SATM vs. GPA shows two possible outliers on the left side. The plot of SATV vs. GPA does not show any obvious outliers.

11.87

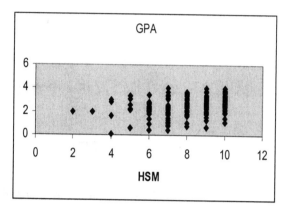

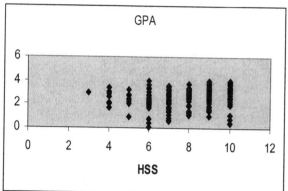

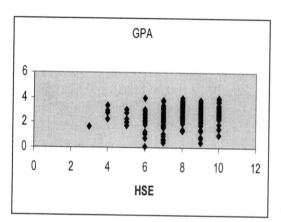

The scatterplots show a possibly increasing trend in GPA as high school grades increase. The variability in GPA also increases with high school grades.

11.88

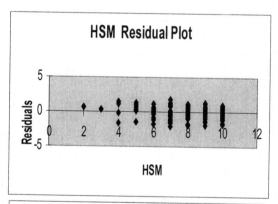

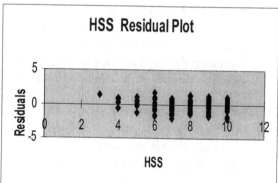

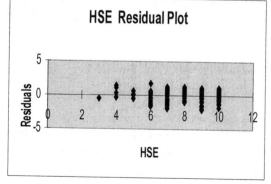

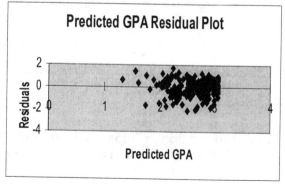

The residuals do not show any obvious patterns.

11.89

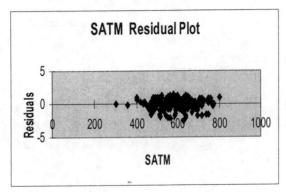

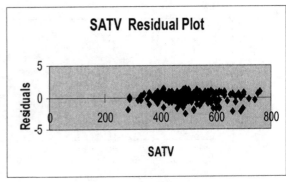

There are no obvious patterns in the residual plots.

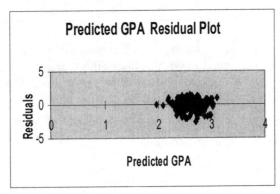

11.90 a) GPA = 0.666 + 0.193 × HSM + 0.00061 × SATM. **b)** H_o: All coefficients in the regression model are zero. H_a: At least one coefficient is not zero. This means that we assume the model is not a significant predictor of GPA and let the data provide evidence that the model is a significant predictor. F = 26.63 and the P-value = 0. This model provides significant prediction of GPA. **c)** HSM: (0.1295, 0.2565) SATM: (−0.00059, 0.001815). Yes, the interval describing the SATM coefficient does contain zero. **d)** HSM: t = 5.99, P-value = 0. SATM: t = 0.999, P-value = 0.319. Based on the large P-value associated with the SATM coefficient one should conclude that SATM does not provide significant prediction of GPA. **e)** s = 0.703. **f)** R^2 = 0.1942.

11.91 While the model with HSE and SATV does provide some prediction of GPA, it is not much. R^2 = 0.086. The explanatory variable SATV is not a significant predictor with HSE in the model. This parallels the results found in 11.90. Note that the model with the math scores: HSM and SATM is a much stronger model than the model with verbal scores.

11.92 Looking at the sample of males only shows the same results when compared to the sample of all students. R^2 = 0.184 (compared to 0.20) and while HSM is a significant predictor, HSS and HSE are not.

11.93 The analysis of the female students also shows similar results to all students. The R^2 value is slightly higher (0.25) but the same explanatory variables are considered insignificant (HSS and HSE).

11.94 a) GPA = 0.582 + 0.155 HSM + 0.050 HSS + 0.044 HSE + 0.067 Gender + 0.05 GHSM − 0.05 GHSS − 0.012 GHSE. The t statistics for each coefficient have P-values greater than 0.10 for all except the explanatory variable HSM. **b)** Verify. **c)** Verify. **d)** F = 0.143, P-value = 0.966. This indicates there is no reason to include gender and the interactions.

Case Study 11.1

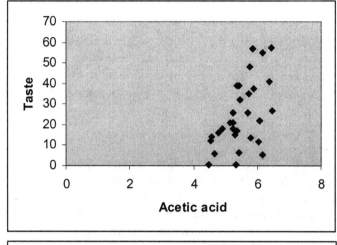

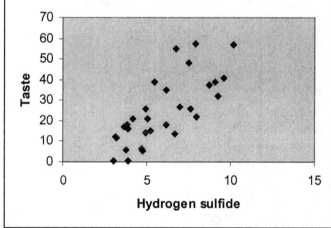

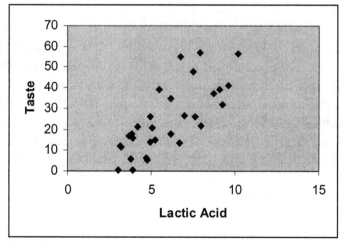

The relationships between Taste and Hydrogen sulfide and Taste and Lactic acid appear slightly stronger than the relationship between Taste and Acetic acid. The correlation coefficient values support this. The values for *r* are: 0.7558, 0.7042, and 0.5500, respectively. After running the analysis with interaction effects, it was found that the strongest model in terms of R^2 was the model

with both the hydrogen sulfide term and the lactic acid term. Interaction did not seem to significantly improve the model's predictive ability. The best model for predicting taste would be:
$\hat{y} = -27.50 + 3.95 \times$ hydrogen sulfide $+ 19.89 \times$ lactic acid.

Case Study 11.2

The model chosen as the best predictor of GPA includes the variables IQ, SC, C1, C3, and C5. The original analysis included all 10 variables. Reviewing the residuals scores and residual plots showed that there were two outliers: cases 51 and 22. After removing these cases and rerunning the analysis with only the variables that appeared significant the resulting model is:
$\hat{y} = -4.0 + 0.09IQ - 0.08SC + 0.29C1 + 0.17C3 + 0.13C5$. $R^2 = 0.62$ and standard error = 1.186. There does not appear to be any reason to question the regression assumptions.

Case Study 11.5

The zip code chosen for analysis was 47905. There were 158 homes in this zip code. After looking at the data, four homes were removed as outliers. Two of the homes had high square footage with very low home prices and two homes had high prices for the square footage. There were two homes that had very high square footage but their prices reflected this and the observations fit the linear trend. The scatterplot below shows the linear trend between price and square footage. The residual plots did not show any reason to believe the relationship was not linear.

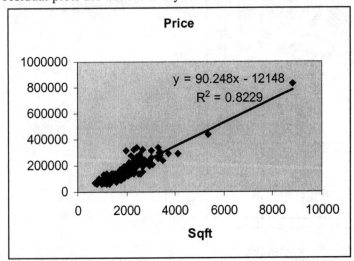

Further analysis was done with the bedroom and bathroom variables. It was found that the number of bedrooms was not a significant predictor of price. This is consistent with the results found in case 11.3. The number of bathrooms did contribute significantly to the price of a home. The indicator variables used were bath25 and bath3. Bath25 was equal to 1 if the home had 2.5 bathrooms and 0 otherwise. Bath3 was equal to 1 if the home had more than 2.5 bathrooms and 0 otherwise. When bath25 and bath3 were both zero this indicated that the home had either one or two bathrooms. The model with sqft, bath25, and bath3 gave the best fit.
$\hat{y} = \$7,539 + 4.234Sqft + 7,532Bath25 + 10,496Bath3$.
$R^2 = 0.8334$ and standard error = 37,202.

Chapter 12
Statistics for Quality: Control and Capability

12.1 Answers will vary.

12.2 Answers will vary.

12.3

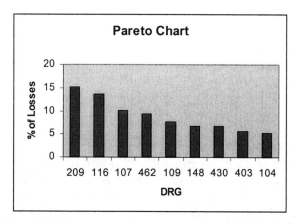

These 9 DRGs account for approximately 80.5% of losses. The hospital should concentrate on DRG 209 first.

12.4 Special causes might be illness or poor weather. A tire blowout or mechanical failure of her bike during a training ride would also be considered a special cause.

12.5 Answers will vary.

12.6 CL = 75, UCL = 75.75, LCL = 74.25.

12.7 a) CL = 11.5, UCL = 11.8, LCL = 11.2. **b)**

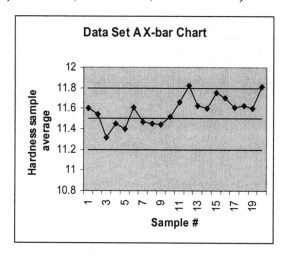

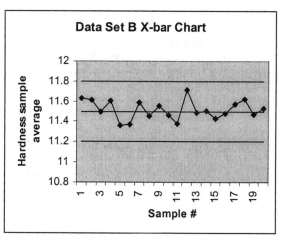

Points 12 and 20 are above the UCL for Data Set A. Data Set B has all points inside the control limits. Data set C shows points 19 and 20 above the UCL.

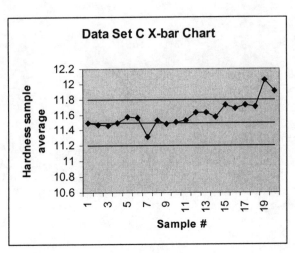

c) Data Set B comes from a process in control. Data Set C shows a process with a gradual drift in the mean. Data Set A shows a process that has shifted suddenly.

12.8 a) number of applications received that day, time of day the application is reviewed. **b)** hiring freeze (no applications reviewed and response time is quick), new employee in human resources (their review time is longer; therefore, response time is longer than other HR employees). **c)** new procedures for review could either increase or decrease the average time, time of year (there may be many applications in May when college graduates hit the job market).

12.9 CL = 0.4607, UCL = 1.044, LCL = 0.

12.10 a)

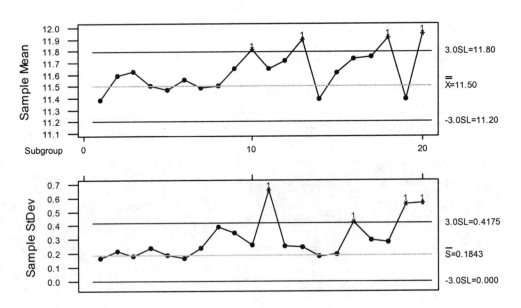

b) It appears that the standard deviation started to move up between sample #10 and #11. The x-bar chart also shows an out of control situation. **c)** The s chart does not reflect the increase in the process mean. The x-bar chart clearly shows the shift in the mean and the increase in the variation by having more scatter in the sample means and several out of control points.

12.11 Answers will vary.

12.12 Answers will vary.

12.13 Answers will vary.

12.14

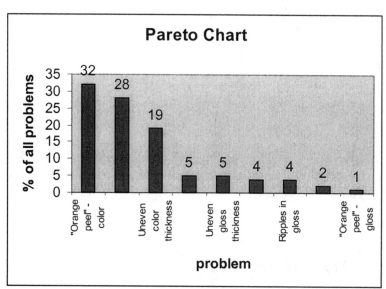

We should look at the "orange peel" texture in color first. It is contributing to 32% of the problems.

12.15 x-bar chart: CL = 0.875, UCL = 0.87661, LCL = 0.87339. s chart: CL = 0.00113, UCL = 0.00236, LCL = 0.

12.16 a) CL = 0.1194, UCL = 0.2494, LCL = 0. **b)** CL = 4.22, UCL = 4.39, LCL = 4.05.

12.17

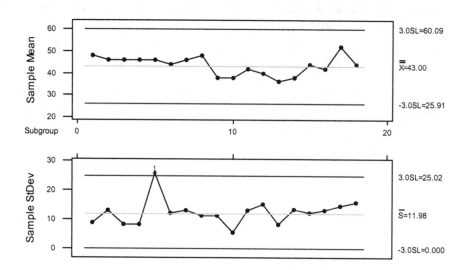

The process appears to be running out of control with respect to variation. Sample five is just above the upper control limit.

12.18 The new type of yarn most likely showed up on the $\bar{x}$ chart. The leaky valve most likely showed up on the s chart.

12.19 $P(\bar{x} > 713 \mid \mu = 693) + P(\bar{x} < 687 \mid \mu = 693) = 0.0004 + 0.1587 = 0.1591$.

12.20 3.3 standard deviations.

12.21 a) $UCL_{\bar{x}} = \mu + 3\dfrac{\sigma}{\sqrt{n}}, LCL_{\bar{x}} = \mu - 3\dfrac{\sigma}{\sqrt{n}}$ **b)** $UCL_s = (c_4 + 2c_5)\sigma, LCL_s = (c_4 - 2c_5)\sigma$.

12.22 a) This would likely show up as one point out on the $\bar{x}$ chart. **b)** This would most likely show up as a run on the $\bar{x}$ chart. **c)** This would likely show up as a run on the $\bar{x}$ chart. **d)** This would likely show up as a single point out on the s chart.

12.23

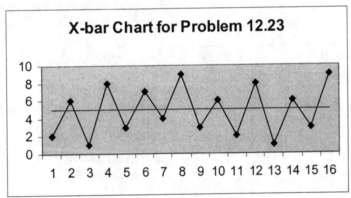

The chart above shows a process that is actually two processes in one. Note that each point alternates above and below the mean of 5. This is an unusual pattern if the process were being operated the same by all operators.

12.24 $\bar{x}$ chart: CL = 48.7, UCL = 50.2, LCL = 47.2. s chart: CL = 0.92, UCL = 2.085, LCL = 0.

12.25 a) $\mu = 275$, $\sigma = 37.5$. **b)** Referring to figure 12.7, almost all of the 20 s values plot below or just slightly above the centerline of the chart. This indicates that σ has most likely decreased.

12.26 a)

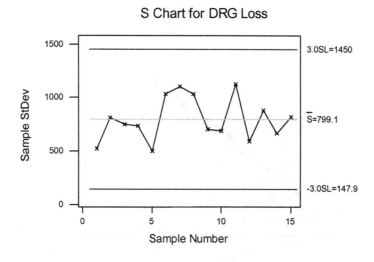

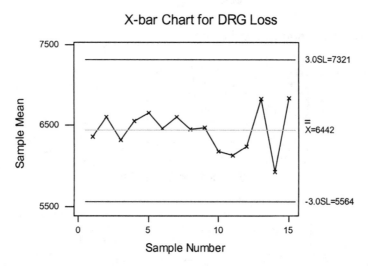

The process appears to be in control with respect to process mean.

12.27 If the computer maker is confident that their monitor manufacturer is operating in control, then they can safely predict the tension on the screens and no longer have to perform incoming inspection.

12.28 Natural tolerances are: $6442 \pm 3(811)$ or $(4009, 8875)$.

12.29

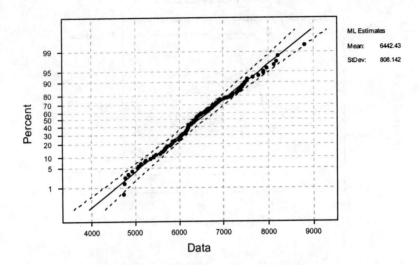

The data appear to have a fairly normal distribution.

12.30 a) 99.94%. **b)** 97.38%.

12.31 99.06%.

12.32 a) Verify.
   b)

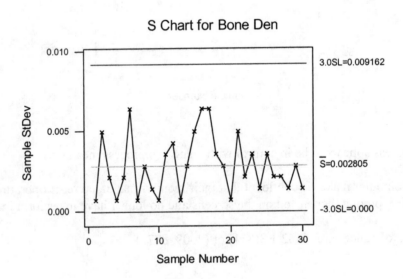

This chart shows process or short run variation. The process appears to be in control with respect to standard deviation.

c)

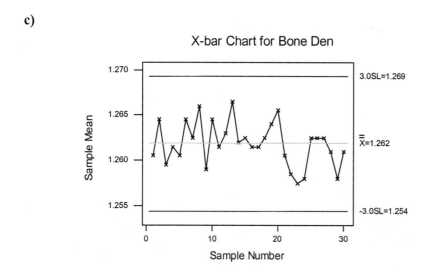

X-bar Chart for Bone Den

Day to day variation will be visible on this chart. It appears that this machine is staying in control with respect to both the variation and the average.

12.33 (6.24, 80.58).

12.34 (1.25191, 1.2719).

12.35 43.16%.

12.36

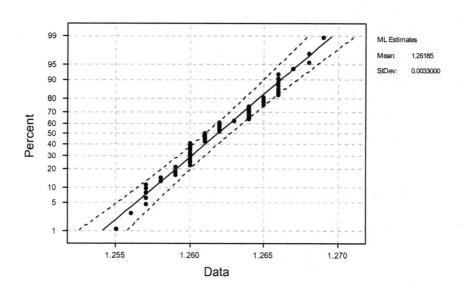

Normal Probability Plot for Bone Density

The data is approximately normal.

12.37

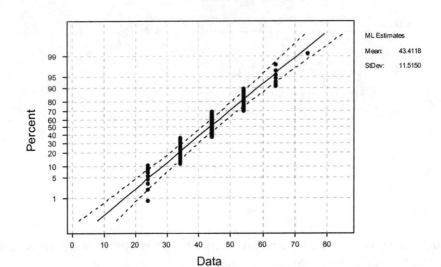

There are no serious departures from normality. The stacks of data appear because of the lack of precision in the measurement.

12.38 a)

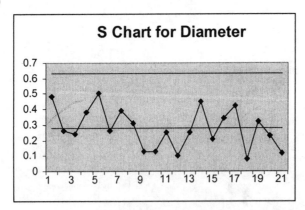

The short-term process variation appears to be in control.

b)

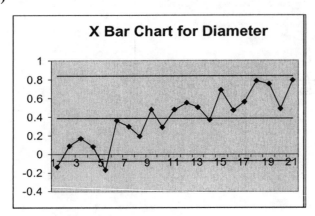

The process average is rising steadily and appears out of control. Tool wear could explain the lack of control.

12.39 a) This would show up as a sudden increase in $\overline{x}$. **b)** This would show up as a sudden change in s or R. **c)** This would show up as a gradual shift in $\overline{x}$.

12.40 a) This speaks to the fact that processes in control may not always be capable but operators can only work with the process management gives them. **b)** Bringing a process into control does not make it capable. **c)** Again, operators can only work with the process that has been provided by management. Pep talks do not make high quality. Capable processes do.

12.41 The control limits include times from the beginning of the Boston Marathon that were highly variable. Since then the variation has decreased and remained steady. Rick should calculate the variation from 1980 on and look at winning times over the past 20 years.

12.42

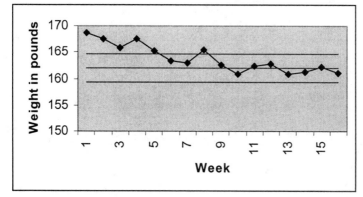

Joe's weight begins well above the UCL but then appears to stabilize towards the end of the 16 weeks.

12.43 Specifications limits start with the customer. When the customer states their product or service requirements, the product/service designer translates those requirements into product/service specifications. These specifications define limits within which the product can function as intended. Control limits, on the other hand, are derived from process behavior. They are independent of product/service specifications. Control limits tell us what the expected variability is in the process with respect to certain product, process, or service characteristics.

12.44 a)

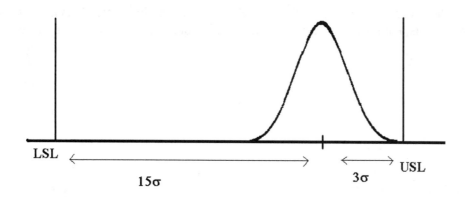

b)

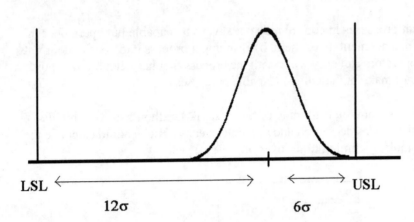

c)

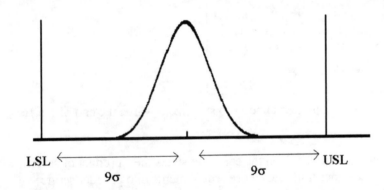

12.45 a) $C_p = 1.3$, $C_{pk} = 1.09$. **b)** $\hat{C}_p = 0.87$, $\hat{C}_{pk} = 0.65$.

12.46 a) $\hat{C}_p = 1.3$, $\hat{C}_{pk} = 1.3$. **b)** $\hat{C}_p = 0.87$, $\hat{C}_{pk} = 0.87$.

12.47 a) $C_{pk} = 1$, 50% meet specifications. **b)** 99.74%. **c)** The capability index formulas make sense for normal distributions, but for distributions that are clearly not normal they will give misleading results.

12.48 $\hat{\sigma} = 37.5$, $\hat{C}_{pk} = 0.67$.

12.49 a) $\hat{\mu} = 43.4, \hat{\sigma} = 11.6$

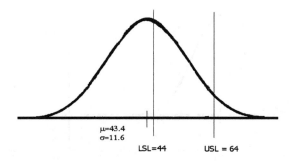

μ=43.4
σ=11.6

LSL=44 USL = 64

b) $\hat{C}_p = 0.29, \hat{C}_{pk} = 0.02$. The process capability is very poor. Not only is the process average below the lower specification but the variability of the process is almost 3 times greater than the width of the specification limits.

12.50 a) 97.12%. **b)** $\hat{C}_p = 0.0.82$. **c)** $\hat{C}_{pk} = 0.64$.

12.51 a) 97.43%. **b)** $\hat{C}_{pk} = 0.73$.

12.52 a) This may show an initial improvement but it won't be lasting. **b)** This will likely show improvements if the operators are trained on the new equipment properly. **c)** This is also a viable solution if in fact the issue is one of not understanding the equipment. **d)** This solution will introduce more variation than is already in the process. **e)** This could be a viable solution also.

12.53 A process is said to be at six-sigma quality when the distance between the mean of the process and each of the specification limits is equal to six times the standard deviation of the process.

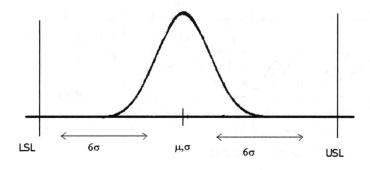

LSL   6σ   μ,σ   6σ   USL

12.54 a)

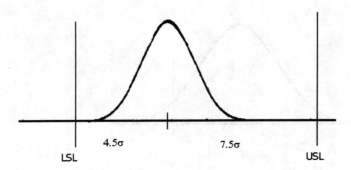

LSL   4.5σ   7.5σ   USL

b) $C_{pk} = 1.5$. No, six-sigma quality is not as strong as requiring $C_{pk} \geq 2$. **c)** The probability of an outcome outside the specification limit is 0.0000034. This means 3.4 parts per million will fail to meet specification.

12.55 The choice to choose six calls at random from each shift makes sense because there are many different people working the call center. The different people add to the common cause variation in the process and we want to include this in our estimate of the process standard deviation. If we did not want to include the variation arising from different workers, then we could choose six consecutive calls.

12.56 a)

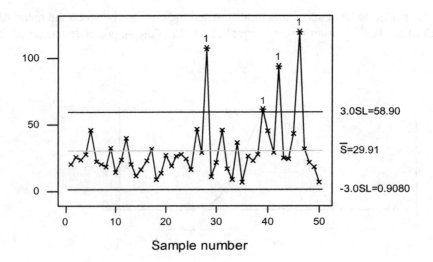

S Chart for Response Time

b)

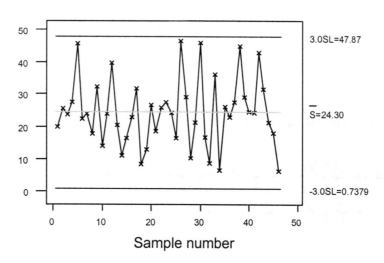

S Chart for Response Time

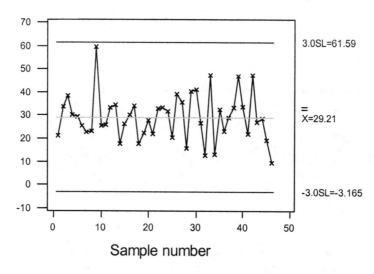

X-bar Chart for Response Time

c) It appears that the process is in control with respect to the process average.

12.57 From sample 28 the outlier is 276. Removing the outlier results in an $s = 9.28$. From sample 42 the outlier is 244 and the resulting $s = 6.71$. From sample 46 the outlier is 333 and the resulting $s = 31.01$.

12.58 CL = 0.0972, UCL = 0.1255, LCL = 0.0689.

12.59 a) 28750, $\overline{p} = 0.0334$. **b)** CL = 0.0334, UCL = 0.0435, LCL = 0.0233.

12.60 CL = 0.005, UCL = 0.0117, LCL = 0.

12.61 CL = 0.006, UCL = 0.0131, LCL = 0.

12.62 For a day with 75,000 prescriptions filled, CL = 0.01, UCL = 0.0111, LCL = 0.0089. For a day with 50,000 prescriptions filled, CL = 0.01, UCL = 0.0113, LCL = 0.0087.

12.63 a) $\overline{p} = 0.3555$, $\overline{n} = 922$.

    b) The process appears to be in control.

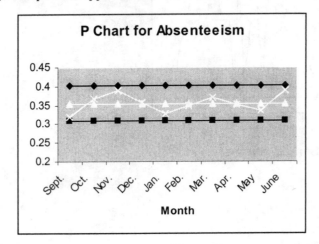

    c)

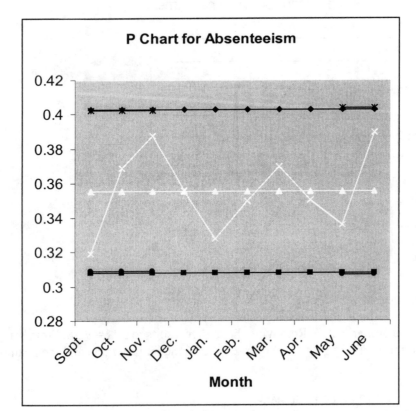

Adding exact limits does not affect the conclusions. The process remains in control.

12.64 a) $\overline{p} = 0.0000035$. One would expect to see 0.0175 defects per day or 0.42 defects per month. **b)** CL = 0.0000035, UCL = 0.000083, LCL = 0. **c)** A p chart is not useful in this circumstance because it will not detect subtle changes in product quality. The probability of observing a defect on any given day is extremely small.

12.65 a) $\overline{p} = 0.008$. One would expect to see 4 bad orders per month. **b)** CL = 0.008, UCL = 0.02, LCL = 0. 11 bad orders would result in an out of control situation.

12.66 When a process is in control it means that the process is predictable. We can anticipate what the output of the process will be. Being predictable does not mean meeting customer requirements. A process can be predictably bad or good.

12.67 a) The percents do not add up to 100 because some customers have more than one complaint.
b)

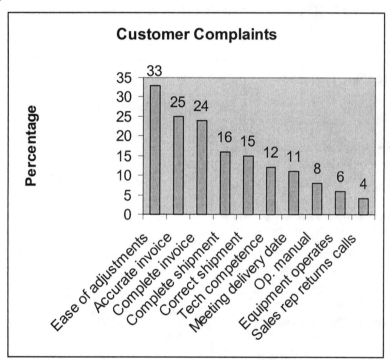

Choose "Ease of adjustments" for focusing your improvement efforts.

12.68 a) $\overline{X} - s$ charts. Time is a continuous variable. **b)** p chart are used for percents. **c)** A p chart would make sense here as well. We can calculate the percentage of employees participating in health screening.

12.69 a) If computer availability is measured as time available, then $\overline{X} - s$ charts make sense because time is a continuous variable. If we measure computer availability as a percentage of total time open for business, then a p chart makes sense. **b)** Again, because time is a continuous variable, $\overline{X} - s$ charts make sense. **c)** Percentages are shown on p charts.

12.70 Use a p chart. CL = 0.005, UCL = 0.0172, LCL = 0.

12.71 CL = 7.65, UCL = 19.642, LCL = 0.

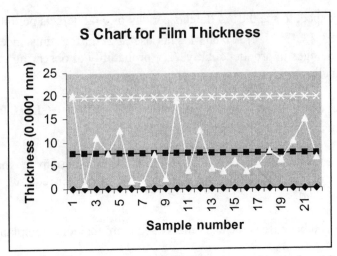

Sample number 1 is above the UCL and sample number 10 is very close to the UCL.

12.72 The new UCL = 16.615.

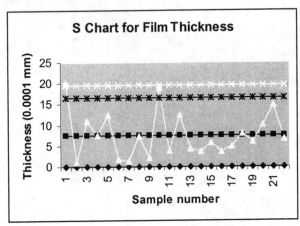

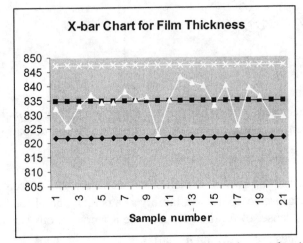

The chart above shows sample means with samples 1 and 10 removed. The process appears to be in control with respect to process average.

12.73 a) $\hat{\sigma} = 7.3$, $C_p = 1.14$. **b)** C_p describes the potential process capability if the process is on target. **c)** Because the process is not on target, the true capability will be less than our estimate for C_p.

12.74 0.0626%.

12.75 a) A p chart would be used with UCL = 0.0194 and LCL = 0. **b)** It is very unlikely that we will observe unsatisfactory films in a sample of 100.

12.76 P(next 15 points will fall within 1σ of μ) = $(0.68)^{15} = 0.0031$.

Chapter 13
Time Series Forecasting

13.1 a) Fourth quarter sales are the highest quarter. The sales also are increasing year by year.
   b)

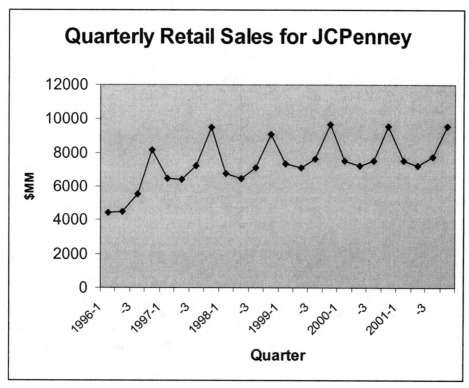

c) There seems to be a positive trend with spikes at every fourth quarter. **d)** The pattern can be seen on a yearly basis. Quarters 1, 2, and 3 are close in value with a slight dip in quarter 2 sales. Quarter 4 shows a strong increase.

13.2 a)

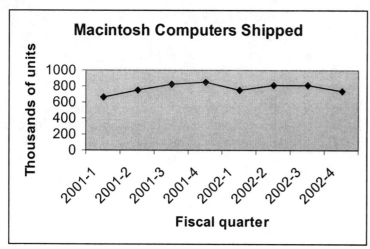

b) $y = 7.9048x + 737.93$. **c)** No, the linear model does not seem appropriate here.

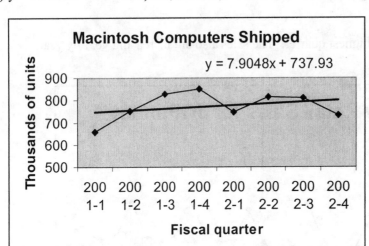

13.3 a) $y = 118.75x + 5903.22$. **b)** The intercept is a prediction for fourth quarter 1995. **c)** The slope tells how much the sales will increase each quarter.

13.4 a) $y = 786.75 + 0.88x - 86.88x_1 - 8.25x_2 + 26.38x_3$. **b)** The fourth quarter is represented by $x_1 = 0$, $x_2 = 0$, and $x_3 = 0$. **c)** The F test indicates that this model is not a good predictor of units shipped.

13.5 a) $y = 7858.8 + 99.54x - 2274.21x_1 - 2564.58x_2 - 2022.79x_3$. **b)** The fourth quarter is represented by $x_1 = 0$, $x_2 = 0$, and $x_3 = 0$. **c)** Yes, fourth quarter 1995. The estimate for the intercept for the second model is 7858. This is greater than the estimate from the first model – 5903. The second estimate is a better estimate.

13.6 a)

1st Q	0.921557
2nd Q	1.015779
3rd Q	1.052191
4th Q	1.010351

b) The average of the four factors is 0.99997. This is close to one. The factor for the first quarter is 0.921557, which means that the seasonal forecast for the number of Macs shipped in the first quarter is approximately 8% below the amount forecasted by the trend model alone.

c)

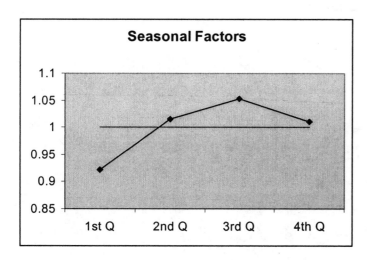

13.7 a)

1st Q	0.922881
2nd Q	0.883456
3rd Q	0.959464
4th Q	1.231493

b) The average of the four factors is 0.99923. This is close to one. The fourth quarter factor is 1.2315, which means that the seasonal forecast for fourth quarter sales is 123% of the trend only forecast.

c)

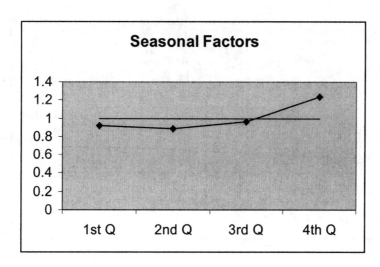

13.8 a) The seasonal pattern shows a steady but small increase during the first three quarters of the year.

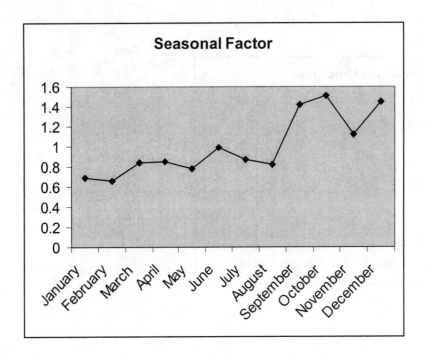

The sales show a dramatic increase in the fourth quarter. **b)** 2,255,508.

13.9 a)

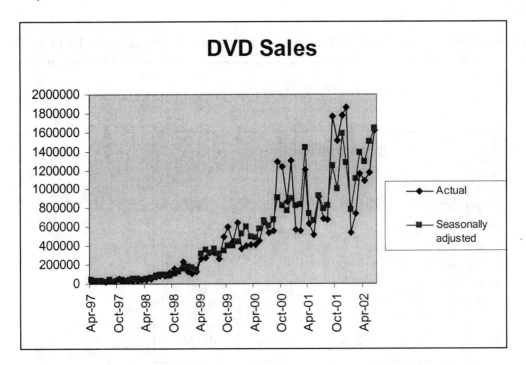

b) No, the seasonal adjustments did not smooth out the time series. The seasonal pattern does not appear to be as strong as the trend.

13.10 c) The residuals appear to be autocorrelated. The residuals are strictly positive from months 26 to

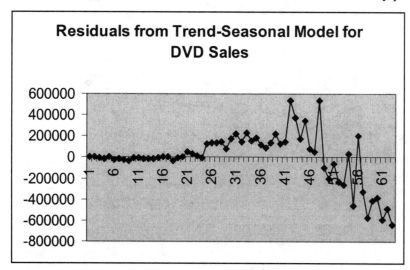

48 and then become mostly negative for the rest of the data set. We should see random scatter around the zero line. It appears that the residuals are positively autocorrelated. **d)** Yes, there is

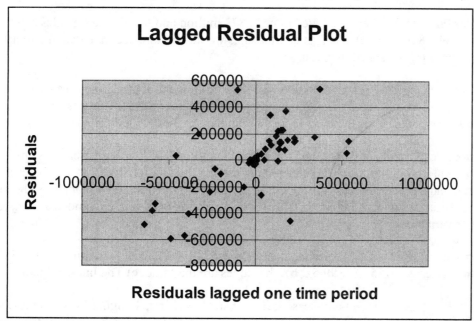

evidence of positive autocorrelation between the residuals. The scatterplot shows a positive trend.

13.11 a) The linear trend model will under predict quarterly sales for the fourth quarter.

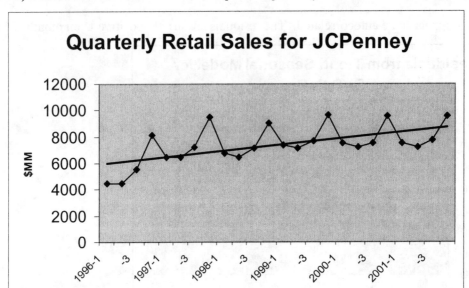

b) First quarter sales for 2002 are predicted to be $8872 million and fourth quarter sales are predicted to be $9228 million. **c)** The first quarter sales would be more accurate than the fourth quarter sales for the reason stated in part a.

13.12 a) First quarter sales for 2002 are predicted to be $8072 million and fourth quarter sales are predicted to be $10,644 million. **b)** The trend-seasonal model gives a lower forecast for the first quarter and a higher forecast for the fourth quarter than the trend-only model.

13.13 a) First quarter sales for 2002 are predicted to be $8,187 million and fourth quarter sales are predicted to be $11,364 million. **b)** The model using seasonality factors gives a lower forecast for the first quarter and a higher forecast for the fourth quarter than the trend only model. **c)** The model using seasonality factors gives a higher forecast for both periods than the trend-and-season model using indicator variables.

13.14 a) First quarter: y = 5584.6 + 99.5x. Second quarter: y = 5294.2 + 99.5x. Third quarter: y = 5836 + 99.5x. Fourth quarter: y = 7858.8 + 99.5x. **b)** The slopes are the same. **c)** The lines are parallel.

13.15 a) Trend-only: R^2 = 0.3501. Trend-and-season: R^2 = 0.8683. R^2 is much higher for the trend-and-season model. **b)** Trend-only: s = 1170. Trend-and-season: s = 567. s is much lower for the trend-and-season model.

c)

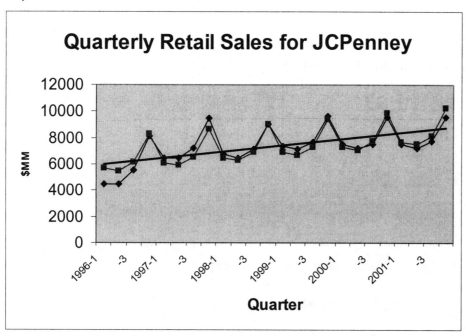

d) The trend-and-season model is a big improvement over the trend-only model.

13.16 a) $7,748.27 million. **b)**

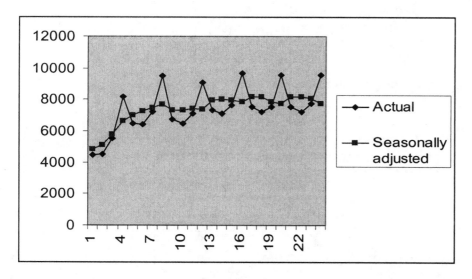

c) Yes, the seasonal adjustment smoothed the sales data. This implies that the seasonal pattern is strong.

13.17 a)

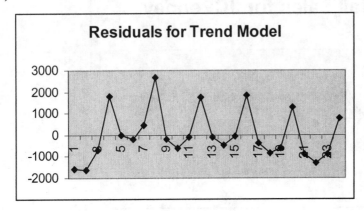

b) It is difficult to detect any autocorrelation from this scatterplot.

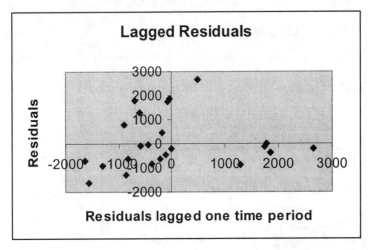

13.18 a)

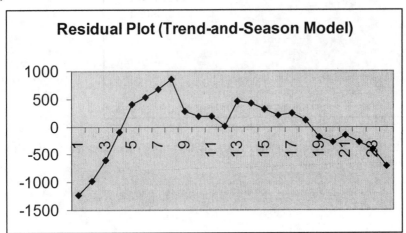

b) There does not appear to be any autocorrelation.

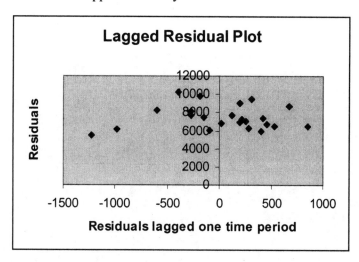

13.19 a) The upper group of ten points would have December sales as the *y*-coordinate. **b)** Yes, the increase in the correlation value indicates a strong autocorrelation in the time series. **c)** We would expect the correlation between the seasonally adjusted time series to be closer to 0.9206. By adjusting the data for seasonal influences we are smoothing out the time series, which should result in a higher correlation.

Chapter 14
One-Way Analysis of Variance

14.1 $x_{ij} = \mu_i + \varepsilon_{ij}$, $i = 1, 2$, and $3, j = 1, \ldots, 60$. $I = 3$. The n_i are all equal to 60 and the parameters are μ_1, μ_2, μ_3, and σ.

14.2 $x_{ij} = \mu_i + \varepsilon_{ij}$, $i = 1, 2, 3, 4$, and $5, j = 1, \ldots, 50$. $I = 5$. The n_i are all equal to 50 and the parameters are μ_1, μ_2, μ_3, μ_4, μ_5, and σ.

14.3 a) Yes, $120 < 2 \times 80$. **b)** $\hat{\mu}_1 = 75, \hat{\mu}_2 = 125, \hat{\mu}_3 = 100, \hat{\sigma} = 101.32$.

14.4 a) No, $14 = 2 \times 7$. **b)** $\hat{\mu}_A = 34, \hat{\mu}_B = 42, \hat{\mu}_C = 20, \hat{\mu}_D = 22, \hat{\mu}_E = 46, \hat{\sigma} = 10.2$.

14.5
0 46	0 6	0 445666
0 7888999	0 777888889999	0 777889
1 012222222	1 00022	1 11122
1 345	1 335	1 33344
1 6	1 6	1

There do not appear to be any systematic differences between the groups.

14.6 It appears that the residuals have a normal distribution with a mean equal to zero.

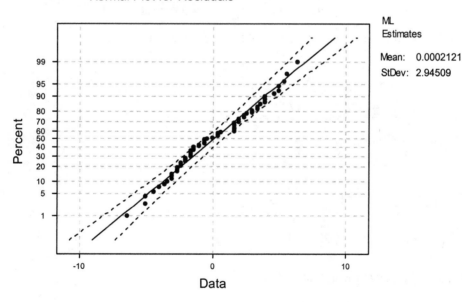

Normal Plot for Residuals

ML Estimates

Mean: 0.0002121
StDev: 2.94509

14.7 $20.58 + 572.45 = 593.03$.

14.8 $I = 3, N = 66$. DFG = 2, DFE = 63, and DFT = 65.

14.9 $2 + 63 = 65$.

14.10 MSG = $20.58/2 = 10.29$. MSE = $572.45/63 = 9.09$.

14.11 MST = 9.1235. This is the value of the sample variance of all 66 responses.

14.12 Verify that MSE = 9.09.

14.13 a) 3 and 20. **b)** 3.10.

14.14 a) 3 and 100. **b)** 2.70.

14.15 a) SAS labels the standard error as Root MSE because the value can be found by taking the square root of the mean square error. **b)** $\sqrt{0.616003} = 0.7849$.

14.16 Applet.

14.17 Applet.

14.18

$$\frac{1}{2}(\mu_1 + \mu_2) = \frac{1}{2}(\mu_4 + \mu_5), \ 0 = \frac{1}{2}(\mu_4 + \mu_5) - \frac{1}{2}(\mu_1 + \mu_2), \ a_1 = a_2 = -\frac{1}{2}, \ a_4 = a_5 = \frac{1}{2}.$$

14.19 $SE_C = s_p \sqrt{\sum \frac{a^2_i}{n_i}} = 10 \sqrt{\frac{1}{25}(\frac{1}{2}^2 + \frac{1}{2}^2 + \frac{1}{2}^2 + \frac{1}{2}^2)} = 2.$

14.20 C = 15. H_o: $\frac{1}{2}(\mu_1 + \mu_2) = \frac{1}{2}(\mu_4 + \mu_5)$, H_a: $\frac{1}{2}(\mu_1 + \mu_2) \neq \frac{1}{2}(\mu_4 + \mu_5)$. $t = 15/2 = 7.5$ with 120 df.
The P-value for this result is less than 0.0005. The contrast is significant.

14.21 (11.032, 18.968).

14.22 $t_{13} = \dfrac{\overline{x}_1 - \overline{x}_2}{s_p \sqrt{\dfrac{1}{n_1} + \dfrac{1}{n_2}}} = \dfrac{41.0455 - 44.2727}{6.31 \sqrt{\dfrac{1}{22} + \dfrac{1}{22}}} = -1.693.$

14.23 $t_{23} = \dfrac{\overline{x}_2 - \overline{x}_3}{s_p \sqrt{\dfrac{1}{n_2} + \dfrac{1}{n_3}}} = \dfrac{46.7273 - 44.2727}{6.31 \sqrt{\dfrac{1}{22} + \dfrac{1}{22}}} = 1.29.$

14.24 We would fail to reject the null hypothesis.

14.25 We would fail to reject the null hypothesis.

14.26 $-3.2273/1.90378 = -1.69$.

14.27 $2.4545/1.90378 = 1.29$.

14.28 Mark groups 1, 2, and 3 with the letter A and mark groups 4 and 5 with the letter B. Groups 1, 2, and 3 do not differ significantly from each other. Groups 4 and 5 do not differ significantly from each other.

14.29 Mark groups 1 and 4 with A, groups 2, 3, and 5 with B, and groups 3 and 4 with C. Groups 1 and 4 do not differ significantly. Groups 2, 3, and 5 do not differ significantly. Groups 3 and 4 do not differ significantly.

14.30 (−7.91, 1.46). Yes, the interval includes 0.

14.31 (−2.23, 7.14). Yes, the interval includes 0.

14.32 a)

Sample size	Power
10	0.2273
20	0.4515
30	0.6445
40	0.7854
50	0.8776
100	0.9959

b)

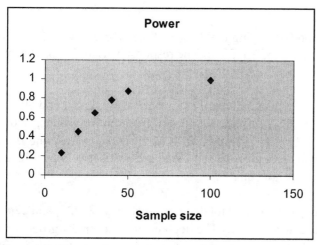

c) Based on the values of *n* selected, I would choose a sample size of 50. The power is fairly high at 0.8776. Increasing the sample size to 100 increases the power so it is very close to one, but to get there the sample size was doubled.

14.33 a)

Sample size	Power
20	0.1366
50	0.3010
75	0.4408
120	0.6569
150	0.7645
200	0.8829

b)

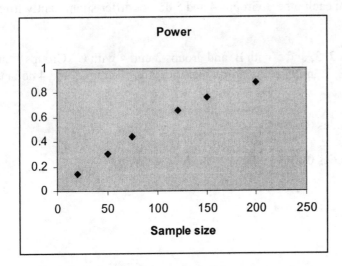

c) The values of the alternative are closer together than in problem 14.32. The sample size needs to be much larger to approximate the same power. A sample size of 200 should be used in this test.

14.34 a) The response variable is program effectiveness rating. $I = 3$, $n_i = 30$, $N = 90$. **b)** The response variable is package attractiveness rating. $I = 6$, $n_i = 50$, $N = 300$. **c)** The response variable is lotion rating. $I = 4$, $n_i = 100$, $N = 400$.

14.35 a) The response variable is likelihood of buying the device. $I = 3$, $n_i = 75$, $N = 225$. **b)** The response variable is strength. $I = 5$, $n_i = 6$, $N = 30$. **c)** The response variable is final exam score. $I = 3$, $n_i = 20$, $N = 60$.

14.36 a) The degrees of freedom for groups, error, and total are, respectively, 2, 87, and 89. H_o: $\mu_1 = \mu_2 = \mu_3$, H_a: at least one μ is not equal. $F^*_{2,87}$. **b)** The degrees of freedom for groups, error, and total are, respectively, 5, 294, and 299. H_o: $\mu_1 = \mu_2 = \mu_3 = \mu_4 = \mu_5 = \mu_6$, H_a: at least one μ is not equal. $F^*_{5,294}$. **c)** The degrees of freedom for groups, error, and total are, respectively, 3, 396, and 399. H_o: $\mu_1 = \mu_2 = \mu_3 = \mu_4$, H_a: at least one μ is not equal. $F^*_{3,396}$.

14.37 a) The degrees of freedom for groups, error, and total are, respectively, 2, 222, and 224. H_o: $\mu_1 = \mu_2 = \mu_3$, H_a: at least one μ is not equal. $F^*_{2,222}$. **b)** The degrees of freedom for groups, error, and total are, respectively, 4, 25, and 29. H_o: $\mu_1 = \mu_2 = \mu_3 = \mu_4 = \mu_5$, H_a: at least one μ is not equal. $F^*_{4,35}$. **c)** The degrees of freedom for groups, error, and total are, respectively, 2, 57, and 59. H_o: $\mu_1 = \mu_2 = \mu_3$, H_a: at least one μ is not equal. $F^*_{2,57}$.

14.38 a) Yes, $24 < 2 \times 18$. **b)** $s_1^2 = 324$, $s_2^2 = 576$, $s_3^2 = 400$, $s_p^2 = 438$. **c)** $s_p = 20.93$.

14.39 a) Yes, it is reasonable. $62 < 2 \times 40$. **b)** $s_1^2 = 3844$, $s_2^2 = 1600$, $s_3^2 = 2704$, $s_4^2 = 2304$, $s_p^2 = 1865$. **c)** $s_p = 43.18$. **d)** The pooled standard deviation is closest to the sample that had the largest sample size.

14.40 a) df $= 2, 21$. P-value $= 0.009748$. **b)** df $= 5, 60$. P-value $= 0.07047$.

14.41 a) df $= 4, 60$. P-value $= 0.183481$, **b)** df $= 9, 30$. P-value $= 0.000629$.

14.42 a) H_o: $\mu_1 = \mu_2 = \mu_3$, H_a: at least one μ is not equal.

b)

Source	Degrees of freedom	Sum of squares	Mean square	F
Groups	2			
Error	253			
Total	255			

c) F will have df = 2 and 253 under the assumption that H_o is true. **d)** 3.00.

14.43 a) H_o: $\mu_1 = \mu_2 = \mu_3 = \mu_4$, H_a: at least one μ is not equal.

b)

Source	Degrees of freedom	Sum of squares	Mean square	F
Groups	3			
Error	196			
Total	199			

c) F will have df = 3 and 196 under the assumption that H_o is true. **d)** 2.65.

14.44 a)

Condition	Vitamin C (mg/100g)		Sample size	Average	Standard deviation
Immediately after baking	47.62	49.79	2	48.71	1.5344
One day after baking	40.45	43.46	2	41.96	2.1284
Three days after baking	21.25	22.34	2	21.80	0.7707
Five days after baking	13.18	11.65	2	12.42	1.0819
Seven days after baking	8.51	8.13	2	8.32	0.2687

b)

ANOVA

Source of Variation	SS	df	MS	F	P-value	F crit
Between Groups	2565.721	4	641.4302	367.742	2.33E–06	5.192163
Within Groups	8.721	5	1.7442			
Total	2574.442	9				

H_o: All μ's are equal. H_a: at least one μ is not equal. $F = 367.742$, P-value = 2.33E–06.

c)

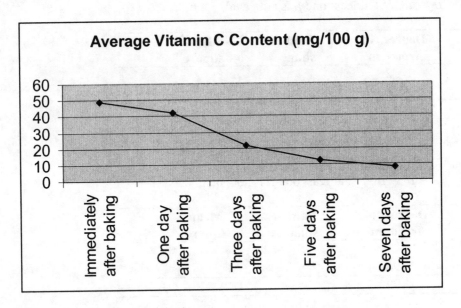

14.45 a) Confidence intervals from Minitab output for comparing means:

```
Tukey's pairwise comparisons

Family error rate = 0.0500
Individual error rate = 0.0102

Critical value = 5.67

Intervals for (column level mean) - (row level mean)

            Five day    Immediate    One day    Seven day

Immediate   -41.585
            -30.995

One day     -34.835       1.455
            -24.245      12.045

Seven day    -1.200      35.090      28.340
              9.390      45.680      38.930

Three day   -14.675      21.615      14.865     -18.770
             -4.085      32.205      25.455      -8.180
```

From the confidence intervals above we can see that there is a significant difference between the Vitamin C content in bread immediately after baking, one day after baking, three days after baking, and five days after baking. The Vitamin C content does not significantly drop between five and seven days after baking.

14.46

```
Analysis of Variance for Vitamin A
Source      DF        SS        MS       F        P
C2           4     0.17894   0.04474   12.09    0.009
Error        5     0.01850   0.00370
Total        9     0.19744
```

```
                                      Individual 95% CIs For Mean
                                      Based on Pooled StDev
Level       N       Mean     StDev   --------+---------+---------+--------
Five day    2     3.3050   0.0778                         (----*-----)
Immediate   2     3.3500   0.0141                          (----*-----)
One day     2     3.2400   0.0566                     (-----*-----)
Seven day   2     2.9650   0.0636     (----*-----)
Three day   2     3.2100   0.0707                 (----*-----)
                                      --------+---------+---------+--------
Pooled StDev =    0.0608                3.00      3.20      3.40
```

```
Analysis of Variance for Vitamin E
Source      DF        SS        MS       F        P
C2           4      9.09      2.27     0.69     0.630
Error        5     16.48      3.30
Total        9     25.56
```

```
                                      Individual 95% CIs For Mean
                                      Based on Pooled StDev
Level       N       Mean     StDev   ---------+---------+---------+-------
Five day    2     96.350    1.909              (------------*-------------)
Immediate   2     95.300    0.990           (------------*------------)
One day     2     94.450    1.768        (------------*------------)
Seven day   2     93.700    1.980     (-----------*------------)
Three day   2     95.850    2.192            (------------*-------------)
                                      ---------+---------+---------+-------
Pooled StDev =    1.815                 92.5      95.0      97.5
```

The ANOVA procedure shows a significant difference in Vitamin A content: $F = 12.9$ and P-value $= 0.009$. The ANOVA procedure shows there is no significant difference in Vitamin E content: $F = 0.69$ and P-value $= 0.63$.

14.47 a) It is not appropriate to perform a multiple comparisons analysis for Vitamin E because the ANOVA procedure showed no significant difference in content after baking.

b) Tukey's pairwise comparisons for Vitamin A content:
```
   Family error rate = 0.0500
   Individual error rate = 0.0102
   Critical value = 5.67
   Intervals for (column level mean) - (row level mean)
```

```
              Five day      Immediate     One day       Seven day

Immediate     -0.28888
               0.19888


One day       -0.17888      -0.13388
               0.30888       0.35388


Seven day      0.09612       0.14112       0.03112
               0.58388       0.62888       0.51888


Three day     -0.14888      -0.10388      -0.21388      -0.48888
               0.33888       0.38388       0.27388      -0.00112
```

Based on the confidence intervals for the mean differences we can see that there is no significant difference in Vitamin A content between immediately after baking, one day after, three days after, and five days after. Once the bread is seven days old, the level of Vitamin A drops significantly.

14.48 Reports will vary by student. The facts are outlined in problems 14.44 to 14.47.

14.49 a)

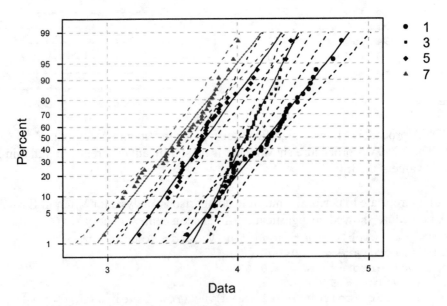

Normal Plot for Expected Price by Promotions

The normal plots do not show obvious departures from normality.

b)

Number of promotions	Average	Standard deviation	Sample size
1	4.224	0.2734	40
3	4.063	0.1742	40
5	3.759	0.2526	40
7	3.549	0.2750	40

c) Yes, the assumption of equal standard deviations is appropriate because $0.2750 < 2 \times 0.1742$.
d) H_o: All μ's are equal. H_a: At least one μ is different from the others. The test statistic is the F statistic with 3 and 156 degrees of freedom. $F = 59.9$ with a P-value $= 0.0$. There is at least one μ that is significantly different than the others.

14.50
```
Tukey's pairwise comparisons
Family error rate = 0.0500
Individual error rate = 0.0104

Critical value = 3.67

Intervals for (column level mean) - (row level mean)

                1               3               5

  3        0.0178
           0.3047

  5        0.3215          0.1603
           0.6085          0.4472

  7        0.5318          0.3705          0.0668
           0.8187          0.6575          0.3537
```

All four means are significantly different from each other.

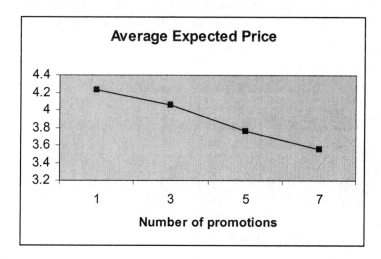

14.51 a)

Type of lesson	Average	Standard deviation	Sample size
Piano	3.62	3.055	34
Singing	-0.30	1.494	10
Computer	0.45	2.212	20
None	0.79	3.072	14

b) H_o: All μ's are equal. H_a: At least one μ is different from the others. The test statistic is the F statistic with 3 and 74 degrees of freedom. $F = 9.24$ with a P-value $= 0.000$. There is at least one μ that is significantly different than the others.

14.52   Tukey's pairwise comparisons
Family error rate = 0.0500
Individual error rate = 0.0104

Critical value = 3.72

Intervals for (column level mean) - (row level mean)

	Computer	None	Piano
None	-2.842		
	2.171		
Piano	-5.195	-5.116	
	-1.140	-0.548	
Singing	-2.036	-1.893	1.330
	3.536	4.064	6.505

Based on the confidence intervals we can see that there is a significant difference in scores between the children that took piano lessons and those that did not. There is no significant difference among the children that took singing lessons, computer lessons, or no lessons.

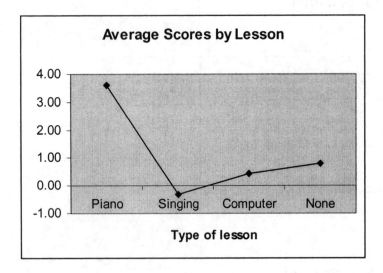

14.53 H_o: $\mu_P = 1/3(\mu_S + \mu_C + \mu_N)$ H_a: $\mu_P > 1/3(\mu_S + \mu_C + \mu_N)$. $c = 3.306$ and $s_P = 0.6356$. $t = 5.20$ with 74 degress of freedom. The P-value is approximately zero. The conclusion is that the average score with piano lessons is greater than the average of the three means without piano lessons.

Group	n	Average	Standard deviation
Control	10	601.1	27.36
High jump	10	638.7	16.59
Low jump	10	612.5	19.33

14.54 a)

Yes, it is reasonable to pool the variances because $27.36 < 2 \times 16.59$. **b)** $F = 7.98$ and P-value = 0.002. There is at least one mean that is significantly different from the rest.

14.55 a)

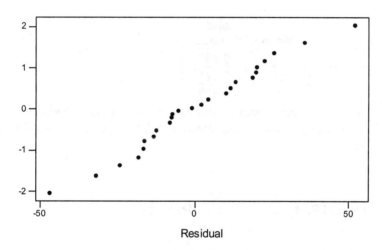

Normal Probability Plot of the Residuals
(response is Bone den)

b) Tukey's pairwise comparisons
Family error rate = 0.0500
Individual error rate = 0.0196
Critical value = 3.51

Intervals for (column level mean) - (row level mean)

```
                Control        High jump

High jump       -61.56
                -13.64

Low jump        -35.36           2.24
                 12.56          50.16
```

Based on the confidence intervals there is a significant difference in bone density between the high jump group and the control and low jump groups. There is no significant difference between the control and low jump groups.

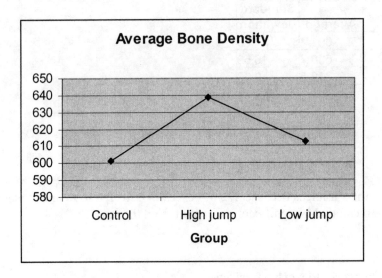

14.56 a)

Type of pot	n	Mean	Standard deviation
Aluminum	4	2.06	0.252
Clay	4	2.18	0.621
Iron	4	4.68	0.628

Because $0.628 < 2 \times 0.252$ it appears unreasonable to pool the standard deviations.

b) $F = 31.16$ with 2 and 9 degrees of freedom. *P*-value = 0.000. At least one of the means is different from the others.

14.57 a)

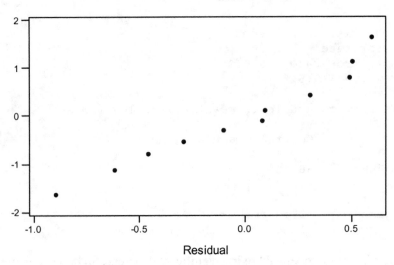

The normal assumption appears reasonable.

b) `Tukey's pairwise comparisons`
`     Family error rate = 0.0500`
`     Individual error rate = 0.0209`

`     Critical value = 3.95`

`     Intervals for (column level mean) - (row level mean)`

```
                      Aluminum        Clay

          Clay          -1.1677
                         0.9277

          Iron          -3.6702      -3.5502
                        -1.5748      -1.4548
```

There does not appear to be a statistically significant difference in iron content between the aluminum and clay pots. Iron pots appear to have a significantly higher iron content than either aluminum or clay pots.

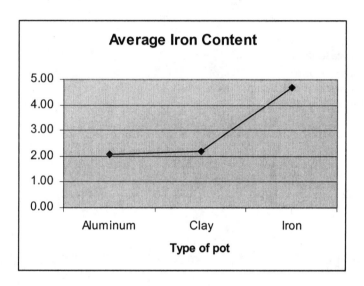

14.58 a)
```
Level          N        Mean       Standard deviation
ECM1           3      65.000         8.660
ECM2           3      63.333         2.887
ECM3           3      73.333         2.887
MAT1           3      23.333         2.887
MAT2           3       6.667         2.887
MAT3           3      11.667         2.887
```

While the largest standard deviation is more than twice the smallest, due to the small sample sizes and the rounding of the data it is reasonable to pool the variances. **b)** $F = 137.94$ with 5 and 12 degrees of freedom. *P*-value = 0.000. At least one μ is different from the rest.

14.59 a)

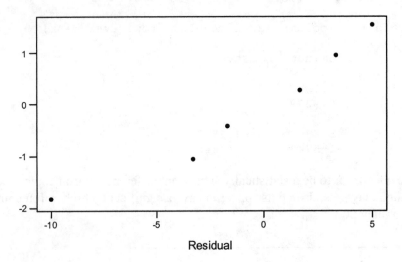

The normal assumption appears reasonable.

b) `Tukey's pairwise comparisons`
`   Family error rate = 0.0500`
`   Individual error rate = 0.00569`

`   Critical value = 4.75`

`   Intervals for (column level mean) - (row level mean)`

	ECM1	ECM2	ECM3	MAT1	MAT2
ECM2	-10.43 13.76				
ECM3	-20.43 3.76	-22.09 2.09			
MAT1	29.57 53.76	27.91 52.09	37.91 62.09		
MAT2	46.24 70.43	44.57 68.76	54.57 78.76	4.57 28.76	
MAT3	41.24 65.43	39.57 63.76	49.57 73.76	-0.43 23.76	-17.09 7.09

There is a significant difference between each of the three ECMs and the MATs. There is a significant difference between MAT1 and MAT2. There is no significant difference between the ECMs or between MAT2 and MAT3 or MAT1 and MAT3.

14.60 $c = 53.333$, $SE_c = 2.079$, $t = 25.653$ with 12 degrees of freedom, and the *P*-value < 0.0005. These results agree with the conclusions found in problem 14.59.

14.61 a)

Level	Mean	Standard deviation
Blue	14.83	5.345
Green	31.50	9.915
Lemon yellow	47.17	6.795
White	15.67	3.327

b) H_o: all μ's are equal H_a: at least one μ is not equal to the rest. **c)** $s_p = 6.784$, $F = 30.55$, P-value $= 0.000$. Conclude that at least one μ is different than the other three.

14.62 The pairs of colors that are significantly different are: Blue and Green, Blue and Lemon yellow, Lemon yellow and Green, Green and White, and Lemon yellow and White. Blue and White are not significantly different. To attract the most insects choose Lemon yellow.

Group (i)	Group (j)	Mean difference (i - j)	t_{ij}
Blue	Green	-16.667	-4.25532
	LY	-32.334	-8.25533
	White	-0.834	-0.21293
Green	Blue	16.667	4.25532
	LY	-15.667	-4.00001
	White	15.833	4.04239
LY	Blue	32.334	8.25533
	Green	15.667	4.00000
	White	31.500	8.04239
White	Blue	0.834	0.21293
	Green	-15.833	-4.04239
	LY	-31.500	-8.04239

14.63 a) 35, 34,951.96, 2,203.14, 15.87. **b)** H_o: all μ's are equal H_a: at least one μ is not equal to the rest. **c)** F with 3 and 32 degrees of freedom. P-value $= 0.000$. At least one μ is different from the others. **d)** $s^2_p = 2,203.14$, $s_p = 46.94$.

14.64 a) 35, 476.88, 2009.92, 2.5308. **b)** H_o: all μ's are equal H_a: at least one μ is not equal to the rest. **c)** F with 3 and 32 degrees of freedom. P-value $= 0.0746$. There is some evidence that at least one μ is different from the rest. **d)** $s^2_p = 62.81$, $s_p = 7.925$.

14.65 a) $s^2_p = 3.8975$, MSE.

b)

Source	Degrees of freedom	Sum of squares	Mean square	F
Groups	2	17.22	8.61	2.2091
Error	206	802.89	3.90	
Total	208			

c) H_o: all μ's are equal H_a: at least one μ is not equal to the rest. **d)** F with 2 and 206 degrees of freedom. P-value $= 0.1124$. There is no strong evidence to support the alternative hypothesis.

14.66 a) $s^2_p = 7{,}2412.12$, MSE.

b)

Source	Degrees of freedom	Sum of squares	Mean square	F
Groups	2	6,572,551	3,286276.00	45.383
Error	230	16,654,788	72,412.12	
Total	232			

c) H_o: all μ's are equal H_a: at least one μ is not equal to the rest. **d)** F with 2 and 230 degrees of freedom. P-value $= 0.000$. There is strong evidence to support the alternative hypothesis. At least one μ is different from the other two.

14.67 a) $\psi_1 = \frac{1}{2}(\mu_1 + \mu_2) - \mu_3$. **b)** $\psi_2 = -\mu_1 + \mu_2$.

14.68 a) $\psi_1 = -\frac{1}{2}(\mu_1 + \mu_2) + \frac{1}{2}(\mu_3 + \mu_4)$. **b)** $\psi_2 = -\mu_1 + \mu_2$. **c)** $\psi_3 = -\mu_3 + \mu_4$.

14.69 a) H_{o1}: $\frac{1}{2}(\mu_1 + \mu_2) = \mu_3$ H_{a1}: $\frac{1}{2}(\mu_1 + \mu_2) > \mu_3$. H_{o2}: $\mu_1 = \mu_2$ H_{a2}: $\mu_1 \neq \mu_2$. **b)** $c_1 = 49$ and $c_2 = 10$. **c)** $s_{c1} = 11.27821$ and $s_{c2} = 16.9008$. **d)** $t_1 = 4.3447$ with 253 degrees of freedom and a P-value < 0.0005. $t_2 = 0.5917$ with 253 degrees of freedom and a P-value $= 0.5546$. It appears that the average SAT math scores for the computer science majors and engineering majors are significantly higher than for the other majors. The computer science and engineering majors do not have significantly different average SAT math scores. **e)** The 95% confidence interval for contrast one is 49 ± 22.59. The 95% confidence interval for contrast two is 10 ± 33.8.

14.70 a) H_{o1}: $\frac{1}{2}(\mu_1 + \mu_2) = \mu_3$ H_{a1}: $\frac{1}{2}(\mu_1 + \mu_2) > \mu_3$. H_{o2}: $\mu_1 = \mu_2$ H_{a2}: $\mu_1 \neq \mu_2$. **b)** $c_1 = 0.93$ and $c_2 = -0.02$. **c)** $s_{c1} = 0.2299$ and $s_{c2} = 0.3421$. **d)** $t_1 = 4.046$ with 221 degrees of freedom and a P-value < 0.0005. $t_2 = -0.058$ with 221 degrees of freedom and a P-value $= 0.9534$. It appears that the average high school math grades for the computer science majors and engineering majors are significantly higher than for the other majors. The computer science and engineering majors do not have significantly different average high school math grades. **e)** The 95% confidence interval for contrast one is 0.93 ± 0.4598. The 95% confidence interval for contrast two is -0.02 ± 0.6842.

14.71 a) $\psi_1 = \mu_1 - \mu_2$ H_{o1}: $\mu_1 = \mu_2$ H_{a1}: $\mu_1 > \mu_2$. $\psi_2 = \mu_1 - \frac{1}{2}(\mu_2 + \mu_4)$ H_{o2}: $\mu_1 = \frac{1}{2}(\mu_2 + \mu_4)$ H_{a2}: $\mu_1 > \frac{1}{2}(\mu_2 + \mu_4)$. $\psi_3 = \mu_3 - 1/3(\mu_1 + \mu_2 + \mu_4)$ H_{o3}: $\mu_3 = 1/3(\mu_1 + \mu_2 + \mu_4)$ H_{a3}: $\mu_3 > 1/3(\mu_1 + \mu_2 + \mu_4)$. **b)** $t_1 = -0.6635$ with a P-value $= 0.2559$. $t_2 = 1.242$ with a P-value $= 0.1116$. $t_3 = 5.282$ with a P-value $= 0.000$. The average score for the joggers groups is significantly higher than the average of the other three groups. **c)** This study does not show causation. There are many lurking variables that could contribute to a low score.

14.72 a) $\psi_1 = \mu_2 - \mu_1$ H_{o1}: $\mu_1 = \mu_2$ H_{a1}: $\mu_1 < \mu_2$. $\psi_2 = -\mu_1 + \frac{1}{2}(\mu_2 + \mu_4)$ H_{02}: $\mu_1 = \frac{1}{2}(\mu_2 + \mu_4)$ H_{a2}: $\mu_1 < \frac{1}{2}(\mu_2 + \mu_4)$. $\psi_3 = -\mu_3 + 1/3(\mu_1 + \mu_2 + \mu_4)$ H_{o3}: $\mu_3 = 1/3(\mu_1 + \mu_2 + \mu_4)$ H_{a3}: $\mu_3 < 1/3(\mu_1 + \mu_2 + \mu_4)$.
b) $t_1 = 1.2663$ with a *P*-value = 0.173. $t_2 = 1.7785$ with a *P*-value = 0.0424. $t_3 = 2.092$ with a *P*-value = 0.0222. The average depression score for the treatment group is significantly lower than for the average of the control and sedentary groups. The average depression score for the joggers groups is significantly lower than the average of the other three groups. **c)** This study does not show causation. There are many lurking variables that could contribute to a low score.

14.73

Group (i)	Group (j)	Mean difference	Standard error	t_{ij}
T	C	−17.06	25.7101	−0.66355
	J	−74.96	20.5096	−3.65488
	S	65.84	20.9922	3.13640
C	T	17.06	25.7101	0.66355
	J	−57.90	25.3176	−2.28695
	S	82.90	25.7101	3.22441
J	T	74.96	20.5096	3.65488
	C	57.90	25.3176	2.28695
	S	140.80	20.5096	6.86509
S	T	−65.84	20.9922	−3.13640
	C	−82.90	25.7101	−3.22441
	J	−140.80	20.5096	−6.86509

The sedentary group is significantly different from the three other groups. The treatment group is significantly different from the jogger group and the sedentary group. There is no significant difference between the jogger group and the control group or between the treatment group and the control group.

14.74

Group (i)	Group (j)	Mean difference	Standard error	t_{ij}
T	C	−5.50	4.3434	−1.26628
	J	2.17	3.4649	0.62629
	S	−6.30	3.5464	−1.77645
C	T	5.50	4.3434	1.26627
	J	7.67	4.2771	1.79326
	S	−0.80	4.3434	−0.18419
J	T	−2.17	3.4649	−0.62629
	C	−7.67	4.2771	−1.79326
	S	−8.47	3.4649	−2.44454
S	T	6.30	3.5464	1.77645
	C	0.80	4.3434	0.18419
	J	8.47	3.4649	2.44454

There do not appear to be any significant differences between groups.

14.75

Sample size	Power
50	0.2948
100	0.5449
150	0.7332
175	0.8014
200	0.8545

A sample size of 200 would give the highest power for these alternative values of μ.

14.76 The results will be the same because the differences are the same.

14.77 a)

Condition	Vitamin C (% of original)		Sample size	Average	Standard deviation
Immediately after baking	74.4063	77.79688	2	76.1094	2.3975
One day after baking	63.2031	67.90625	2	65.5625	3.3256
Three days after baking	33.2031	34.90625	2	34.0625	1.2042
Five days after baking	20.5938	18.20313	2	19.4063	1.6905
Seven days after baking	13.2969	12.70313	2	13	0.4198

b) You could have performed the transformation directly on the means and standard deviations by using the relationships described in Chapter 4.

ANOVA

Source of Variation	SS	df	MS	F	P-value	F crit
Between Groups	6263.967	4	1565.992	367.742	2.33E-06	5.192163
Within Groups	21.292	5	4.258			
Total	6285.259	9				

c)

The F statistic has the same value as the one found in problem 14.44.

14.78 In general the F statistic, degrees of freedom, and P-value stay the same when changing the units of measure.

14.79 a) $F = 2.0$ with a P-value $= 0.146$. The test does not show a statistically significant result. **b)** The result found in 14.61 did show a statistically significant result. Outliers can change the conclusion of an ANOVA test.

c)

Level	N	Mean	StDev
Blue	6	14.83	5.34
Green	6	31.50	9.91
Lemon yellow	6	114.67	164.42
White	6	15.67	3.33

One can see that the outlier would be in the Lemon Yellow level because the high value of the mean and standard deviation stand out.

Level	n	Mean	StDev
Blue	6	3.7931	0.7312
Green	6	5.5435	0.9613
Lemon yellow	6	6.8533	0.4882
White	6	3.9400	0.4142

14.80 a)

b) $F = 27$ with a P-value = 0.000. This result indicates there is at least one μ that is significantly different than the rest. This is the same result we found in 14.61.

14.81 a)

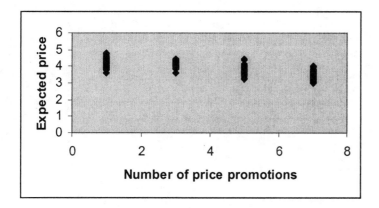

The pattern is roughly linear. **b)** The test for $\beta = 0$ is the test for no linear relationship between explanatory variable and response variable. **c)** The results of the regression analysis show that there is a significant linear relationship between the number of promotions and the expected price. The ANOVA results state that there is at least one μ that is different from the other three. Regression analysis gives more information because we know that there is a linear relationship. ANOVA does not tell us the type of relationship between the variables.

Chapter 15
Two-Way Analysis of Variance

15.1 Response variable: Effectiveness rating. Factors: Training program and Delivery method. I = 3, J = 2, and N = 120.

15.2 Response variable: Attractiveness rating. Factors: Type of packaging and Color. I = 4, J = 3, and N = 480.

15.3 Response variable: Lotion rating. Factors: Formulation and Fragrance.   I = 5, J = 3, and N = 1800.

15.4 Verify.

15.5 The difference increases with age until the age of 65.

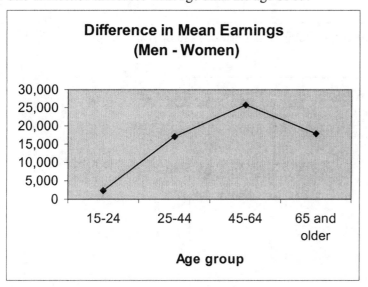

15.6 The two mean plots follow each other. Figure 15.2 shows divergent plots.

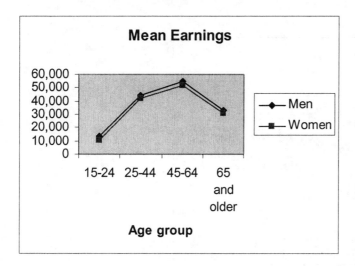

15.7 a)

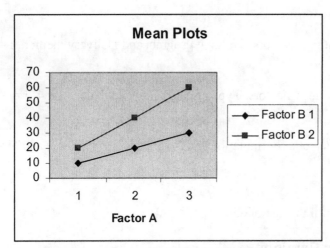

Yes, there is an interaction. The effect of factor B increases as factor A increases.

b)

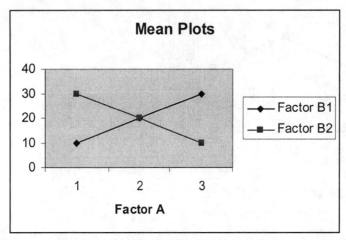

Yes, there is an interaction. The effect of factor B decreases as factor A increases.

c)

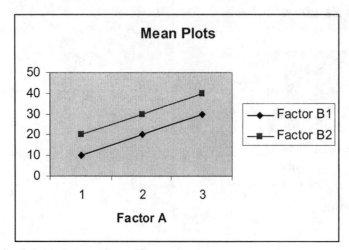

No, there is no interaction effect.

d)

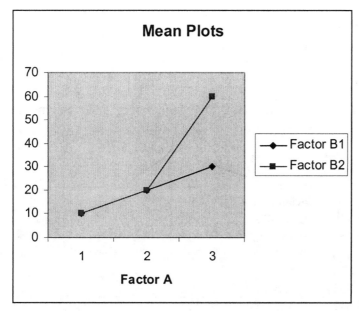

Yes, there is an interaction effect. The effect is not apparent until we reach level 3 of factor A.

15.8 The effect of the training program: 2 and 114 degrees of freedom. The effect of the delivery method: 1 and 114 degrees of freedom. The interaction effect: 2 and 114 degrees of freedom.

15.9 3 and 468. 2 and 468. 6 and 468.

15.10 4 and 1785. 2 and 1785. 8 and 1785.

15.11

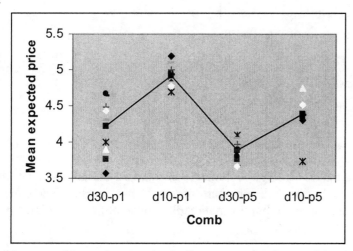

The spread in each group is similar except for the combination d10-p5. There may be an outlier on the low side. The treatment means appear to be different.

15.12

	Discount		
Promotions	**20%**	**40%**	**Total**
1	4.689	4.423	4.556
3	4.524	4.284	4.404
Total	4.6065	4.3535	

Excel agrees with the SPSS output except for one thing. Excel does not give the total mean for the entire set of observations.

15.13

Promo	Discount	Mean	Standard deviation	N
1	30%	4.225	0.385609	10
1	10%	4.920	0.152023	10
	Total	4.573	0.456611	20
5	30%	3.890	0.162891	10
5	10%	4.393	0.268537	10
	Total	4.142	0.336613	20
Total	30%	4.058	0.335463	20
	10%	4.657	0.343791	20
	Total	4.357	0.452113	40

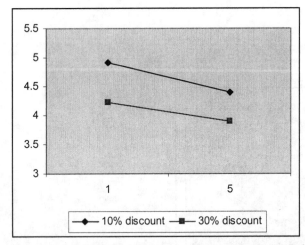

Based on the standard deviations it makes sense to pool the group standard deviations to get MSE. There is a difference in mean expected price as the number of promotions decrease. There may be an interaction effect due to percentage discount but it is not readily apparent from the plot.

15.14 Verify.

15.15 Answers will vary.

15.16 There is a significant drop in expected price when the number of promotions increases from 1 to 5. ($F = 27.47$, df = 1 and 36, $P = 0.0$). When the discount increases from 10% to 30% there is a significant drop in expected price ($F = 53.07$, df = 1 and 36, $P = 0.0$). There is no significant interaction effect ($F = 0.09$, df = 1 and 36, $P = 0.2507$).

15.17 a) Response variable: number of hours of sleep each night. Factors: Type of smoker and Gender. I = 3, J = 2, and N = 480. **b)** Response variable: strength of concrete. Factors: Concrete formula and Number of freezing cycles. I = 6, J = 3, and N = 54. **c)** Response variable: Final exam score. Factors: Teaching method and Major area of study. I = 4, J = 2, and N = 32.

15.18 a)

Source	Degrees of freedom	Sum of squares	Mean square	F
A	2			
B	1			
AB	2			
Error	474			
Total	479			

b)

Source	Degrees of freedom	Sum of squares	Mean square	F
A	5			
B	2			
AB	10			
Error	36			
Total	53			

c)

Source	Degrees of freedom	Sum of squares	Mean square	F
A	3			
B	1			
AB	3			
Error	24			
Total	31			

15.19 a) 2 and 60. 3 and 60. 6 and 60. **b)** 3.15, 2.76, and 2.25. **c)** 4.98, 4.13, 3.12.

15.20 a) 1 and 30. 2 and 30. 2 and 30. **b)** 4.17, 3.32, 3.32. **c)** 7.56, 5.39, 5.39.

15.21 a)

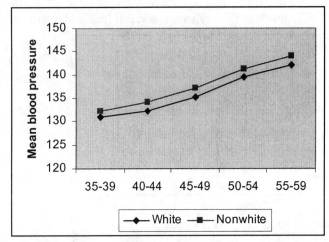

b) There does appear to be a pattern. Blood pressure increases as age increases. The blood pressure for the nonwhite group is greater than for the white group. There is no interaction between race and age.

c)

	35-39	40-44	45-49	50-54	55-59	Total means
White	131.0	132.3	135.2	139.4	142.0	135.98
Nonwhite	132.3	134.2	137.2	141.3	144.1	137.82
Means difference	1.3	1.9	2	1.9	2.1	1.84

The differences in means for each group are very close together. This supports the observation that there is no significant interaction effect.

15.22 a)

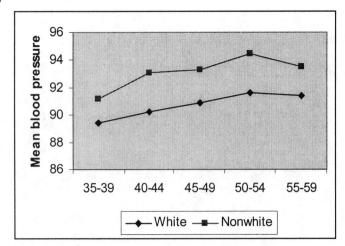

b) There does appear to be a difference between the two groups. Nonwhites have higher blood pressure than whites. Diastolic blood pressure increases with age. The interaction between race and age is not obvious in the plot.

c)

	35-39	40-44	45-49	50-54	55-59	Total means
White	89.4	90.2	90.9	91.6	91.4	90.70
Nonwhite	91.2	93.1	93.3	94.5	93.5	93.12
Means difference	1.8	2.9	2.4	2.9	2.1	2.42

The difference in means appears to be greater for the age groups 40-44 and 50-54.

15.23 a)

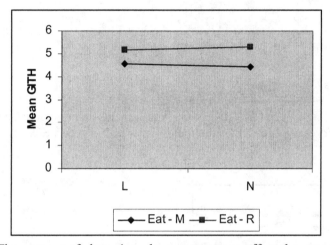

b) The amount of chromium does not seem to affect the mean GITH. Restricting the diet does seem to increase the amount of GITH. No interaction is obvious.

c)

Chromium	Eat - M	Eat - R	Means difference
L	4.545	5.175	0.630
N	4.425	5.317	0.892
Total Means	4.485	5.246	0.761

The differences in means are similar. No interaction is obvious.

15.24

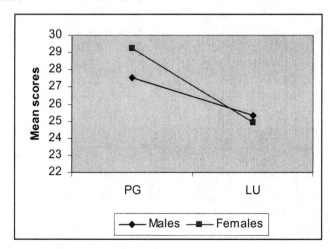

The scores decrease from the PG group to the LU group. The interaction effect is evident but because of the type of interaction the main effect of gender does not mean anything without the information about the individuals tested.

15.25

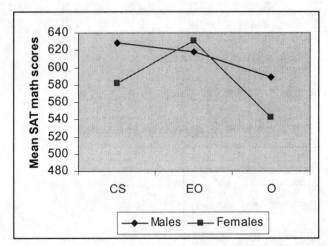

The males' SAT math scores decrease from CS to EO to O. The females' scores increase and then decrease. In fact, the females' scores are greater for the males' only in the group EO.

15.26

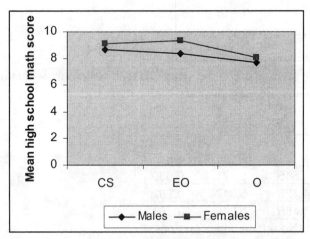

The mean high school math scores decrease from the groups CS to EO to O. The males' scores tend to be slightly lower than the females'. There does not appear to be an interaction.

15.27 Excel output:

Anova: Two-Factor with Replication

SUMMARY	4 weeks	8 weeks	Total
ECM1			
Count	3	3	6
Sum	195	190	385
Average	65	63.33333	64.16667
Variance	75	8.333333	34.16667

ECM2			
Count	3	3	6
Sum	190	190	380
Average	63.33333	63.33333	63.33333
Variance	8.333333	33.33333	16.66667

ECM3			
Count	3	3	6
Sum	220	220	440
Average	73.33333	73.33333	73.33333
Variance	8.333333	33.33333	16.66667

MAT1			
Count	3	3	6
Sum	70	65	135
Average	23.33333	21.66667	22.5
Variance	8.333333	33.33333	17.5

MAT2			
Count	3	3	6
Sum	20	20	40
Average	6.666667	6.666667	6.666667
Variance	8.333333	8.333333	6.666667

MAT3			
Count	3	3	6
Sum	35	30	65
Average	11.66667	10	10.83333
Variance	8.333333	25	14.16667

b)

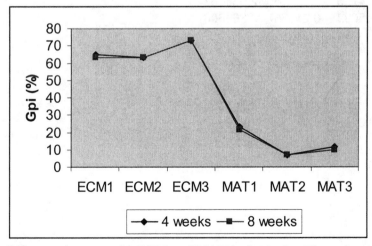

The difference between the ECM and MAT is dramatic. There does not seem to be a difference in mean Gpi between the two times. **c)** For the scaffold material effect: $F = 251.26$ with df = 5 and 24. $P = 0.0$. For the time effect: $F = 0.29$ with df = 1 and 24. $P = 0.595$. For the interaction effect: $F =$

0.058 with df = 5 and 24. P = 0.998. The main effect of type of material used as a scaffold was significant. The effect of time and the interaction effect showed no significant differences in means.

15.28 The two main effects, material and time, are both significant now. The interaction effect is also significant. The percent of Gpi drops for each type of material between the 2-week period and the 4-week period. For the ECM groups 1 and 2 the drop is relatively small. For ECM3 there is actually an increase in percent of Gpi. For the MAT groups, the drop in percent Gpi is almost half of what the value is at the 2-week period. Material: F = 280.09 with df = 5 and 36. P = 0.0. Time: F = 17.04 with df = 2 and 36. P = 0.0. Interaction: F = 4.25 with df = 10 and 36. P = 0.00061.

15.29 For the 2-week period: There is a significant difference (using Tukey's comparison with alpha = 0.05) between all three MAT groups and between the MAT groups and each of the ECM groups. There is no significant difference between the three ECM groups. For the 4-week period: There is a significant difference (using Tukey's comparison with alpha = 0.05) between the three MAT groups and the three ECM groups. There is no significant difference among the MAT groups or the ECM groups. For the 8-week period: The same result holds as for the 4-week period.

15.30 a) Excel output:

Anova: Two-Factor With Replication

SUMMARY	Meat	Legumes	Vegetables	Total
Aluminum				
Count	4	4	4	12
Sum	8.23	9.32	4.93	22.48
Average	2.0575	2.33	1.2325	1.873333
Variance	0.063492	0.012333	0.053492	0.27277
Clay				
Count	4	4	4	12
Sum	8.71	9.89	5.84	24.44
Average	2.1775	2.4725	1.46	2.036667
Variance	0.386025	0.005092	0.211667	0.361606
Iron				
Count	4	4	4	12
Sum	18.72	14.68	11.16	44.56
Average	4.68	3.67	2.79	3.713333
Variance	0.394733	0.0298	0.057533	0.78197

b)

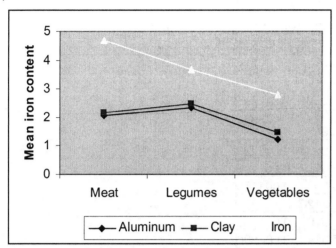

The iron content of foods appears to be much higher for the iron pot when compared to the aluminum and clay pots. There is a noticeable decrease in mean iron content as the food type changes from meat to legumes and vegetables.

c)

ANOVA

Source of Variation	SS	df	MS	F	P-value	F crit
Sample (type of pot)	24.89396	2	12.44698	92.26312	8.53E-13	3.354131
Columns (type of food)	9.296872	2	4.648436	34.45649	3.7E-08	3.354131
Interaction	2.640428	4	0.660107	4.893037	0.004247	2.727766
Within	3.6425	27	0.134907			
Total	40.47376	35				

Both of the main effects and the interaction effect are significant.

15.31 Yes, in general, this data support the hypothesis that foods cooked in iron pots contain a significantly higher iron content than foods cooked in aluminum or clay pots. The interaction effect is small compared to the main effect of type of pot.

15.32

```
                                   Based on Pooled StDev
   Level    N     Mean    StDev   ---+---------+---------+---------+---
   L-A      4    2.3300   0.1111             (--*---)
   L-C      4    2.4725   0.0714             (---*--)
   L-I      4    3.6700   0.1726                         (---*--)
   M-A      4    2.0575   0.2520         (--*--)
   M-C      4    2.1775   0.6213         (--*--)
   M-I      4    4.6800   0.6283                                  (--*--)
   V-A      4    1.2325   0.2313    (--*--)
   V-C      4    1.4675   0.4681     (--*--)
   V-I      4    2.7900   0.2399               (--*--)
```

Based on Tukey's comparison with alpha = 0.05, the clay and aluminum pots do not show significant differences in iron content for meat, legumes, and vegetables. However, there are significant differences between iron and aluminum and iron and clay. There are also significant differences across the three food types.

15.33 a)

Tool	Time	Mean	Standard deviation
1	1	25.0307	0.001155
	2	25.0280	0
	3	25.0260	0
2	1	25.0167	0.001155
	2	25.0200	0.002000
	3	25.0160	0
3	1	25.0063	0.001528
	2	25.0127	0.001155
	3	25.0093	0.001155
4	1	25.0120	0
	2	25.0193	0.001155
	3	25.0140	0.004000
5	1	24.9973	0.001155
	2	25.0060	0
	3	25.0003	0.001528

b)

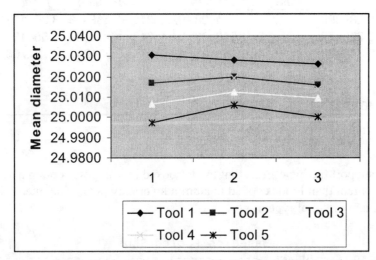

The means change with each tool and with time but the times the measurements were taken does not appear as dramatic. There may be a slight interaction effect.

c)

ANOVA

Source of Variation	SS	df	MS	F	P-value	F crit
Sample	0.003597	4	0.000899	412.9439	9.27E-26	2.689632
Columns	0.00019	2	9.5E-05	43.60204	1.33E-09	3.315833
Interaction	0.000133	8	1.67E-05	7.645409	1.55E-05	2.266162
Within	6.53E-05	30	2.18E-06			
Total	0.003986	44				

Both the main effects of time and tool type were significant, as well as the interaction effect.

15.34

ANOVA

Source of Variation	SS	df	MS	F	P-value	F crit
Sample	5.76E-06	4	1.44E-06	412.9439	9.27E-26	2.689632
Columns	3.04E-07	2	1.52E-07	43.60204	1.33E-09	3.315833
Interaction	2.13E-07	8	2.66E-08	7.645408	1.55E-05	2.266162
Within	1.05E-07	30	3.48E-09			
Total	6.38E-06	44				

The SS values changed but the F values, degrees of freedom and P-values did not change.

15.35 a)

Number of promotions	Percent discount	Mean	Standard deviation
1	40	4.423	0.184755
	30	4.225	0.385609
	20	4.689	0.233069
	10	4.920	0.152023
3	40	4.284	0.204026
	30	4.097	0.234618
	20	4.524	0.270727
	10	4.756	0.242908
5	40	4.058	0.175992
	30	3.890	0.162891
	20	4.251	0.264846
	10	4.393	0.268537
7	40	3.780	0.214372
	30	3.760	0.261789
	20	4.094	0.240749
	10	4.269	0.269916

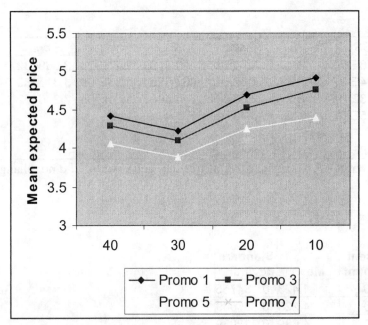

There is a main effect from the number of promotions offered. As the number of promotions offered increases, the expected price decreases. There is also a main effect from the percent discount. As the percent discount increases, the expected price tends to decrease. There does not appear to be an interaction effect.

b)

ANOVA

Source of Variation	SS	df	MS	F	P-value	F crit
Sample	8.360502	3	2.786834	47.72504	1.78E-21	2.667441
Columns	8.306937	3	2.768979	47.41927	2.24E-21	2.667441
Interaction	0.230586	9	0.025621	0.438758	0.9121	1.945452
Within	8.40867	144	0.058394			
Total	25.30669	159				

The main effects of promotions offered ($F = 47.72$ with df = 3 and 144 and $P = 0.0$) and percent discount ($F = 47.42$ with df = 3 and 144 and $P = 0.0$) are both statistically significant. The interaction effect is not statistically significant ($F = 0.4388$ with df = 9 and 144 and $P = 0.9121$).

15.36

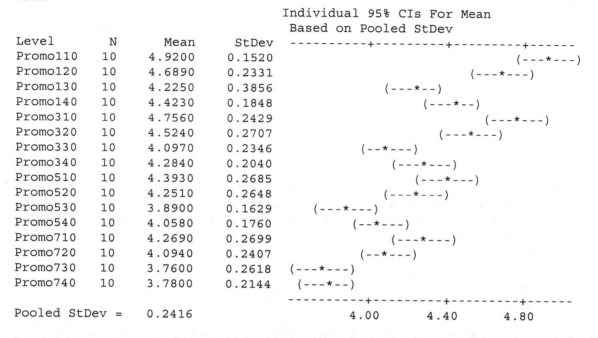

```
                                    Individual 95% CIs For Mean
                                    Based on Pooled StDev
Level        N      Mean    StDev  ----------+---------+---------+------
Promo110    10     4.9200   0.1520                                 (---*---)
Promo120    10     4.6890   0.2331                           (---*---)
Promo130    10     4.2250   0.3856              (---*--)
Promo140    10     4.4230   0.1848                  (---*--)
Promo310    10     4.7560   0.2429                              (---*---)
Promo320    10     4.5240   0.2707                         (---*---)
Promo330    10     4.0970   0.2346            (--*---)
Promo340    10     4.2840   0.2040               (---*---)
Promo510    10     4.3930   0.2685                    (---*---)
Promo520    10     4.2510   0.2648                 (---*---)
Promo530    10     3.8900   0.1629         (---*---)
Promo540    10     4.0580   0.1760          (--*---)
Promo710    10     4.2690   0.2699               (---*---)
Promo720    10     4.0940   0.2407          (--*---)
Promo730    10     3.7600   0.2618    (---*---)
Promo740    10     3.7800   0.2144     (---*--)
                                    ----------+---------+---------+------
Pooled StDev =     0.2416            4.00      4.40      4.80
```

The ANOVA tool on Minitab generated the confidence intervals above. One can see a decreasing trend in expected price as the number of promotions increases. It is also possible to see that within each promotion group, the lowest expected price occurs at a 30% discount. (Note: Minitab does not calculate the Bonferroni multiple comparisons.)

15.37 a)

ANOVA				
Source of Variation	*df*	*SS*	*MS*	*F*
A (Chromium)	1	0.00121	0.00121	0.04031
B (Eat)	1	5.79121	5.79121	192.91173
AB	1	0.17161	0.17161	5.71652
Error	36	1.08084	0.03002	
Total	39	7.04487		

b) $F = 5.71652$. The distribution has df = 1 and 36. $P = 0.022125$. **c)** Chromium: $F = 0.04031$ with df = 1 and 36. $P = 0.842006$. Eat: $F = 192.91173$ with df = 1 and 36. $P = 0.0$. **d)** $s_p^2 = 0.03002$ and $s_p = 0.17326$. **e)** The results of this ANOVA test are consistent with the observations made in 15.23. The chromium level does not affect the level of GITH. There is a significant difference in GITH between the restricted diet and unrestricted diet. There is no significant interaction effect.

15.38 a)

ANOVA

Source of Variation	df	SS	MS	F
A (Chromium)	1	62.40	62.40	0.668
B (Eat)	1	1,599.03	1,599.03	17.124
AB	1	163.80	163.80	1.754
Error	146	13,633.29	93.38	
Total	149	15,458.52		

b) $F = 1.754$. The distribution has df = 1 and 146. **c)** Gender: $F = 0.668$ with df = 1 and 146 and $P = 0.41508$. Group: $F = 17.124$ with df = 1 and 146 and $P = 0.00006$. **d)** $s_p^2 = 93.38$ and $s_p = 9.66$. **e)** The main effect of Group is significant. The main effect of gender and the interaction effect are not significant. This is consistent with the observations from problem 15.24.

15.39 a) $F = 22.36$ with df = 1 and 945: $P = 0.0$. $F = 37.44$ with df = 1 and 945: $P = 0.0$. $F = 2.10$ with df = 1 and 945: $P = 0.1476$. **b)** The main effects of gender and handedness are significant but the interaction effect is not.

15.40 a) $F = 7.02$ with df = 3 and 56: $P = 0.00043$. $F = 1.96$ with df = 1 and 56: $P = 0.16703$. $F = 1.24$ with df = 3 and 56: $P = 0.3039$. **b)** The main effect of series is significant but the effects of holder and interaction are not. The difference in average readings from the four production series was important because it is typically assumed that the detectors are all the same whereas this study shows that they are not. The different production series actually detected different average levels even though they were exposed to the same level of radon.

15.41 The main effects of group and gender are both significant. The interaction effect is shown to be statistically significant even though it is not apparent in a plot of the means. This is most likely due to the large sample sizes used in the study. One might ask if this interaction effect is of practical significance as well as statistical significance.

Chapter 16
Nonparametric Tests

16.1

Rate Asia	2.3	8.8	3.9	4.1	6.4	5.9	4.2	2.9	1.3	5.1	5.6	6.2	
Rank	9	25	14	15	23	20	16	10	7	18	19	22	
Rate Europe	6	-5.2	-1	3.5	3.2	-1.7	-1.5	1	4.9	1.4	7	3.7	-12
Rank	21	2	5	12	11	3	4	6	17	8	24	13	1

The European rates appear to have lower ranks than the Asian rates.

16.2 $W = 198$, $\mu_W = 156$, $\sigma_W = 18.385$. Minitab reports the P-value = 0.012.

16.3 Using the normal approximation with the continuity correction for a one-tailed test, the P-value = 0.012.

16.4 The rank sum for Europe is 127. $198 + 127 = 325$. The Minitab output is below. Note that the P-value is the same as that in 16.2.

```
Europe      N =   13     Median =        1.400
Asia        N =   12     Median =        4.650
Point estimate for ETA1-ETA2 is      -2.950
95.3 Percent CI for ETA1-ETA2 is  (-6.599,-0.398)
W = 127.0
Test of ETA1 = ETA2   vs   ETA1 < ETA2 is significant at 0.0120
```

16.5

MPG	24	24	23	30	28	26	23	22	24	24	24
Rank	7	7	2.5	27.5	21.5	15	2.5	1	7	7	7
Brand (A or F)	F	F	F	F	F	F	F	F	F	F	F
MPG	28	28	25	24	25	28	26	28	32	31	26
Rank	21.5	21.5	12	7	12	21.5	15	21.5	31	30	15
Brand (A or F)	F	F	F	F	F	F	F	F	F	F	F
MPG	30	24	27	29	30	30	25	27	28	33	
Rank	27.5	7	17.5	25	27.5	27.5	12	17.5	21.5	32	
Brand (A or F)	A	A	A	A	A	A	A	A	A	A	

16.6 $W = 215$, P-value = 0.042. Yes, there is a significant difference between the mileages of domestic and foreign brands.

16.7 a)

Price	2.92	2.92	2.93	2.93	2.97	3.57	3.58	3.59	3.6	3.62
Rank	1	2	3	4	5	6	7	8	9	10

b) $W = 40$, $\mu_W = 27.5$, $\sigma_W = 4.787$. **c)** P-value = 0.012.

16.8 a) The data primarily depart from normality because they are integer valued. **b)** Yes, there is significant evidence (P-value = 0.0000) that Malathion significantly reduces larvae per stem.

16.9 a)

```
      8    09
          10
   0 0    11    8
     4    12    0 6  6 9
          13
     0    14
```

b) We do not have strong evidence that breaking strengths are lower for strips buried longer (*P* = 0.1467).

16.10 a) Answers may vary.

b) The mean difference for the treatment group is 11.4 and for the control group is 8.25. The control group is skewed to the right.

```
          0
     6    0    455
     7    0    78
  2110    1    12
   533    1    4
     6    1
```

c) Minitab calculated the *P*-value for a one-tailed test at 0.0494. This is significant at the 0.05 level.

16.11 a) Yes, there appears to be a difference in species counts.

```
          0
          0    4
          0
          1    02
 55333    1    455
   998    1    788
  2210    2
          2
          2
```

b) H_o: there is no difference in the number of tree species in unlogged forests and logged forests
H_a: logged forests have a significantly lower number of tree species
$W = 159$ with a *P*-value = 0.29. The results show a significantly lower number of tree species in logged forests.

16.12 The results are significant (*P*-value = 0.0000) and we can conclude that piano lessons increase spatial-temporal reasoning.

16.13 Yes, it appears that women are more concerned than men about food safety in restaurants. $W = 32267.5$ with a *P*-value = 0.0001.

16.14 The responses "srest" and "sfair" are not independent samples with different subjects. The responses are dependent on the subjects. We cannot conduct a two sample test using these results.

16.15 a) $\chi^2 = 3.955$, df = 4, *P*-value = 0.412. There is no strong evidence to indicate a relationship between income and city. **b)** No, there is no strong evidence to indicate a systematically higher income level in one city over the other. ($W = 56370$, *P*-value = 0.4949.)

16.16 a) The differences (control − treatment) are: −0.01622, −0.01102, −0.01607. Yes, it appears that the treated plots have faster growth. **b)** H_o: $\mu_D = 0$ H_a: $\mu_D < 0$. $t = -8.45$ with df = 2 and *P*-value = 0.007. Yes, the mean difference between control and treatment is less than zero. **c)** Conducting a Wilcoxon signed rank test results in a *P*-value = 0.091. There is no strong evidence to indicate the difference is negative.

16.17 The Wilcoxon signed rank test results in a *P*-value = 0.05. This test is just significant at the 0.05 level.

16.18 a) H_o: median$_{low}$ = median$_{medium}$ H_a: median$_{low}$ > median$_{medium}$ where the median is the difference resting − final. The proper test is the Wilcoxon rank sum test. **b)** $W = 39$ with *P*-value = 0.0098. There is significant evidence that the medium rate has a systematically higher difference than the low rate.

16.19 H_o: The distributions of the test scores are the same before and after a course. H_a: The scores are systematically higher after the course. $W^+ = 138.5$ with a *P*-value = 0.002. Conclude that the scores are higher after the course.

16.20

Score	1	1	2	2	2	3	3	3	3	3	3	6	6	6	6	6	**6**
Rank	1.5	1.5	4	4	4	8.5	8.5	8.5	8.5	8.5	8.5	15	15	15	15	15	**15**

$W^+ = 138.5$. The bold-faced column represents the one negative value.

16.21 Yes, there is evidence of a loss in vitamin C. $W^+ = 341$, *P*-value = 0.000.

16.22 $W^+ = 1552.5$ with a *P*-value = 0.000. The conclusion is that restaurant food is perceived to be safer than fair food.

16.23 *P*-value = 0.206. There is no strong evidence of a systematic difference between the perceived safety of fast food and fair food.

16.24 a) The data appears skewed to the right.

```
9 2578
10 2455
11 19
12 2
```

b) $W^+ = 31$ with a *P*-value = 0.556. There is no strong evidence to indicate that the median ≠ 105.

16.25 $W^+ = 88$ with a *P*-value = 0.059. The evidence is not significant at the 0.05 level.

16.26 The 94.5% confidence level is (98.1, 110.5).

16.27 The 95% confidence level is (26.3, 38.6).

16.28 b) H_o: consumer responses have the same distribution for each type of ad. H_a: consumer responses are systematically higher in some groups than others. **c)** $H = 23.24$ (adjusted for ties) and *P*-value = 0.000. The conclusion is that the responses are higher for some of the ad types.

16.29 a) $H = 8.73$ with a *P*-value = 0.068. The results of this test are not significant at the 0.05 level. It appears that there is not a significant difference in vitamin C loss over time. **b)** Yes, the difference in *P*-values would lead to different conclusions.

16.30 b) Control

```
          5 5
          5 6
          5 99
          6 0011
          6 2
          6 5
```

Low jump

```
          58 8
          59 469
          60 57
          61
          62
          63 1258
```

High jump

```
          62 2266
          63 1
          64 33
          65 00
          66
          67 4
```

c) $H = 10.68$ with a *P*-value = 0.005. The findings show a systematically higher bone density in some groups over others. The Kruskal-Wallis tests the hypothesis that the distributions of bone density are the same and the ANOVA test looks at the means of the distributions.

16.31 a) The ANOVA tests the hypothesis that the four means are the same. The Kruskal-Wallis tests the hypothesis that the four distributions are the same. **b)** The Minitab output containing the medians and the *H* statistic is below. Lemon Yellow appears most effective. The results of the test indicate a significant difference in the number of insects attracted by each color.

Kruskal-Wallis Test

```
C9              N    Median    Ave Rank         Z
Blue            6     15.00         6.7     -2.33
Green           6     34.50        14.8      0.93
LYellow         6     46.50        21.2      3.47
White           6     15.50         7.3     -2.07
Overall        24                  12.5

H = 16.95  DF = 3  P = 0.001
H = 16.98  DF = 3  P = 0.001 (adjusted for ties)
```

16.32 Verify with above value of *H*.

16.33 a) 4.6, 6.54, 9.53, 16.09. **b)** 126, 126, 135, 110. The hypothesis tested is that the medians are all equal. **c)** $H = 5.63$ with a *P*-value = 0.131. The conclusion is that there is not a significant difference in the decay medians between the four lengths of time.

16.34 The responses for "srest" and "sfast" are dependent on the subject. They are not independent samples.

16.35 a) Unlogged

```
13  000
14
15  00
16
17
18  0
19  00
20  0
21  0
22  00
```

Logged(1)

```
0  2
0
0  7
0  8
1  11
1  23
1  4555
1
1  8
```

Logged(8)

```
0  4
0
0
1  0
1  2
1  455
1  7
1  88
```

The stemplots show many outliers for each of the distributions. The medians are: 18.5, 12.5, and 15. **b)** $H = 9.44$ with a P-value = 0.009. The conclusion would be that there is a significant difference in medians between the three groups.

16.36 a) This relationship is shown in the data. 76% of those in the higher SES group have never smoked or are former smokers. Only 58% in the middle SES and 54% in the lower SES have never smoked or are former smokers. **b)** $\chi^2 = 18.51$ with df = 4 and P-value = 0.001. This indicates there is a significant relationship between SES groups and smoking status. **c)** $H = 6.88$ with a P-value = 0.032. Some SES classes smoke more heavily than others.

16.37 P-value = 0.042. The results show a significant difference between the right-hand times and left-hand times. Right-hand times are faster than left-hand times

16.38 The 95% confidence interval for the median is (19, 24). Problem 7.13 gave the interval on μ as (19.98, 27.14).

16.39 a) A graphs shows that the data are right-skewed with a large outlier. **b)** $W^+ = 378$ with P-value = 0.695. **c)** $t = 0.83$ with df = 49 and P-value = 0.41. The conclusions are the same. There is no reason to reject the hypothesis that the mean is equal to 20.

16.40 Yes, $W^+ = 154.5$ with a P-value = 0.034.

16.41 a)

Beef hot dogs	Meat hot dogs	Poultry hot dogs
8	8	8 67
9	9	9 49
10	10 7	10 226
11 1	11	11 3
12	12	12 9
13 1259	13 5689	13 25
14 1899	14 067	14 2346
15 2378	15 3	15 2
16	16	16
17 56	17 2359	17 0
18 146	18 2	18
19 00	19 015	19

The five-number summaries are:

Hot dog type	Minimum	Q_1	Median	Q_3	Maximum
Beef	111	139.5	152.5	179.8	190
Meat	107	138.5	153.0	180.5	195
Poultry	86	100.5	129.0	143.5	170

b) The distributions of the beef and meat hot dogs appear nonnormal. They are not symmetrical, have a gap in the data at 160 calories, and both have one low outlier. The poultry hot dogs have one high outlier. **c)** $H = 15.89$ with a P-value = 0.000. There is a systematically higher calorie content for the beef and meat hot dogs.

16.42 a)

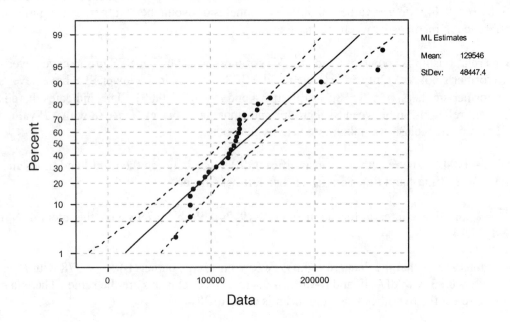

Normal Probability Plot for 3 Bedrooms

b) Use a two-sample t test. $H_o: \mu_1 = \mu_2$ $H_a: \mu_1 \neq \mu_2$. $t = 3.08$ with df = 12 and P-value = 0.0095. There is a significant difference between the mean price of four bedroom homes and the mean price of three bedroom homes. **c)** H_o: The distribution of prices is the same. H_a: The distributions of prices are different. $H = 9.06$ with df = 1 and P-value = 0.003. There is a significant difference between the distribution of prices of four bedroom homes and the distribution of prices of three bedroom homes.

16.43 a)

Beef hot dogs	Meat hot dogs	Poultry hot dogs
1	1 4	1
1	1	1
2	2	2
2 59	2	2
3 011223	3 3	3
3 778	3 67889	3 557889
4 024	4 002	4 23
4 7789	4 579	4
5	5 0014	5 112244
5 8	5	5 8
6 4	6	6

The five-number summaries are:

Hot dog type	Minimum	Q_1	Median	Q_3	Maximum
Beef	253	319.8	380.5	478.5	645
Meat	144	379.0	405.0	501.0	545
Poultry	357	379.0	430.0	535.0	588

b) The distributions all have outliers and the poultry sodium distribution appears to have two distinct groups of data. **c)** $H = 4.71$ with a P-value = 0.095. The evidence of systematically higher sodium content for some types of hot dogs is not strong.

16.44 a) With such small sample sizes it is difficulty to establish normality; however, the sample standard deviations are all quite different. **b)** For meat: $H = 9.98$ with P-value = 0.007. For legumes: $H = 7.04$ with P-value = 0.03. For vegetables: $H = 5.6$ with P-value = 0.061. The median values show little difference in iron content between food cooked in aluminum pots and food cooked in clay pots.

16.45 The difference in iron content between food cooked in aluminum and clay pots was not significant for either meat or legumes. ($H = 1.32$ with P-value = 0.251 and $H = 2.08$ with P-value = 0.149, respectively.)

16.46 Yes, there appears to be a significant difference in iron content between the three food groups cooked in an iron pot. $H = 7.0$ with a P-value = 0.03.

Problems 16.47 through 16.50 cannot be done with the student version of Minitab because the data set is too large.

16.51 a) Let W_1 be the sum of the ranks from n_1. Let W_2 be the sum of the ranks from n_2. $W_1 + W_2 = \sum_{i=1}^{N} i$.

$$\mu_{W_1} + \mu_{W_2} = \mu_{W_1 + W_2} = \mu_{\sum_{i=1}^{N} i} = \sum_{i=1}^{N} i . \quad \sum_{i=1}^{N} i = \frac{n_1(N+1)}{2} + \frac{n_2(N+1)}{2} = \frac{N(N+1)}{2} .$$

b) For N = 27, $(27 \times 28)/2 = 378$. **c)** $(62 \times 63)/2 = 1953$. $308 + 350 + 745 + 550 = 1953$.

Chapter 17
Logistic Regression

17.1 0.7606, 3.176. 0.536, 1.154.

17.2 Men: 0.1076, 0.1206. Women: 0.2128, 0.2703.

17.3 1.156, 0.143.

17.4 Men: −2.1161, Women: −1.3082.

17.5 $b_o = 0.143$, $b_1 = 1.013$. $\log(\text{ODDS}) = 0.143 + 1.013x$. The odds ratio of exclusive territories to non-exclusive is 2.754.

17.6 $b_o = -2.1161$, $b_1 = 0.8079$. $\log(\text{ODDS}) = -2.1161 + 0.8079x$. The odds ratio of women label users to men label users is 2.243.

17.7 $\dfrac{\text{ODDS}_{x+1}}{\text{ODDS}_x} = \dfrac{e^{-13.71}e^{2.25(x+1)}}{e^{-13.71}e^{2.25x}} = \dfrac{e^{2.25x}e^{2.25}}{e^{2.25x}} = e^{2.25} = 9.49.$

17.8 β_o: −1.586, 0.0267. β_1: 0.3617, 0.0388. The estimate of the odds ratio of men to women is 1.436 with a 95% confidence interval of (1.33, 1.549).

17.9 $\log(\text{ODDS}) = 0.1431 + 1.0127x$, where $x = 1$ if the franchise has an exclusive territory and $x = 0$ otherwise. The odds ratio of exclusive territories to nonexclusive territories is 2.75 with a 95% confidence interval of (1.19, 6.36).

17.10 $\log(\text{ODDS}) = -2.1158 + 0.8079x$, where $x = 1$ for women and $x = 0$ for men. The odds ratio of female label users to male label users is 2.24 with a 95% confidence interval of (1.38, 3.65).

17.11 (2.3485, 3.8691).

17.12 Verify.

17.13 Verify.

17.14 a) 0.60. **b)** 3 to 2. **c)** 0.40. **d)** 2 to 3. **e)** The results are reciprocals of each other.

17.15 a) 0.80, 4 to 1. **b)** 0.69, 2.23. **c)** 1.84.

17.16 a) 1.3863, 0.8020. **b)** 0.7911, 0.609. **c)** $e^{0.609} = 1.84$.

17.17 a) (−0.047, 1.265). **b)** (0.95, 3.54). **c)** There does not seem to be a difference in the proportions of high tech companies and non-high tech companies that offer stock options.

17.18 The analysis stays the same for the estimates until we get to the inference portion. Because the sample sizes increased, the standard error decreased. This results in the confidence intervals for both β_1 and the odds showing significant results. The 95% confidence interval for β_1 is (0.1453, 1.0727) and for the odds ratio is (1.16, 2.92).

17.19 a) 0.32. **b)** 0.47 or approximately 1 to 2. **c)** 0.68. **d)** 2.13 or approximately 2 to 1. **e)** They are reciprocals of each other.

17.20 a) log(ODDS) = −2.6293 + 2.6865x. **b)** The *P*-value for the significance test shows that there is strong evidence that the slope is not equal to 0. **c)** (4.87, 44.27).

17.21 a) 0.165. 0.0168 or approximately 2 to 100. **b)** 0.0078. 0.0079. **c)** 2.12. Men with high-blood pressure are 2.12 time more likely to die of cardiovascular disease than men with low-blood pressure.

17.22 a) (0.2452, 1.2558). **b)** χ^2 = 8.4681. *P*-value = 0.004.

17.23 a) 2.12, (1.28, 3.51).

17.24 a) 0.80, 4 to 1. **b)** 0.40, 0.67. **c)** 6.15.

17.25 a) (1.0946, 2.5396). **b)** 24.30, *P*-value = 0.000. **c)** A female reference is 6.15 times more likely to a juvenile reference than a male reference is juvenile.

17.26 a) 6.15, (2.99, 12.67). **b)** The confidence interval shows that the odds are significantly greater than one.

17.27 a) log(ODDS) = −4.2767 + 1.3504x. **b)** For a binomial distribution we would assume that each employee is an independent trial and each employee has the same chance of being terminated. This may not be realistic because the employee's performance is likely to play a role in their termination. **c)** 3.86, (1.72, 8.67). An employee that is over 40 years old is 3.86 times more likely to be terminated than an employee that is 40 or younger. The confidence interval on the odds estimate shows that the odds are significantly greater than 1. **d)** You can also incorporate performance evaluations as an explanatory variable by creating a multiple logistic regression model.

17.28 The odds ratio of orders filled in 5 days or less before improvement and orders filled in 5 days or less after improvement are 47.25 with a 95% confidence interval of (26.01, 85.83). This is strong evidence that there is a true improvement.

17.29 log(ODDS) = −0.0282 + 0.6393x. χ^2 = 48.30 with a *P*-value = 0.000. The odds ratio estimate is 1.90. There are significantly greater odds for a college graduate to use the Internet to make travel arrangements than a non-college graduate.

17.30 log(ODDS) = 0.033 + 0.604x. χ^2 = 5.56 with a *P*-value = 0.000. The odds ratio estimate is 1.83. There are significantly greater odds for someone with an income greater than or equal to $50,000 to use the Internet to make travel arrangements than those who make less.

17.31 log(ODDS) = −1.804 + 1.136x. χ^2 = 5.29 with a *P*-value = 0.000. The odds ratio estimate is 3.11. There are significantly greater odds for a male who died in a bicycle accident to test positive for alcohol than a female who died in a bicycle accident.

Chapter 18
Bootstrap Methods and Permutation Tests

Preface to the instructor:

This chapter uses computationally demanding resampling procedures, for which the use of a computer is critical. We used S-PLUS while writing this chapter, and give commands below for performing the analyses in S-PLUS. Our goal is to make it as easy as possible for you, and students, to focus on the statistical aspects of this chapter. You will probably find it easiest to use S-PLUS for this chapter even if you use other software for other chapters.

To use S-PLUS you need:
- a copy of S-PLUS: there is a free version for students and instructors, see
  `http://elms03.e-academy.com/splus`
- the new S+Resample library: for this and the following items, see
  `http://www.insightful.com/Hesterberg/bootstrap`
- the data: if using the student version of S-PLUS, some of the datasets are too large to read in, so you'll need the PBSdata library, and
- other materials, such as a student guide to using the graphical interface for resampling (optional).

Your answers to most questions in this chapter may differ slightly from ours due to random sampling. Here we specify random number seeds to make results reproducible, but we do not do that in materials we supply to students because we want them to experience randomness.

18.1 a) and **b)** Students' answers will vary. **c)** Here is a stemplot for 200 resamples (the students do 20):
```
 0 : 677889999
 1 : 0000111112222344444455555566678889999
 2 : 000001122236
 3 : 4678899
 4 : 000111111112222222233333344444455555555555555556666677777788888888899
 5 : 001122455579
 6 : 899
 7 : 00112222333444556666777788899
 8 : 00001234
 9 :
10 : 122244467779
11 : 002
12 :
13 : 4
```
d) The standard error for 1000 resamples is 2.8.
This is normally done by hand, but the following commands would work:
```
boot1 <- bootstrap(Exercise18.1, mean, B=20, seed=0)
stem(boot1$replicates)
boot1  # The standard error is the printed "SE"
```

18.2 a) It is approximately Normal, but with some positive skewness. This amount of skewness would not be a concern in raw data, but here it occurs in a bootstrap distribution, after the central limit theorem has already acted. The departures from Normality would translate directly into errors in coverage-level or P-values. **b)** 986 **c)** 19609, 23517
```
boot2 <- bootstrap(Exercise18.2, mean, seed=0)
plot(boot2)
qqnorm(boot2)
boot2  # the SE is printed
limits.percentile(boot2)
```

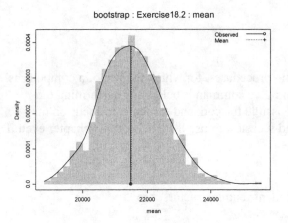

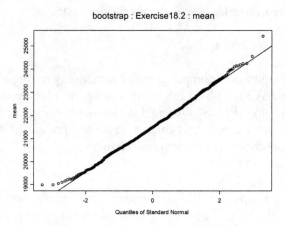

18.3 a) See figures below. **b)** The distribution is symmetric and bell-shaped, and the quantile plot shows a small amount of right skewness. While this amount of skewness would not be a concern in raw data, here it occurs in a bootstrap distribution, after the central limit theorem has had a chance to work. The departures from Normality would translate directly into errors in coverage-level or *P*-values.

```
hist(Exercise18.3)
qqnorm(Exercise18.3)
boot3 <- bootstrap(Exercise18.3, mean, seed=0)
plot(boot3)
qqnorm(boot3)
```

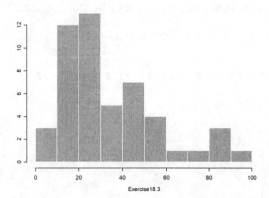

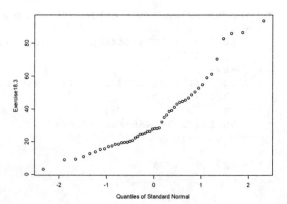

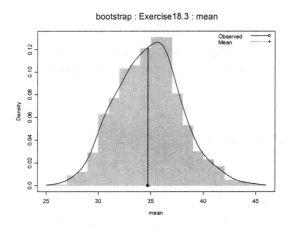

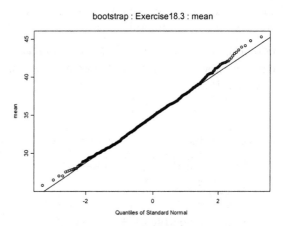

18.4 a) See figures below. **b)** There is right skewness, but much less than for the data distribution.

```
hist(Exercise18.4)
qqnorm(Exercise18.4)
boot4 <- bootstrap(Exercise18.4, mean, seed=0)
plot(boot4)
qqnorm(boot4)
```

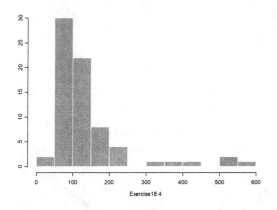

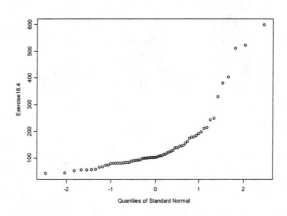

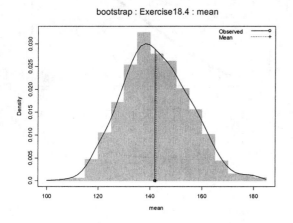

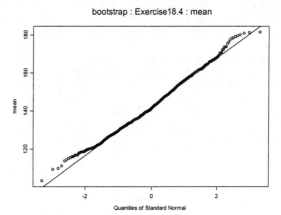

18.5 a) It is roughly Normal, but with positive skewness. The skewness is greater than for Exercise 18.3.
b) The bootstrap standard error for Exercise 18.3 is 3.07, and for the data in this exercise the
bootstrap standard error is 7.45. The standard error of the sample mean is $s/\sqrt{n}$; here the
denominator is substantially larger, and the numerator s is slightly larger (25.6, compared to 21.7 in
Exercise 18.3).

```
hist(Exercise18.5)
qqnorm(Exercise18.5)
boot5 <- bootstrap(Exercise18.5, mean, seed=0)
par(mfrow=c(2,2))  # two rows and two columns of plots
plot(boot5); qqnorm(boot5)
plot(boot3); qqnorm(boot3)
par(mfrow=c(1,1))
boot5
boot3
stdev(Exercise18.5)
stdev(Exercise18.3)
```

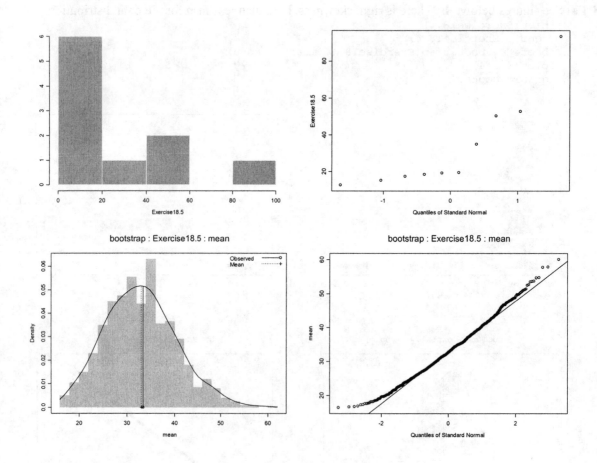

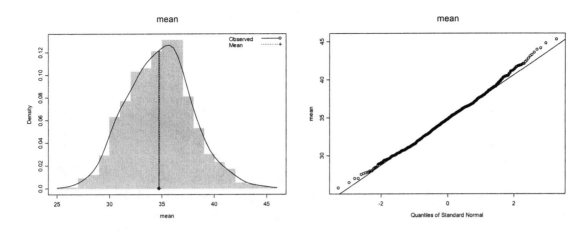

18.6 a) This bootstrap distribution is less Normal, with stronger right skewness.

b) The bootstrap standard error for Exercise 18.4 is 12.8, and for the data in this exercise the bootstrap standard error is 33.1. The standard error of the sample mean is $s/\sqrt{n}$; here the denominator is substantially larger, and the numerator s is slightly larger (153, compared to 109 in Exercise 18.4).

```
hist(Exercise18.6)
qqnorm(Exercise18.6)
boot6 <- bootstrap(Exercise18.6, mean, seed=0)
par(mfrow=c(2,2))   # two rows and two columns of plots
plot(boot6); qqnorm(boot6)
plot(boot4); qqnorm(boot4)
par(mfrow=c(1,1))
boot6
boot4
stdev(Exercise18.6)
stdev(Exercise18.4)
```

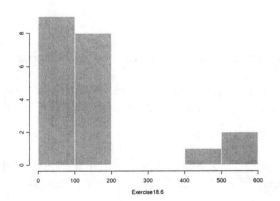

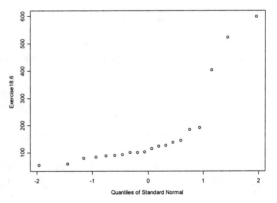

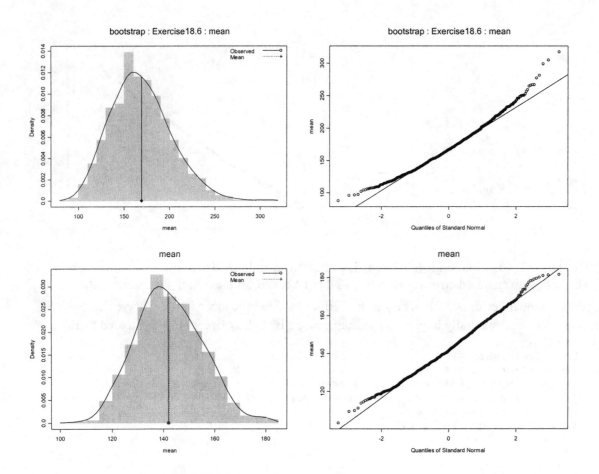

18.7 $s = 21.7$, so $s/\sqrt{n} = 3.07$. The bootstrap standard error in Exercise 18.3 is 3.07, which agrees with $s/\sqrt{n} = 3.07$.

```
stdev(Exercise18.3)
stdev(Exercise18.3) / sqrt(50)
boot3
stdev(boot3$replicates) # another way to get the bootstrap standard error
```

18.8 The estimated bias is 0.08 (this answer will vary randomly above or below zero, but should be close to zero). This is small compared to the standard error of 3.1. This indicates that the bias is small.

```
boot3
mean(boot3$replicates) - boot3$observed  # another way to get bootstrap bias
```

18.9 The estimated bias is 0.45 (this answer will vary randomly above or below zero, but should be close to zero). This is small compared to the standard error of 12.8. This indicates that the bias is small.

```
boot4
mean(boot4$replicates) - boot4$observed  # another way
```

18.10 a) c(28.5, 40.9) **b)** c(28.5, 40.9). The intervals are very similar.

```
limits.t(boot3)
t.test(Exercise18.3)
```

18.11 a) The 25% trimmed mean is 30.1, which is smaller than the sample mean of 34.7. If we examine the histogram of the data for the 50 we see that the data are right skewed. The trimmed mean eliminates much of the large right tail (i.e., the very large values that cause the sample mean to be large), and hence the trimmed mean is smaller than the sample mean. **b)** The 95% confidence interval for the 25% trimmed mean spending in the population of all shoppers is (23.7, 36.5).

```
mean(Exercise18.3, trim=.25)
mean(Exercise18.3)
hist(Exercise18.3)
qqnorm(Exercise18.3)
boot11 <- bootstrap(Exercise18.3, mean(Exercise18.3, trim=.25), seed=0)
limits.t(boot11)
```

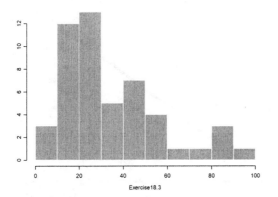 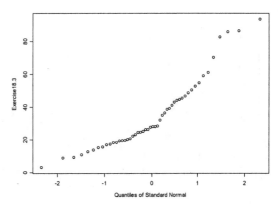

18.12 The distribution is not Normal; it has gaps, spikes, and a long right tail. The shape is not Normal so it is not appropriate to use a *t* interval, which is based on Normal distributions.

```
boot12 <- bootstrap(Exercise18.3, median, seed=0)
plot(boot12)
qqnorm(boot12)
```

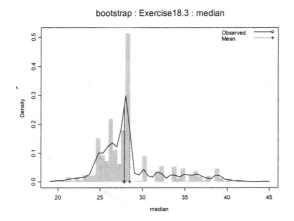 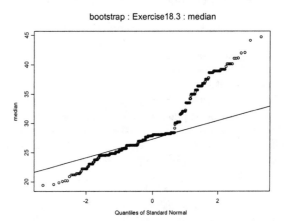

18.13 The formula-based standard error is 4.08. The bootstrap standard error in Example 18.7 is 4.052, which is close to the formula-based value.

```
sqrt( stdev(ILEC)^2 / length(ILEC) + stdev(CLEC)^2 / length(CLEC))
```

18.14 a) 4.3 **b)** Yes—the distribution appears to be very close to Normal, with no appreciable bias. **c)** The bootstrap *t* interval calculated with the conservative rule for degrees of freedom is (1.01, 18.90), which is very close to the formula *t* interval calculated with the conservative rule (0.97, 18.94).

```
Exercise18.14  # has columns score and group
boot14 <- bootstrap2(Exercise18.14$score, mean,
                treatment = Exercise18.14$group, seed=0)
```

```
boot14
plot(boot14)
qqnorm(boot14)
limits.t(boot14)
x <- Exercise18.14$score[Exercise18.14$group == "Treatment"]
y <- Exercise18.14$score[Exercise18.14$group == "Control"]
mean(x) - mean(y) + qt(c(.025,.975), min(length(x), length(y))-1) *
          sqrt(var(x)/length(x) + var(y)/length(y))
```

bootstrap : Exercise18.14$score : mean : Treatment - Control

18.15 a) Yes, the distribution appears to be quite close to Normal (the Normal quantile plot shows this better than the histogram does), with no appreciable bias.

b) The observed difference is 0.902 and the standard error is SE = 0.113. The bootstrap t confidence interval is (0.67, 1.13).

c) The two-sample t confidence interval reported on page 479 is (0.65, 1.15), slightly wider than the bootstrap t confidence interval in part (b).

```
Exercise18.15  # has columns status and ratio
boot15 <- bootstrap2(Exercise18.15$ratio, mean,
                treatment = Exercise18.15$status, seed=0)
plot(boot15)
qqnorm(boot15)
boot15
limits.t(boot15)
```

bootstrap : Exercise18.15$ratio : mean : Healthy - Failed

18.16 The standard deviation of a sample measures how spread a sample is. The standard error estimates how much a sample mean would vary, if you take the means of many samples from the same population. The standard error is smaller by a factor of $\sqrt{n}$.

18.17 a) The two bootstrap distributions look similar.

b) The bootstrap standard error of the mean is 45.0. In Example 18.5, the bootstrap standard error of the 25% trimmed mean is 16.83. We see that the bootstrap standard error of the mean is almost three times as large as the bootstrap standard error of the 25% trimmed mean. The bootstrap distribution for the mean has greater spread (the histogram covers a range from about 225 to 475) than the bootstrap distribution for the 25% trimmed mean (the histogram covers a range from about 200 to 300).

```
boot17 <- bootstrap(Exercise18.17, mean, seed=0)
plot(boot17)
qqnorm(boot17)
boot17
```

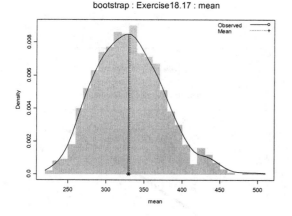
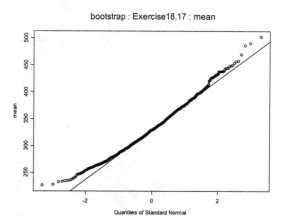

18.18 a) 16.5 **b)** The bootstrap distribution does not appear Normal (it is bimodal, and has gaps).

```
boot18 <- bootstrap(Exercise18.18, median, seed=0)
plot(boot18)
qqnorm(boot18)
boot18
```

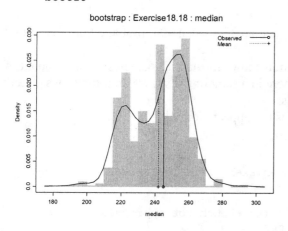
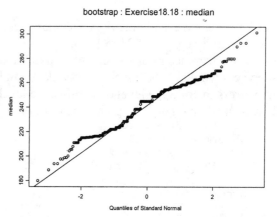

18.19 a) There do not appear to be any significant departures from Normality. The histogram is centered at about 0 and the spread is approximately what we would expect for the N(0, 1) distribution.

b) The standard error of the bootstrap mean is 0.128.

c) Yes, the distribution appears very close to Normal, with no appreciable bias. The interval is (−0.129, 0.379).

```
hist(Exercise18.19)
qqnorm(Exercise18.19)
boot19 <- bootstrap(Exercise18.19, mean, seed=0)
boot19
```

```
plot(boot19)
qqnorm(boot19)
limits.t(boot19)
```

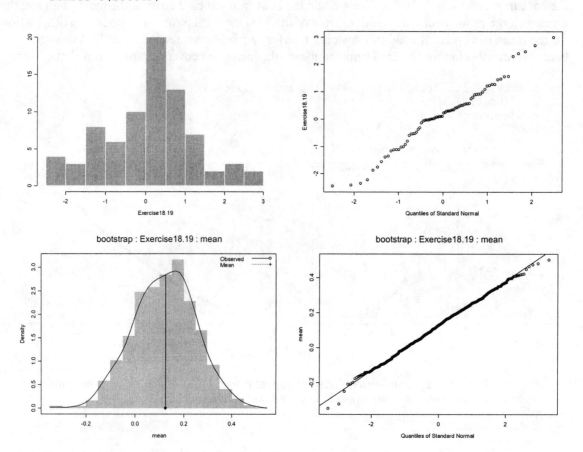

18.20 a) The data have moderate right skewness, with median 350, mean 404, first and third quartiles 250 and 539, and range from 21 to 1103.

b) For the trimmed mean—the bootstrap distribution shows substantial skewness. This amount of skewness would not be a worry in raw data, but here in a sampling distribution it translates directly into errors in coverage level or significance levels.

For the median—not appropriate, distribution does not appear Normal.

```
hist(Exercise18.20)
qqnorm(Exercise18.20)
summary(Exercise18.20)
boot20 <- bootstrap(Exercise18.20, mean(Exercise18.20, trim=.25), seed=0)
plot(boot20)
qqnorm(boot20)
limits.t(boot20)   # This is how to do it, though not appropriate
boot20b <- bootstrap(Exercise18.20, median, seed=0)
plot(boot20b)
qqnorm(boot20b)
limits.t(boot20b)  # This is how to do it, though not appropriate
```

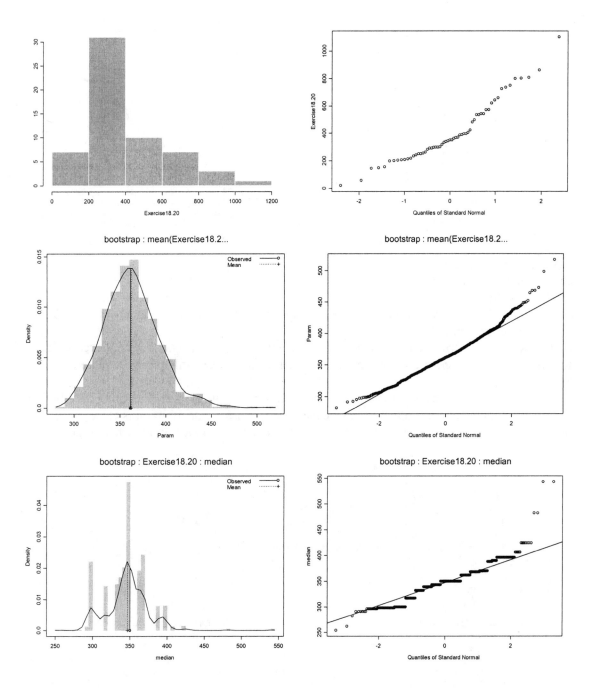

18.21 a) $s = 7.71$.

b) The bootstrap standard error for s is SE = 2.23.

c) The bootstrap standard error is almost one-third the value of the sample standard deviation. This suggests that the sample standard deviation is only moderately accurate as an estimate of the population standard deviation.

d) The bootstrap distribution is not Normal. Thus, it would not be appropriate to give a bootstrap t interval for the population standard deviation.

```
stdev(Exercise18.21)
boot21 <- bootstrap(Exercise18.21, stdev, seed=0)
boot21
plot(boot21)
```

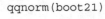

```
qqnorm(boot21)
```

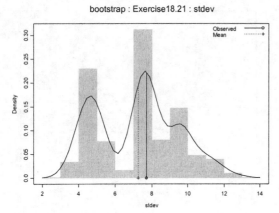

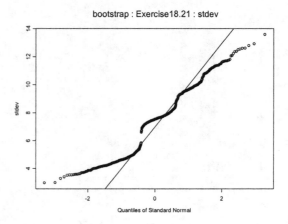

18.22 a) The interquartile range is 6.7.

b) The bootstrap standard error is 2.0.

c) The bootstrap standard error is almost one-third the value of the sample interquartile range. This suggests that the sample interquartile range is only moderately accurate as an estimate of the population interquartile range.

d) The bootstrap distribution has some positive skewness; it also has gaps and repeated values, which make the histogram appear very non-Normal (a Normal quantile plot gives a better picture of the distribution).

While this amount of skewness would not be a concern in raw data, in a sampling distribution it results in errors in coverage level or significance level. Here the distribution is close enough to Normal that a bootstrap *t* interval would be acceptable for most applications, where high accuracy is not needed.

The bootstrap *t* interval is (2.6, 10.8).

```
summary(Exercise18.21)
quantile(Exercise18.21)
# simplify things by defining our own function
interQuartile <- function(x) { a <- quantile(x); a[4] - a[2] }
interQuartile(Exercise18.21)
boot22 <- bootstrap(Exercise18.21, interQuartile, seed=0)
boot22
plot(boot22)
qqnorm(boot22)
limits.t(boot22)
```

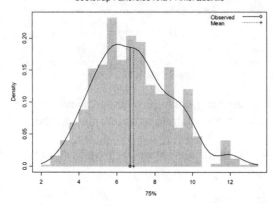

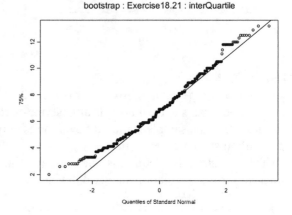

18.23 a) The plots do not show any significant departures from Normality, so there is nothing in the plots to suggest that the difference in means might be non-Normal.

b) A 95% paired *t* confidence interval for the difference in population means is (17.4, 25.1). The interval does not contain 0 and only includes positive values. This is evidence that the minority refusal rate is larger than the white refusal rate.

c) The bootstrap distribution looks reasonably Normal. The bias is small. Thus, a bootstrap *t* confidence interval is appropriate here. A 95% bootstrap *t* confidence interval is (17.6, 24.9). This is close to the formula-based interval calculated in (b).

```
Exercise18.23  # columns Minority and White
par(mfrow=c(2,2))  # two rows and two columns of plots
hist(Exercise18.23$Minority); qqnorm(Exercise18.23$Minority)
hist(Exercise18.23$White);    qqnorm(Exercise18.23$White)
par(mfrow=c(1,1))
t.test(Exercise18.23$Minority, Exercise18.23$White, paired=T)
difference <- Exercise18.23$Minority - Exercise18.23$White
t.test(difference)
boot23 <- bootstrap(difference, mean, seed=0)
# another way:
# boot23 <- bootstrap(Exercise18.23, mean(Minority) - mean(White), seed=0)
plot(boot23)
qqnorm(boot23)
limits.t(boot23)
```

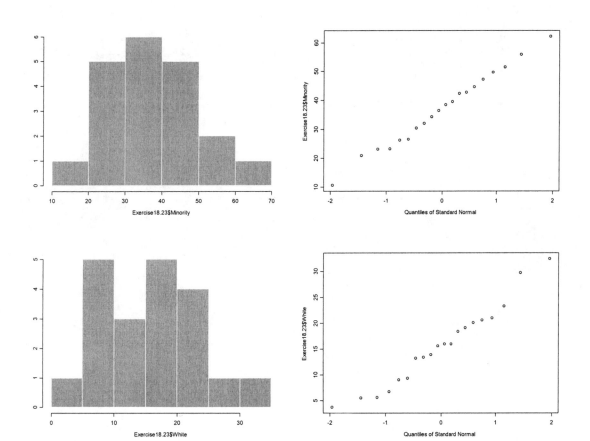

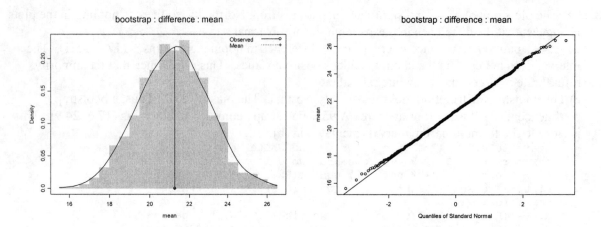

18.24 The distribution is right skewed, so we will use a trimmed mean rather than an ordinary mean. The trimmed mean is 1.95, standard error is 0.37, and estimated bias is 0.08—note that the bias is a substantial fraction of the standard error. The bootstrap distribution is very skewed, so a bootstrap t interval would not be appropriate if high accuracy is important. We'll learn more accurate methods later. For now we will do one anyway in order to get a rough idea; it gives a 95% confidence limit of (1.17, 2.72) for the average wealth of the middle 50% of billionaires.

```
sort(Exercise18.24)
hist(Exercise18.24)
qqnorm(Exercise18.24)
boot24 <- bootstrap(Exercise18.24, mean(Exercise18.24, trim=.25), seed=0)
plot(boot24)
qqnorm(boot24)
boot24
limits.t(boot24)
```

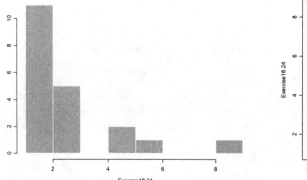

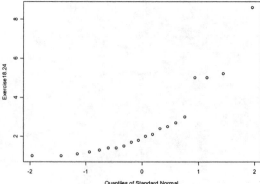

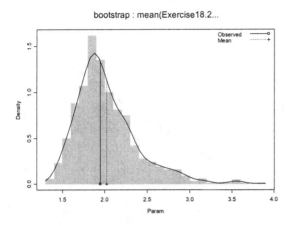

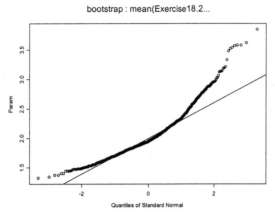

18.25 a) This bootstrap distribution is right-skewed. The bootstrap distribution of the Verizon repair times appears to be approximately Normal. The standard error for the CLEC mean is 4.1, much larger than the standard error for the Verizon mean, 0.37.

b) Because the Verizon bootstrap means vary so little, what really matters when you take (ILEC mean) – (CLEC mean) is the CLEC mean. Because of the "–" sign, the right skewness of the CLEC means makes the difference have less skewness.

```
boot25 <- bootstrap(CLEC, mean, seed=0)
plot(boot25)
qqnorm(boot25)
boot25
boot25b _ bootstrap(ILEC, mean, seed = 36)  # This was used for Figure 18.3
boot25b
plot(boot25b)
qqnorm(boot25b)    # CLEC is more skewed, and much larger standard error
```

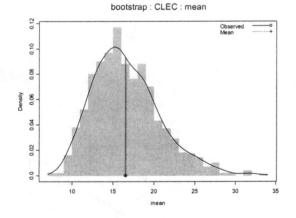

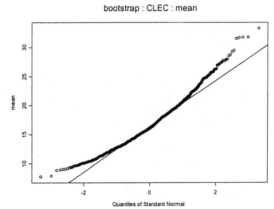

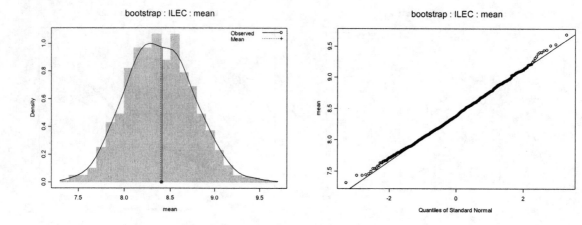

18.26 a) Normal with mean 8.4 and standard deviation $14.7/\sqrt{n}$.

  b) and **c)** See figures.

  d) Students' answers may vary, depending on their samples. May see some skewness for smaller samples. Should have almost no bias, and standard deviation decreasing by a factor of 2 each time the sample size increases by a factor of 4.

```
set.seed(1)   # So can reproduce results (but do not use seed 0, use that
below)
x10 <- rnorm(10, mean = 8.4, sd = 14.7)
boot26a <- bootstrap(x10, mean, seed=0)
plot(boot26a)
qqnorm(boot26a)
boot26a
set.seed(1)
x40 <- rnorm(40, mean = 8.4, sd = 14.7)
boot26b <- bootstrap(x40, mean, seed=0)
plot(boot26b)
qqnorm(boot26b)
boot26b
set.seed(1)
x160 <- rnorm(160, mean = 8.4, sd = 14.7)
boot26c <- bootstrap(x160, mean, seed=0)
plot(boot26c)
qqnorm(boot26c)
boot26c
```

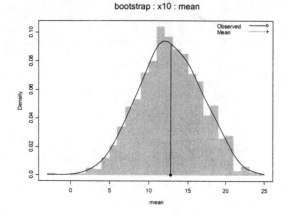
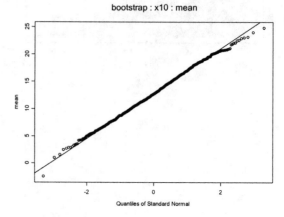

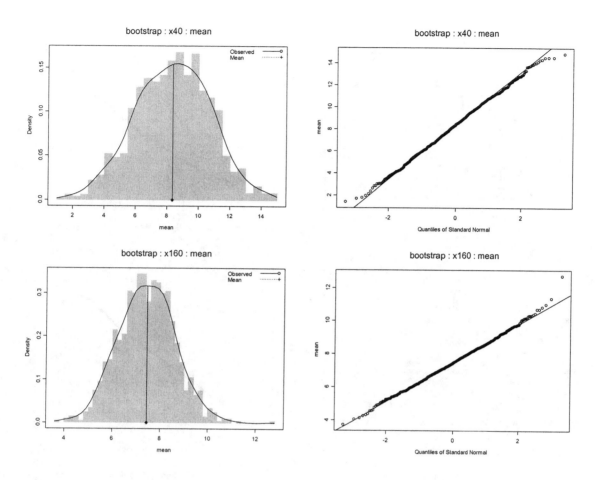

18.27 a) mean is 8.4, standard deviation is $14.7/\sqrt{n}$.

b) and **c)** See figures.

d) Students' answers may vary, depending on their samples. Should see substantial right skewness for smaller samples, closer to Normal for large samples. Should have almost no bias, and standard deviation decreasing by a factor of 2 each time the sample size increases by a factor of 4.

```
set.seed(1)  # different seed than zero
y10 <- sample(ILEC, size=10)
boot27a <- bootstrap(y10, mean, seed=0)
plot(boot27a)
qqnorm(boot27a)
boot27a
set.seed(1)  # different seed than zero
y40 <- sample(ILEC, size=40)
boot27b <- bootstrap(y40, mean, seed=0)
plot(boot27b)
qqnorm(boot27b)
boot27b
set.seed(1)  # different seed than zero
y160 <- sample(ILEC, size=160)
boot27c <- bootstrap(y160, mean, seed=0)
plot(boot27c)
qqnorm(boot27c)
boot27c
```

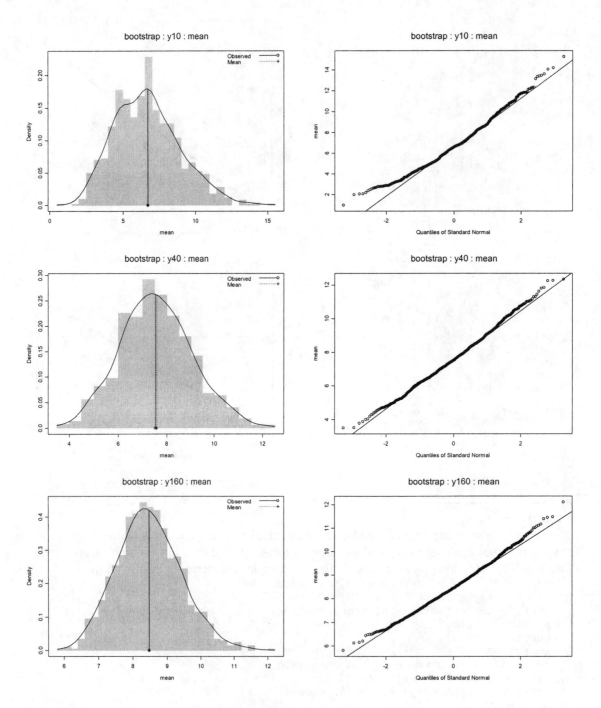

18.28 Students' answers should vary depending on their samples. They should notice that the bootstrap distributions are approximately Normal for larger sample sizes; for small samples, the sample could be skewed one way or the other, and that would be reflected in the bootstrap distribution.

18.29 5% and 95%.

18.30 a) Yes, approximately Normal. There is a small amount of left skewness.
b) 1.49, (106.0, 111.9).
c) See figures. The distribution appears very close to Normal, with no appreciable bias. The standard error is 1.46, and the 95% bootstrap *t* confidence interval is (106.0, 111.8).

d) (105.9, 111.7). All three intervals agree quite closely. The formula confidence interval is good enough.

```
qqnorm(Exercise18.30)
stdev(Exercise18.30)/sqrt(length(Exercise18.30))
t.test(Exercise18.30)
boot30 <- bootstrap(Exercise18.30, mean, seed=0)
plot(boot30)
qqnorm(boot30)
boot30
limits.t(boot30)
limits.percentile(boot30)
```

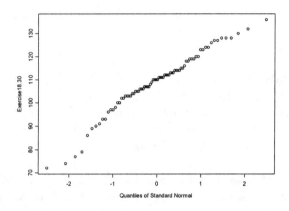

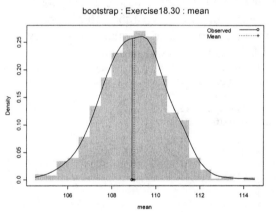

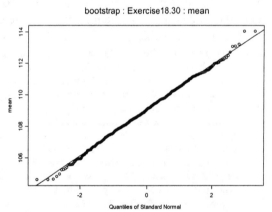

18.31 The 95% bootstrap *t* interval is (–0.144, 0.358) and the bootstrap percentile interval is (–0.128, 0.356). There is very close agreement between the upper endpoints of both intervals. However, the lower endpoints differ somewhat and this may indicate skewness, or just randomness in the bootstrap distribution.

18.32 The bootstrap *t* interval is (0.12, 0.59) and the percentile interval is (0.11, 0.57). These are reasonably close, and the bootstrap distribution appears approximately Normal, so these intervals appear trustworthy.

```
Exercise18.32  # columns Wages LOS Size
boot32 <- bootstrap(Exercise18.32, cor(Wages, LOS), seed=0)
boot32
plot(boot32)
qqnorm(boot32)
limits.t(boot32)
limits.percentile(boot32)
```

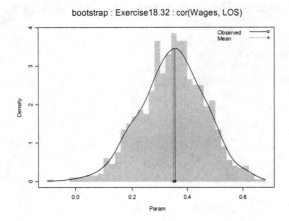
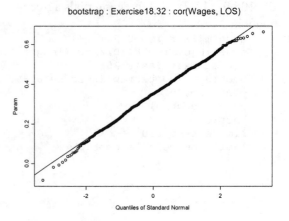

18.33 The 95% bootstrap *t* confidence interval is (241.1, 417.5).

The 95% bootstrap percentile confidence interval is (252.5, 433.1).

The 95% formula-based one-sample *t* confidence interval is (239.3, 419.3).

The BCa 95% confidence interval is (270, 455.7)

A tilting 95% confidence interval is (265.0, 458.7).

Students should draw a picture.

The bootstrap *t* and traditional intervals are centered approximately on the sample mean. The bootstrap percentile interval is shifted to the right of these two. A BCa and tilting intervals are shifted even further to the right. The latter two better reflect the skewed nature of the data. Using a *t* interval or the bootstap percentile interval, we get a biased picture of what the value of the population mean is likely to be. In particular, we would underestimate its value. Any policy decisions based on these data, such as tax rates, would reflect this underestimate.

```
# Numbers are from Figure 18.18, page 18-46.  See Example18.11.
# The bootstrap t interval answer in the back of the book differs
# (was based on different bootstrap samples).
329.3 + qt(c(.025, .975), 49) * 43.9  # (241.1, 417.5)
boot33 <- bootstrap(Example18.11, mean, B=1000, seed= 0)
plot(boot33)
segments(x1 = 241.1, x2 = 417.5, y1 = 0.008)
text(470, 0.008, "bootstrap t")
segments(x1 = 252.5, x2 = 433.1, y1 = 0.0075)
text(470, 0.0075, "percentile")
segments(x1 = 239.3, x2 = 419.3, y1 = 0.0070)
text(470, 0.0070, "traditional")
segments(x1 = 270, x2 = 455.7, y1 = 0.0065)
text(470, 0.0065, "BCa")
segments(x1 = 265, x2 = 458.7, y1 = 0.0060)
text(470, 0.0060, "tilting")
```

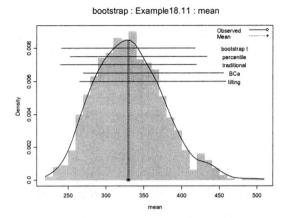

18.34 The intervals are:
bootstrap t: (209.3, 278.7)
percentile: (212.3, 280.3)
BCa: (212.3, 280.7)
Tilting: (212.9, 278.7)
The intervals are very similar. The percentile, BCa, and tilting intervals
have endpoints slightly to the right of the bootstrap *t* interval.

```
boot34 <- bootstrap(Seattle2002, mean(Seattle2002, trim = .25), seed=0)
limits.t(boot34)
limits.percentile(boot34)
limits.bca(boot34)
limits.tilt(boot34)
plot(boot34)
segments(x1 = 209.3, x2 = 278.7, y1 = .020); text(300, .020, "bootstrap t")
segments(x1 = 212.3, x2 = 280.3, y1 = .018); text(300, .018, "percentile")
segments(x1 = 212.3, x2 = 280.7, y1 = .016); text(300, .016, "BCa")
segments(x1 = 212.9, x2 = 278.7, y1 = .014); text(300, .014, "tilting")
```

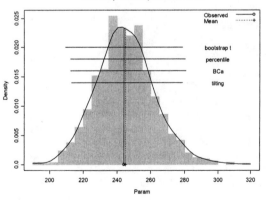

18.35 The bootstrap *t* confidence interval is (0.122, 0.585).
The bootstrap percentile interval is (0.110, 0.573).
The 95% BCa interval is (0.133, 0.594).
The tilting interval is (0.118, 0.555).
The BCa and tilting intervals have a larger lower endpoint and are narrower than the bootstrap *t* and
percentile intervals.

These intervals should differ slightly from Exercise 18.32 because they use different random bootstrap samples.

```
# We did this bootstrap in Exercise 32.  See figures there.
boot32 <- bootstrap(Exercise18.32, cor(Wages, LOS), seed=0)
boot32
plot(boot32)
qqnorm(boot32)
limits.t(boot32)
limits.percentile(boot32)
limits.bca(boot32)
limits.tilt(boot32)
```

18.36 a) The sample mean is 16.5; the histogram and Normal quantile plot show strong right skewness, with one large observation.

b) The bootstrap distribution shows strong right skewness. The formula t, bootstrap t, and (to a lesser extent) the percentile intervals would not be accurate. The BCa and tilting intervals adjust for skewness and so should be accurate. (*See Exercise 25 for figures.*)

c) The standard error is 4.1, the bootstrap t interval is (8.0, 25.0).

d) The percentile interval is (10.1, 26.2).
The BCa interval is (11.4, 31.7).
The tilting interval is (10.7, 29.1).

e) The tilting and BCa interval have both endpoints substantially to the right of the bootstrap t interval because they adjust for skewness. The percentile interval is in the middle; it partially adjusts for skewness.

f) You would tend to underestimate the requirements.

```
hist(CLEC)
qqnorm(CLEC)
mean(CLEC)
# We did this bootstrap in Exercise 25.  See figures there.
boot25 <- bootstrap(CLEC, mean, seed=0)
plot(boot25)
qqnorm(boot25)
boot25
limits.t(boot25)
limits.percentile(boot25)
limits.bca(boot25)
limits.tilt(boot25)
```

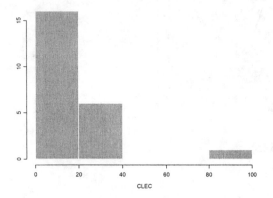 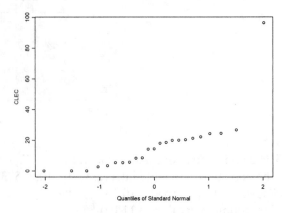

18.37 a) and **b)** The 95% BCa confidence interval is (–18.89, –2.48). This interval does not include 0, so we would conclude that the mean repair times for all Verizon customers are lower than the mean repair times for all CLEC customers.

c) Using a *t* or percentile interval, we would tend to understate the difference in mean repair times.

```
# boot37 <- bootstrap2(Verizon, mean(Time), treatment = Group, seed=0)
# Previous works, but the BCa calculations below are much slower
boot37 <- bootstrap2(Verizon$Time, mean, treatment = Verizon$Group, seed=0)
limits.bca(boot37)
# limits.tilt(boot37)
# limits.tilt doesn't yet support the new bootstrap2 procedure.  It may
# by the time you read this.  In the meantime, do this:
diffMean _ function(x, group, ..., weights = NULL){
  # calculate the difference in means for two groups
  set1 _ group == group[1]
  (mean(x[set1], ..., weights = weights[set1]) -
    mean(x[!set1], ..., weights = weights[!set1]))
}
boot37b <- bootstrap(Verizon, diffMean(Time, Group), group = Group, seed=0)
boot37b$L <- boot37$L  # this is optional, but makes next steps faster
limits.bca(boot37b)
limits.tilt(boot37b)
```

18.38 a) (–0.13, 0.37). This interval does include zero (students' intervals might not).

    b) (–0.13, 0.38). The two intervals agree closely.

```
limits.percentile(boot19)  # see problem19, where boot19 was created
limits.t(boot19)
```

18.39 a) A 95% traditional one-sample *t* confidence interval is (59.83, 66.19).

    b) The value 92.3 is an outlier and might strongly influence the traditional confidence interval.

    c) The 95% bootstrap percentile interval is (60.43, 66.32). Both ends are to the right of the interval in (a), due to skewness in the sampling distribution. This is also slightly narrower.

    d) A 95% confidence interval for the mean weights of male runners (in kilograms) is (60.43, 66.19).

```
t.test(Exercise18.21)
hist(Exercise18.21)
qqnorm(Exercise18.21)
boot39 <- bootstrap(Exercise18.21, mean, seed=0 ,
                    label="Exercise 39, mean")
limits.percentile(boot39)
plot(boot39)
qqnorm(boot39)
```

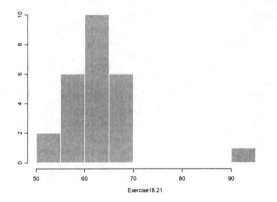

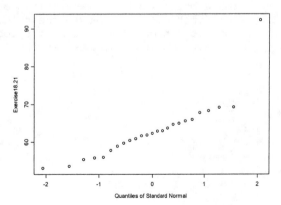

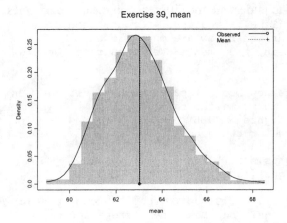
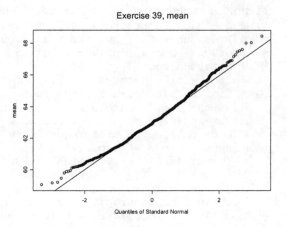

18.40 a) The data are right skewed. A robust statistic like a trimmed mean would be more representative of the bulk of the data than a simple mean would be.

b) The standard error for the trimmed mean is 1031. (The standard error for the mean is only slightly larger, 1074).

c) Students should pick a statistic and report an interval. Both bootstrap distributions are skewed, so they would report a BCa or tilting interval.

Some intervals for the trimmed mean: BCa (17321, 21321), tilting (17368, 21391), bootstrap *t* (16343, 20880), percentile (17221, 21071).

For the simple mean: BCa (18251, 22920), tilting (18243, 22612), bootstrap *t* (17440, 22168), percentile (17862, 22070).

The intervals for the mean lie above those for the trimmed mean (the observed mean is larger than the trimmed mean).

```
hist(Exercise18.40)
qqnorm(Exercise18.40)
boot40 <- bootstrap(Exercise18.40, mean(Exercise18.40, trim=.25), seed=0)
boot40
boot40b <- bootstrap(Exercise18.40, mean, seed=0)
boot40b
plot(boot40)
qqnorm(boot40)
limits.bca(boot40); limits.tilt(boot40)
limits.t(boot40); limits.percentile(boot40)
limits.bca(boot40b); limits.tilt(boot40b)
limits.t(boot40b); limits.percentile(boot40b)
```

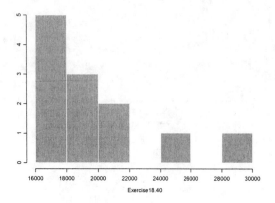
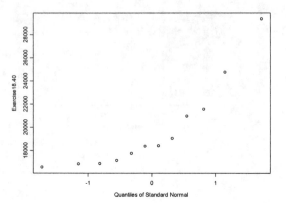

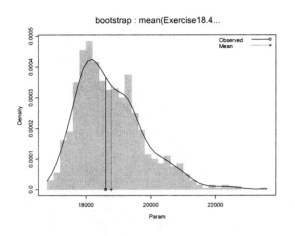
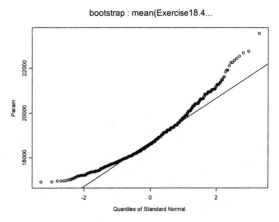

18.41 a) There are two large outliers present. *t* procedures can be used even for skewed distributions when the sample size is large enough. In this example, *n* = 43, so one-sample *t* procedures may be safe, but we should check.

b) A 95% traditional one-sample *t* confidence interval is (116.3, 124.8).

c) The bootstrap distribution shows moderate skewness to the right, so a bootstrap *t* interval should be moderately accurate.

d) The 95% bootstrap percentile interval is (116.9, 124.4). This agrees closely with the interval found in (b), so we conclude that the one-sample *t* interval is reasonably accurate here.

```
hist(Exercise18.41)
qqnorm(Exercise18.41)
t.test(Exercise18.41)
boot41 <- bootstrap(Exercise18.41, mean, seed=0)
plot(boot41)
qqnorm(boot41)
limits.percentile(boot41)
```

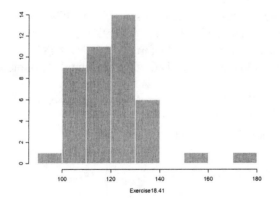
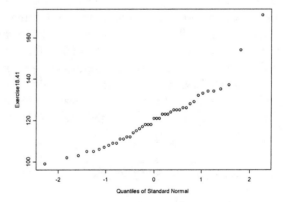

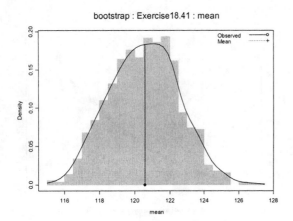
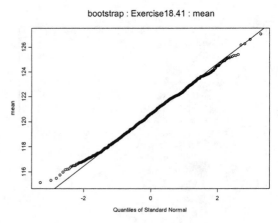

18.42 a) The BCa limit is (117.0, 124.7) and the tilting interval is (116.7, 125.6).

b) These intervals are similar to the percentile interval. However, if we look more closely, we notice that these intervals extend farther to the right than to the left of the observed value (−3.5, 4.0) and (−3.8, 5.0). The percentile interval captured only part of this asymmetry (−3.7, 3.9).

c) We would generally use the percentile interval as a quick check, or the BCa or tilting interval as a more accurate check.

```
limits.bca(boot41)
limits.bca(boot41) - boot41$observed
limits.tilt(boot41)
limits.tilt(boot41) - boot41$observed
limits.percentile(boot41) - boot41$observed
```

18.43 a) The data are clearly right-skewed. The mean would not be a useful measure of the price of a typical house in Ames. The trimmed mean or median might be more useful. We examine the trimmed mean.

b) The standard error of our bootstrap statistic is SE = 6797.

c) The distribution looks approximately Normal and the bias is relatively small. The 95% bootstrap *t* interval and the 95% bootstrap percentile interval are reasonable choices. The 95% bootstrap percentile interval is (119,677, 144,161). For comparison, the 95% BCa interval is (120,484, 147,562), the 95% maximum-likelihood tilting interval is (120,496, 146,665), and the 95% bootstrap *t* interval is (119,058, 146,375).

d) We are 95% confident that the mean selling price of all homes sold in Ames for the period represented by these data is in the interval ($119,677, $144,161).

```
Exercise18.43  # variables Price, SquareFootage, Age
hist(Exercise18.43$Price)
qqnorm(Exercise18.43$Price)
boot43 <- bootstrap(Exercise18.43, mean(Price, trim=.25), seed=0)
boot43
plot(boot43)
qqnorm(boot43)
limits.percentile(boot43)
limits.bca(boot43)
limits.tilt(boot43)
limits.t(boot43)
```

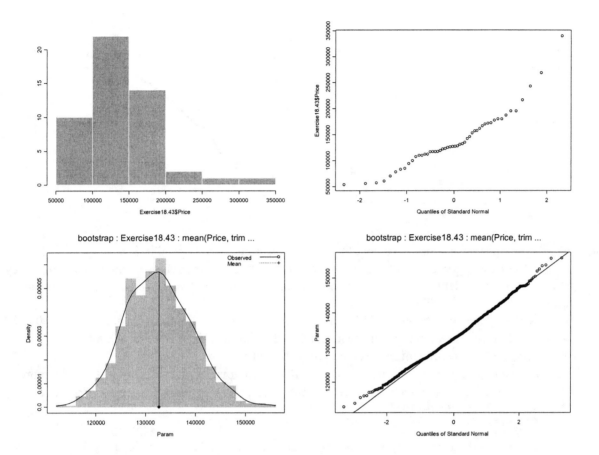

18.44 The bootstrap distribution is clearly non-Normal; a *t* or percentile interval would not be accurate. The 95% BCa interval is (0.70, 0.90), and tilting interval is (0.71, 0.90). In contrast, the bootstrap *t* interval is (0.73, 0.93); the *t* interval is symmetric about the observed correlation, while the BCa interval extends to the left and right (−0.13, 0.07) (more than twice as far to the left, before rounding).

```
boot44 <- bootstrap(Exercise18.44, cor(Price, SquareFootage), seed=0)
plot(boot44)
qqnorm(boot44)
limits.t(boot44)  # should not use this as final answer, only as check
limits.percentile(boot44) # ditto
limits.bca(boot44)
limits.tilt(boot44)
limits.bca(boot44) - boot44$observed
```

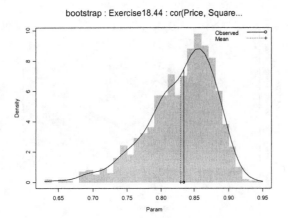

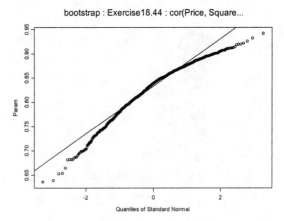

18.45 a) The relationship appears linear and the association is negative. r = −0.848.

b) The 95% BCa interval is (−0.898, −0.769) and the 95% tilting interval is (−0.900, −0.776). They provide a 95% confidence interval for the population correlation between weight and gas mileage in miles per gallon for all 1990 model year cars.

c) The least-squares regression line to predict gas mileage from weight is Mileage = 48.35 − 0.0082 (Weight). The traditional 95% *t* confidence interval for the slope is (−0.0096, −0.0068).

d) The bootstrap percentile interval is (−0.0095, −0.0068).

In this and following regression problems I'll give command-line code, but it would be more natural to do this using menus, under: `Statistics/Regression/LinearBootstrap`

```
Exercise18.45 # variables Weight, Mileage
plot(Exercise18.45$Weight, Exercise18.45$Mileage)
cor(Exercise18.45)
boot45a <- bootstrap(Exercise18.45, cor(Weight, Mileage), seed=0)
limits.bca(boot45a)
limits.tilt(boot45a)
lm45 <- lm(Mileage ~ Weight, data=Exercise18.45)
lm45
summary(lm45)
-.0082 + qt( c(.025, .975), df=58) * .0007
boot45b <- bootstrap(lm45, coef, seed=0)
limits.percentile(boot45b)
# The problem doesn't ask students to do this, but it is interesting to put
# regression lines on the plot.  Not too many or it gets busy.
bootstrap(lm45, abline(lm45, col=2), B=20)
abline(lm45, lwd=2)  # Add the original line with a wider line
```

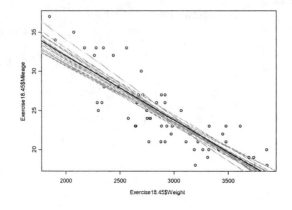

18.46 a) The line is (predicted BA) = 0.253 + 0.00147(salary). Each $1 million in salary increases the predicted batting average by 0.00147.

b) The bootstrap distribution suggests that any of the intervals would be reasonably accurate. The 95% intervals are bootstrap t: (−0.0022, 0.0052), percentile (−0.0023, 0.0050), BCa (−0.0023, 0.0050), tilting (−0.0021, 0.0050).

c) This agrees; all intervals include zero, which corresponds to no (linear) relationship between batting average and salary.

```
Exercise18.46 # variables Salary, Average
plot(Exercise18.46$Salary/10^6, Exercise18.46$Average)
lm46 <- lm(Average ~ I(Salary/10^6), data=Exercise18.46)
lm46
# .0014 increase in batting average per extra $milllion salary
abline(lm46)
boot46 <- bootstrap(lm46, coef, seed=0)
plot(boot46)
qqnorm(boot46 , subset.statistic=2)
limits.t(boot46); limits.percentile(boot46)
limits.bca(boot46); limits.tilt(boot46)
```

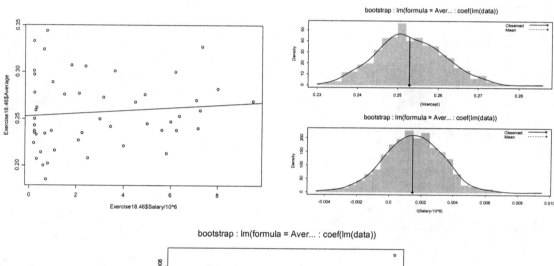

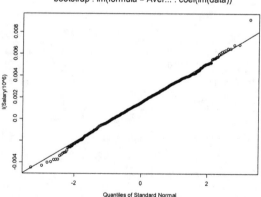

18.47 a) Examining the plots, we see that the bootstrap distribution with the outlier included is shifted significantly to the left (centered at a smaller value) of the bootstrap distribution with the outlier excluded. Also, the bootstrap distribution with the outlier included appears to be slightly left-skewed. There is little bias in either case (in fact, any apparent bias is due to random resampling, because the sample mean has no true bias).

b) A 95% BCa interval for the mean with the outlier included is (16504, 18322). A 95% BCa interval for the mean with the outlier removed is (17241, 18614). The lower confidence limit for the interval based on the data that includes the outlier is much smaller than the lower confidence limit for the interval based on the data with the outlier excluded. The outlier was an unusually low value, so it appears that the effect of the outlier is to pull the lower limit down. The upper confidence limits for both intervals are more nearly equal, but the upper confidence limit for the interval based on the data that includes the outlier is smaller than the lower confidence limit for the interval based on the data with the outlier excluded. Thus, the low value of the outlier also pulls the upper confidence limit down.

```
hist(Exercise18.47)
qqnorm(Exercise18.47)
stem(Exercise18.47)
which( Exercise18.47 < 14000 ) # observation 10
Exercise18.47[ -10 ] # omit observation 10
boot47a <- bootstrap(Exercise18.47, mean, seed=0)
boot47b <- bootstrap(Exercise18.47[ -10 ], mean, seed=0)
par(mfrow=c(2,2))
plot(boot47a); plot(boot47b)
qqnorm(boot47a); qqnorm(boot47b)
par(mfrow=c(1,1))
boot47a
boot47b
limits.bca(boot47a)
limits.bca(boot47b)
```

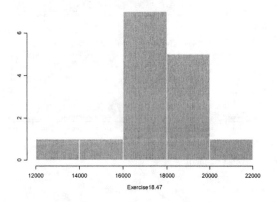

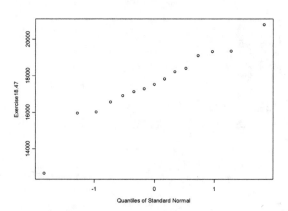

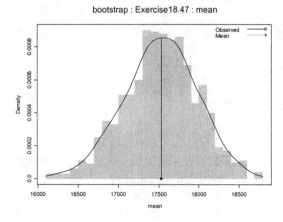

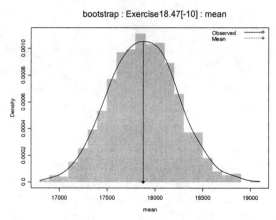

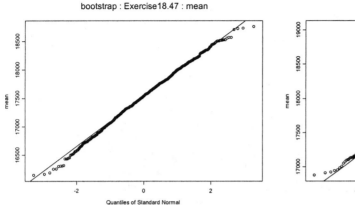
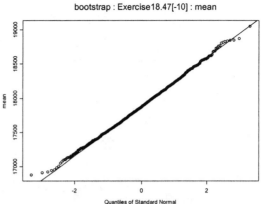

18.48 a) 3. **b), c),** and **d)** Answers will vary. In this example there are only 15 possible combinations, which give differences in means equal to (-18.00, -15.00, -11.25, -8.25, -8.25, -4.50, -1.50, -1.50, 1.50, 3.00, 5.25, 9.75, 12.75, 16.50, 19.50), and the exact *P*-value is 0.4.

This is normally done by hand, but the following commands would work:

```
mean( c(24, 61)) - mean( c(42, 33, 46, 37))
perm48 <- permutationTestMeans(c(24,61), data2=c(42,33,46,37), seed=0,
                        alternative="greater")
perm48
sort(unique(perm48$replicates))
perm48b _ bootstrap(c(24,61,42,33,46,37), diffMean(data, c(1,1,2,2,2,2)),
                B = 15, sampler = samp.combinations(k=2, both=T))
sort(perm48b$replicates)
mean(perm48b$replicates >= 3)
```

18.49 a) Let μ_1 denote the mean selling price for all Seattle real estate transactions in 2001, and μ_2 the mean selling price for all Seattle real estate transactions in 2002. We test H_0: $\mu_1 = \mu_2$ vs. H_a: $\mu_1 \neq \mu_2$.

b) 0.423 (not pooling variances).

c) The *P*-value is 0.462. This is consistent with the *P*-value we computed in (b). We conclude that there is little evidence that the population means μ_1 and μ_2 differ.

d) A BCa 95% confidence interval for the change from 2001 to 2002 is (−40.1, 164.8). This interval includes 0 and suggests that the two means are not significantly different at the 0.05 level. This is consistent with the conclusions in (c).

```
Exercise18.49 # variables Price and Year
t.test(Exercise18.49$Price[Exercise18.49$Year == 2002],
       y=Exercise18.49$Price[Exercise18.49$Year == 2001], var.equal=F)
perm49 <- permutationTestMeans(Exercise18.49, treatment = Year, seed=0)
perm49
plot(perm49)
# boot49 <- bootstrap2(Exercise18.49, mean(Price), treatment=Year, seed=0)
boot49 <- bootstrap2(Exercise18.49$Price, mean, treatment=Exercise18.49$Year,
               seed=0) # this is quicker
plot(boot49)
limits.bca(boot49)
# limits.tilt(boot49) # not yet implemented; do the following for now:
boot49b <- bootstrap(Exercise18.49, diffMean(Price, Year), group = Year,
seed=0)
boot49b$L <- boot49$L  # this is optional, but makes next steps faster
limits.bca(boot49b)
limits.tilt(boot49b)
```

```
# The two BCa intervals differ; the BCa varies quite a lot under
# random sampling (37 times higher variance than tilting).
# While the initial seed is the same in boot49 and boot49b, the random
# numbers are used in a different order in bootstrap and bootstrap2.
```

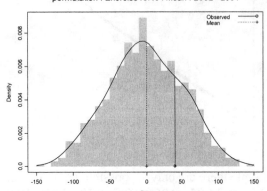

permutation : Exercise18.49 : mean : 2002 - 2001

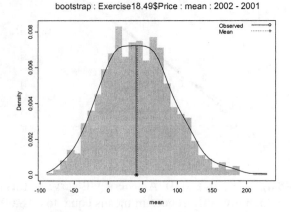

bootstrap : Exercise18.49$Price : mean : 2002 - 2001

18.50 a) H_0: $\mu_1 = \mu_2$, H_a: $\mu_1 > \mu_2$, where μ_1 is the mean ratio among healthy firms.

b) The *t* statistic is 7.9, and the *P*-value is about 10^{-11}.

c) The estimated *P*-value is 0.001, which is the smallest possible value with 1000 replications. This result is consistent with the formula-based *t* test.

d) A 95% BCa confidence interval is (0.67, 1.11). The interval does not include zero, so this agrees with the conclusion from the significance tests that the data are not consistent with the hypothesis that the difference in means is zero.

```
Exercise18.50  # variables status and ratio
t.test(Exercise18.50$ratio[Exercise18.50$status == "Healthy"],
       Exercise18.50$ratio[Exercise18.50$status == "Failed"],
       alternative="greater", var.equal=F)
perm50 <- permutationTestMeans(Exercise18.50, treatment=status,
                        alternative="greater", seed=0)
perm50
plot(perm50)
# boot50 <- bootstrap2(Exercise18.50, mean(ratio), treatment=status, seed=0)
boot50 <- bootstrap2(Exercise18.50$ratio, mean, # faster than previous
                treatment=Exercise18.50$status, seed=0)
plot(boot50)
limits.bca(boot50)
# limits.tilt(boot50) # not yet implemented; do the following for now:
boot50b <- bootstrap(Exercise18.50, diffMean(ratio, status), group = status,
seed=0)
boot50b$L <- boot50$L  # this is optional, but makes next steps faster
limits.bca(boot50b)
limits.tilt(boot50b)
```

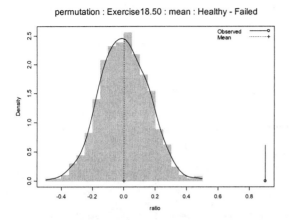

permutation : Exercise18.50 : mean : Healthy - Failed

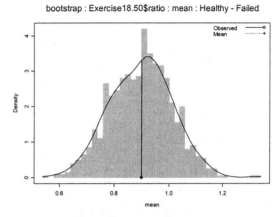

bootstrap : Exercise18.50$ratio : mean : Healthy - Failed

18.51 The standard deviation for the estimated *P*-value of 0.015 for the DRP study, based on 999 resamples is 0.00385. The standard deviation for the estimated *P*-value of 0.0183 based on the 500,000 resamples in the Verizon study is 0.000190.

```
sqrt(.015 * (1-.015)/999)
sqrt(.0183 * (1-.0183) / 500000)
```

18.52 a) The two populations should be the same, but may be skewed (or differ otherwise from Normality). **b)** The two populations are the same, and are Normal. **c)** Two Normal populations with the same mean but different variances.

18.53 a) Let p_1 denote the probability of success of new franchise firms with exclusive territory clauses and p_2 the probability of success of new franchise firms with no exclusive territory clause. We test the hypotheses $H_0: p_1 = p_2$ vs. $H_a: p_1 > p_2$.
b) The *z* statistic is 2.43. The *P*-value for the test is 0.0075.
c) Under the null hypothesis, all 170 firms are equally likely to be a success. In this case, successes occur for reasons that have nothing to do with whether the firm has an exclusive territory clause. We can resample in a way consistent with the null hypothesis by choosing an ordinary SRS of 142 of the firms without replacement and assigning them to the exclusive territory clause group.
The *P*-value for the permutation test is 0.018. This *P*-value is larger than that found in part (b), largely because the *z*-test fails to take ties into account.
d) There is evidence at the 0.05 level, that exclusive territory clauses increase the chance of success. There is not evidence that exclusive territory clauses increase the chance of success at the 0.01 level.
e) A 95% BCa confidence interval for the difference between the two population proportions is (0.033, 0.426). This interval does not include 0 and lies to the positive side of 0. This is consistent with the results of the permutation test in part (d), which rejected the null hypothesis at the 0.05 level.

```
Exercise18.53 # variables Exclusive and Success
p1 <- 108/142
p2 <- 15/28
p <- (108+15)/(142+28)
#(p1-p2)/sqrt(p1*(1-p1)/142 + p2*(1-p2)/28)  # not appropriate for testing
(p1-p2)/sqrt(p*(1-p)/142 + p*(1-p)/28)
# Note - by recording success and failure as 1 and 0, we can compute
# proportions by calculating means
1 - pnorm( (p1-p2)/sqrt(p*(1-p)/142 + p*(1-p)/28) ) # for one-sided test
perm53 <- permutationTestMeans(Exercise18.53, treatment=Exclusive, seed=0,
                    alternative="greater")
perm53
permutationTestMeans(Exercise18.53, treatment=Exclusive, seed=0,
                alternative="greater", B=99999)
```

…

```
# increae number of replications for greater accuracy: p-value = .01667
plot(perm53)
# Note - z-test fails to take ties into account.
#boot53 <- bootstrap2(Exercise18.53, mean(Success), treatment=Exclusive,
seed=0)
boot53 <- bootstrap2(Exercise18.53$Success, mean,
                treatment=Exercise18.53$Exclusive, seed=0)
plot(boot53)
limits.bca(boot53)
#limits.tilt(boot53) # not yet implemented; do the following for now:
boot53b <- bootstrap(Exercise18.53, diffMean(Success, Exclusive),
                group = Exclusive, seed=0)
boot53b$L <- boot53$L   # this is optional, but makes next steps faster
limits.bca(boot53b)
limits.tilt(boot53b)
```

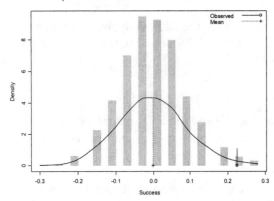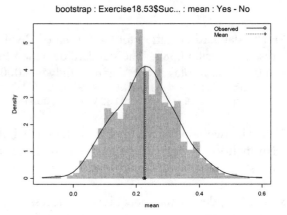

18.54 a) H_0: $\mu_1 = \mu_2$, H_a: $\mu_1 < \mu_2$, where μ_1 is the mean response time for turning the knob clockwise (to the right). (A two-sided alternative would also be reasonable.) **b)** *P*-value = 0.0043. **c)** See figure; the area to the left of the vertical line segment on the left side of the figure.

```
Exercise18.54 # variables Right and Left
perm54 <- permutationTestMeans(Exercise18.54$Right, data2=Exercise18.54$Left,
                paired=T, seed=0, alternative="less")
perm54
permutationTestMeans(Exercise18.54$Right, data2=Exercise18.54$Left, B=99999,
                paired=T, seed=0, alternative="less")
# more samples for higher accuracy:  P-value = 0.00434
plot(perm54)
```

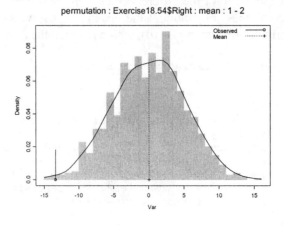

18.55 a) Let r denote the correlation between the salaries and batting averages of all major league baseball players. We test the hypotheses H_0: $r = 0$ vs. H_a: $r > 0$.

b) The *P*-value is 0.257. We conclude that there is not strong evidence that salaries and batting averages are correlated in the population of all major league players.

```
Exercise18.55 # variables Salary and Average
# must permute only one of the variables
perm55 <- permutationTest(Exercise18.55$Salary, seed=0,
              cor(data, Exercise18.55$Average), alternative="greater")
perm55
plot(perm55)
```

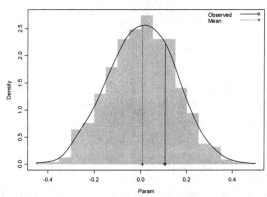

permutation : Exercise18.55$Salary : cor(data, Exercis...

18.56 a) The averages of the two groups appear about the same; the heights of the forwards are a bit more spread out.

```
        Forwards          Centers
              45 : 6 :
          666677 : 6 : 6
         8888999 : 6 : 888889
 000000011111 : 7 : 000111
          222223 : 7 : 222333
           44555 : 7 : 5
                 6 : 7
```

b) H_0: $\mu_1 = \mu_2$, H_a: $\mu_1 < \mu_2$, where μ_1 is the mean height of forwards. (Could also do a two-sided test.)

c) The *P*-value is 0.35. We conclude that there is not significant evidence that the mean height of forwards is less than that of centers.

```
Exercise18.56 # variables Height and Position
stem(Exercise18.56$Height[ Exercise18.56$Position == "Forward" ],
     scale = -1, nl=2)
stem(Exercise18.56$Height[ Exercise18.56$Position == "Center" ],
     scale = -1, nl=2)
# Put those together back-to-back by hand.
perm56 <- permutationTestMeans(Exercise18.56, treatment = Position, seed=0,
                        alternative="less")
perm56
plot(perm56)
```

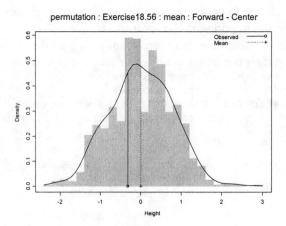

18.57 a) For the median we test the hypotheses H_0: $\mu_1 = \mu_2$ vs. H_a: $\mu_1 \neq \mu_2$, where μ_1 and μ_2 are mean response times for the right and left hands, respectively. For the 25% trimmed mean we test the hypotheses H_0: $m_1 = m_2$ vs. H_a: $m_1 \neq m_2$, where m_1 and m_2 are the 25% trimmed means for the right and left hands, respectively.

b) The permutation distribution is clearly not Normal. The *P*-value for the permutation test for the difference in medians is 0.002.

c) The permutation distribution looks much more like a Normal distribution than the permutation distribution in (b) for the difference in medians. The *P*-value for the permutation test for the difference in 25% trimmed means is 0.002.

d) There is strong evidence that there is a difference in the population median times when using the right hand versus the left hand. Similarly for 25% trimmed means.

```
Exercise18.57 # variables Time, Distance, Hand; latter "right" or "left"
perm57a <- permutationTest2(Exercise18.57, median(Time),
                    treatment=Hand, seed=0)
plot(perm57a)
perm57a
perm57b <- permutationTest2(Exercise18.57, mean(Time, trim=.25),
                    treatment=Hand, seed=0)
plot(perm57b)
perm57b
```

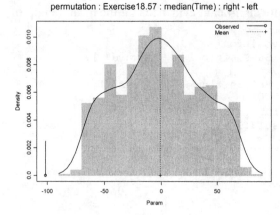 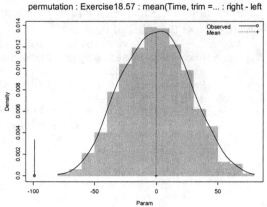

18.58 a) It appears that the weights are somewhat larger for the younger customers.

```
      Age < 60        Age >= 60
          9 : 6 : 8
        34 : 7 : 1234
```

```
55678 : 7 : 5778
   01 : 8 : 0
```

b) Greater, because the goal of this significance test is to test the hypothesis that the weight given to younger customers is greater than that for older customers.

c) The *P*-value is 0.223. This does not provide significant evidence against the null hypothesis. We would fail to reject the null hypothesis of equality. However, it is possible that there is an effect, just not large enough to be detected with a sample of this size.

```
Exercise18.58  # variables Weight and Age, either "<60" or ">=60"
stem(Exercise18.58$Weight[ Exercise18.58$Age == "<60" ])
stem(Exercise18.58$Weight[ Exercise18.58$Age == ">=60" ])
# do back-to-back by hand
perm58 <- permutationTestMeans(Exercise18.58, treatment=Age,
          alternative="greater", seed=0)
plot(perm58)
qqnorm(perm58)
perm58
```

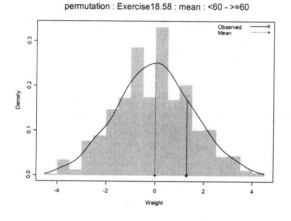

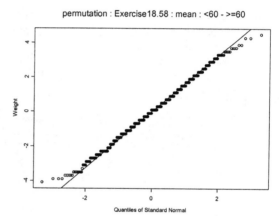

18.59 a) Let p_1 denote the proportion of women in the population who pay attention to a "No Sweat" label when buying a garment and p_2 denote the proportion of men in the population who pay attention to a "No Sweat" label when buying a garment. We test the hypotheses H$_0$: $p_1 = p_2$ vs. Ha: $p_1 \neq p_2$.

b) The *P*-value for the permutation test is 0.002.

c) The permutation distribution is approximately Normal (except that it is discrete; you can see this using a Normal quantile plot or by observing spikes in the histogram) and thus it is not surprising that the permutation test agrees closely with the *z* test in Example 8.6.

```
names(Exercise18.59)  # variables Sex and LabelUser
perm59 <- permutationTestMeans(Exercise18.59, treatment=Sex, seed=0)
perm59
plot(perm59)
qqnorm(perm59)
```

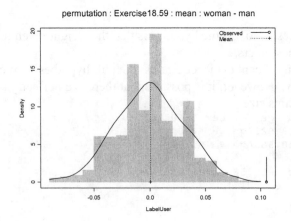
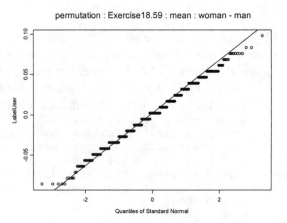

18.60 The median for 2002 is 244.9, and for 2001 is 260.8. The *P*-value for the two-sided alternative is 0.576; we conclude that there is not significant evidence of a change in price.

```
names(Exercise18.60)  # Price and Year
perm60 <- permutationTest2(Exercise18.60, median(Price),
                  treatment = Year, seed=0)
plot(perm60)
perm60
```

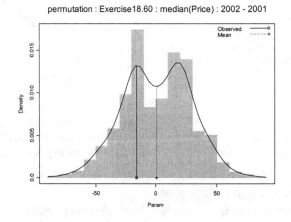

18.61 A two-sided permutation test of the hypothesis has *P*-value = 0.002, and we conclude that there is strong evidence of a correlation between square footage and age of a house in Ames, Iowa.

```
names(Exercise18.61) # variables Price, SquareFootage, Age
perm61 <- permutationTest(Exercise18.61$SquareFootage,
                  cor(data, Exercise18.61$Age), seed=0)
plot(perm61)
perm61
```

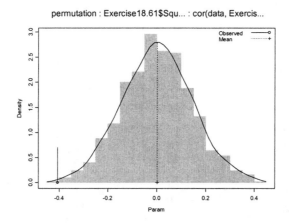

18.62 For the one-sided alternative that the success probability is greater for subjects receiving calcium, the *P*-value is 0.273. We conclude that there is not significant evidence that calcium gives an improvement.

```
Exercise18.62 # variables Treatment (calcium or placebo) and Success 1 or 0
perm62 <- permutationTestMeans(Exercise18.62, treatment=Treatment,
                alternative = "greater", seed=0)
plot(perm62)
perm62
```

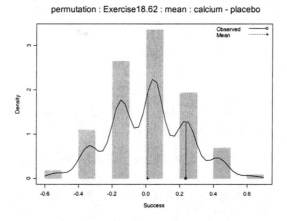

18.63 A 95% bootstrap *z* interval using the observed difference in proportions (0.2364) and the bootstrap standard error (SE = 0.215) is (−0.185, 0.657).

```
boot63 <- bootstrap2(Exercise18.62$Success, mean,
                treatment = Exercise18.62$Treatment, seed=0)
plot(boot63)  # unusual plot -- high-low pattern.  This is because
# histograms are sensitive to the width of bins.
plot(boot63, nclass=10)  # more reasonable
plot(boot63, nclass=40)  # shows gaps
qqnorm(boot63)# note the bunching & gaps, explains the high-low pattern
boot63
limits.t(boot63, z=T)
```

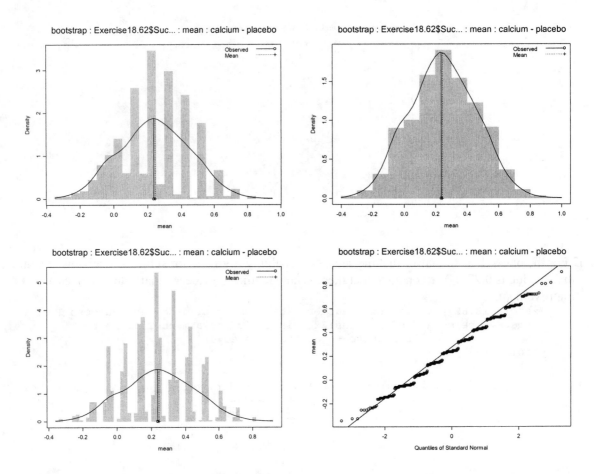

18.64 a) The ILEC distribution is clearly skewed to the right. The CLEC distribution appears if anything to be skewed to the left, but it is hard to tell with this little data. The means and spreads appear to be similar.

b) The *P*-value is 0.004 for a one-sided test against the alternative that the mean for the CLEC distribution is greater.

c) The *P*-value is 0.0073. The permutation test does not require Normal distributions, and gives more accurate answers in the case of skewness.

d) The difference is significant at both the 5% and 1% levels.

```
Exercise18.64 # variables Time and Group (ILEC or CLEC)
histogram(~Time | Group, data=Exercise18.64)
t.test(Exercise18.64$Time[Exercise18.64$Group == "ILEC"],
       Exercise18.64$Time[Exercise18.64$Group == "CLEC"],
       alternative="less", var.equal=F)
# Easy to do perm test for difference in means:
perm64a <- permutationTestMeans(Exercise18.64, treatment=Group,
                        alternative="less", seed=0)
perm64a
permutationTestMeans(Exercise18.64, treatment=Group, B=99999,
                        alternative="less", seed=0)
# P-value based on 100K replications is 0.00729.
```

It is harder to do a perm test where the test statistics is a pooled-variance t;
need to ensure that only one variable is permuted.
As a side note, there is a one-to-one relationship between the difference
in means and the pooled-variance, so tests based on these statistics
are equivalent; hence we usually test based on the simpler statistic.

```
perm64b <- permutationTest(Exercise18.64$Time,
```

```
                        alternative="less", seed=0,
            t.test(data[Exercise18.64$Group == "ILEC"],
                data[Exercise18.64$Group == "CLEC"],
                alternative="less", var.equal=T)$statistic)
perm64b
plot(perm64a)
plot(perm64b)
# permutation distributions are very skewed
```

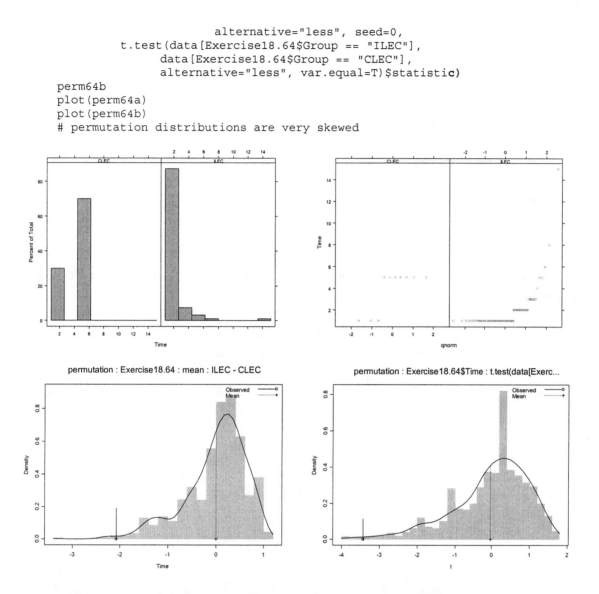

18.65 a) We performed a two-sided permutation test on the ratio of standard deviations. Some of the ratios were infinite because the permutation test produced a standard deviation of 0 in the denominator. The mean and SE of the permutation distribution are undefined, but we can still obtain the P-value = 0.386 based on the permutation distribution. This P-value tells us that there is not strong evidence that the variability in the repair times for ILEC and CLEC customers differ.
b) The P-value for the permutation test differs from that obtained by the F statistic. This suggests that the test based on the F statistic is not very accurate.

```
perm65 <- permutationTest(Exercise18.64$Time,
        function(data) {stdev(data[Exercise18.64$Group == "ILEC"]) /
                    stdev(data[Exercise18.64$Group == "CLEC"])},
                    seed=0)
perm65
plot(perm65)
```

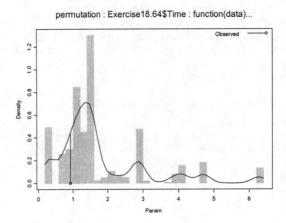

18.66 a) H_0: $\sigma_1 = \sigma_2$ vs. H_a: $\sigma_1 \neq \sigma_2$. **b)** The *P*-value is 0.042. **c)** For these data, the F test is reasonable.

```
Exercise18.66 # variables status (Healthy or Failed) and ratio
qqmath(~ratio | status, data=Exercise18.66)
perm66 <- permutationTest(Exercise18.66$ratio,
     function(data) {var(data[Exercise18.66$status == "Healthy"]) /
                     var(data[Exercise18.66$status == "Failed"])},
                 seed=0)

perm66
```

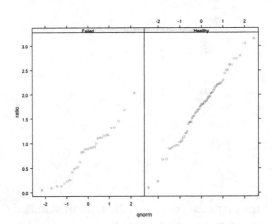

18.67 a) We test the hypotheses H_0: $\mu = 0$ vs. H_a: $\mu > 0$, where μ is the mean change (posttest – pretest). Note that positive values of μ indicate that mean posttest scores are higher than mean pretest scores, and hence that test scores have improved.

b) The *P*-value is 0.026, so there is evidence (significant at the 0.05 level but not at the 0.01 level) that the mean change (posttest - pretest) is positive.

c) The area to the right of 1.45 is the *P*-value.

```
Exercise18.67 # variables Pretest and Posttest
perm67 <- permutationTestMeans(Exercise18.67$Posttest,
                      data2 = Exercise18.67$Pretest,
                      paired = T, alternative = "greater", seed = 0)

perm67
plot(perm67)
```

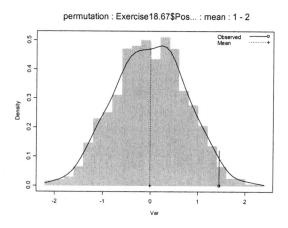

18.68 a) The distribution is approximately Normal, aside from being discrete.

b) The mean is 3.62, and formula standard error is 0.52.

c) The bootstrap standard error is 0.51. This is close to the formula standard error.

```
hist(Exercise18.68)
qqnorm(Exercise18.68)
mean(Exercise18.68)
stdev(Exercise18.68)/sqrt(length(Exercise18.68))
boot68 <- bootstrap(Exercise18.68, mean, seed=0)
boot68
```

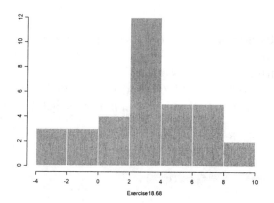

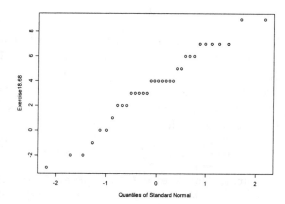

18.69 In this problem, the answers will depend strongly on the random sample drawn.

a) For a Uniform distribution on 0 to 1, the population median is 0.5.
The shape of the bootstrap distribution will depend on the sample drawn.

b) The bootstrap standard error is 0.072. A 95% bootstrap *t* confidence interval is (0.373, 0.572). (Both depend heavily on the sample drawn.)

c) The bootstrap BCa 95% confidence interval is (0.369, 0.620). A tilting 95% interval is (0.373, 0.572). The bootstrap *t* 95% confidence interval is the same as the 95% tilting interval, slightly narrower than the 95% BCa interval. Although the bootstrap distribution for the median is not Normal, the bootstrap *t* interval is reasonably reliable here.

```
set.seed(1)
x69 <- runif(50)
median(x69)
boot69 <- bootstrap(x69, median, seed=0)
plot(boot69)
qqnorm(boot69)
boot69
```

```
limits.t(boot69)
limits.bca(boot69)
limits.tilt(boot69)
```

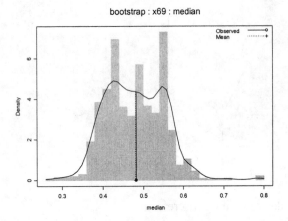

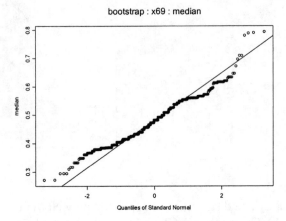

18.70 a) The difference appears quite significant.

```
          : 1 : 9
          : 2 : 01
      3 : 2 : 2233
      5 : 2 : 4
      6 : 2 :
    899 : 2 :
     01 : 3 :
     22 : 3 :
      5 : 3 :
```

b) The *P*-value is about 0.00056 (based on 100,000 resamples). For 1000 resamples, the answer will usually be either 0.002 or 0.004 (round up, then double).

c) We conclude that there is significant evidence that the mean ages differ.

Note: with enough resamples we see that the permutation test *P*-value is consistent with the answer form a *t* test, but students doing only 1000 resamples may get an answer that indicates that the *t* test *P*-value is too small.

```
Exercise18.70 # variables Age and Sex (male or female)
stem(Exercise18.70$Age[ Exercise18.70$Sex == "male" ],
    scale = -1, nl=2)
stem(Exercise18.70$Age[ Exercise18.70$Sex == "female" ],
    scale = -1, nl=2)
# have to do back-to-back stemplot by hand
perm70 <- permutationTestMeans(Exercise18.70, treatment=Sex, seed=0)
perm70
permutationTestMeans(Exercise18.70, treatment=Sex, seed=0, B=99999)
# p-value 0.00056
plot(perm70)
```

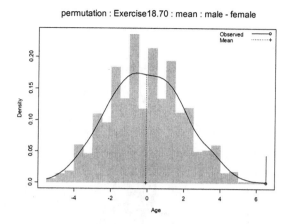

permutation : Exercise18.70 : mean : male - female

18.71 a) The bootstrap distribution is left-skewed and does not appear to be approximately Normal. The bootstrap standard error is 0.134.

b) The bootstrap *t* confidence interval is not appropriate here because the bootstrap distribution is not approximately Normal.

c) A 95% BCa confidence interval is (0.179, 0.710) and a 95% tilting interval is (0.218, 0.698).

```
Exercise18.71 # variables Year, Overseas, U.S.
boot71 <- bootstrap(Exercise18.71, cor(Overseas, U.S.), seed=0)
plot(boot71)
boot71
limits.bca(boot71)
limits.tilt(boot71)
```

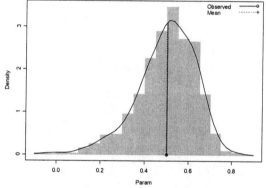

bootstrap : Exercise18.71 : cor(Overseas, U.S.)

18.72 a) The standard deviation of daily changes is 2.21

b) 0.31 **c)** (1.56, 2.87) **d)** BCa (1.69, 2.96), tilting (1.65, 2.89).

The two more accurate intervals reach farther to the right than the left, for example (−0.52, 0.75) for the BCa and (−0.56, 0.68) for tilting. This asymmetry suggests that *t* intervals would not be accurate.

```
Exercise18.72 # variables Day, Close, Change
x72 <- 100 * Exercise18.72$Change / Exercise18.72$Close  # percent change
# There we divided by the close, because it was easy.  Really should divide
# by the previous day's close:
x72b <- 100 * Exercise18.72$Change / (Exercise18.72$Close -
Exercise18.72$Change)
stdev(x72) # 2.21
stdev(x72b)# also 2.21
boot72 <- bootstrap(x72, stdev, seed=0)
```

```
boot72
plot(boot72)
limits.t(boot72)
limits.bca(boot72)
.Last.value - boot72$observed
limits.tilt(boot72)
.Last.value - boot72$observed
```

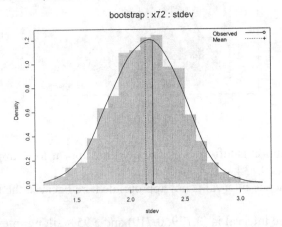

18.73 a) The histogram of the 2000 data is strongly right-skewed with two outliers, one of which is extreme. This violates the guideline for using the *t* procedure given in Section 17.1, namely for a sample size of at least 15, that *t* procedures can be used except in the presence of outliers or strong skewness. The histogram of the 2001 is right-skewed, but less strongly than that of the 2000 data. **b)** The *P*-value for the permutation test for the difference in means is 0.292. We conclude that there is not strong evidence that the mean selling prices for all Seattle real estate in 2000 and in 2001 are different.

```
Exercise18.73 # univariate
par(mfrow=c(2,2))
hist(Table18.5); qqnorm(Table18.5)
hist(Exercise18.73); qqnorm(Exercise18.73)
par(mfrow=c(1,1))
perm73 <- permutationTestMeans(Table18.5, data2 = Exercise18.73, seed=0)
perm73
plot(perm73)
```

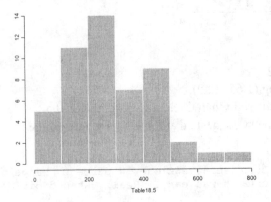

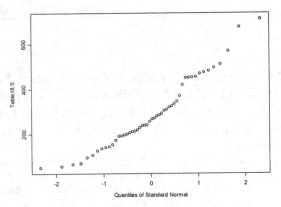

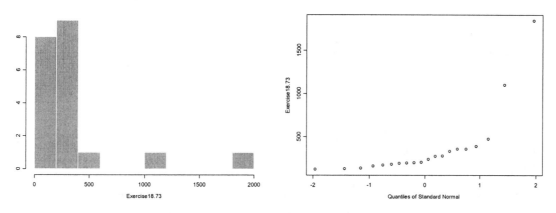

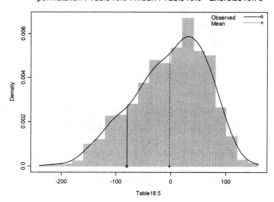

18.74 a) The formula-based *t* interval is (78.8, 115.7).

b) The tilting interval is (72.4, 108.1) or, in other words, the observed value plus (-24.9, 10.9).

c) The bootstrap distribution shows strong left skewness (note that we are looking at a sampling distribution, as opposed to the distribution of a dataset; the skewness observed here is after the effect of the central limit theorem).

d) The *t* interval is not robust in this case. It indicates that the value 105 is well within the range of the interval, while a more accurate interval suggests that it is barely within the range of the interval.

```
t.test(Exercise18.74)
boot74 <- bootstrap(Exercise18.74, mean, seed=0)
limits.tilt(boot74)
.Last.value - boot74$observed
plot(boot74)
qqnorm(boot74)
```

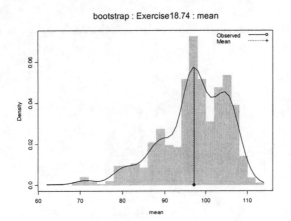

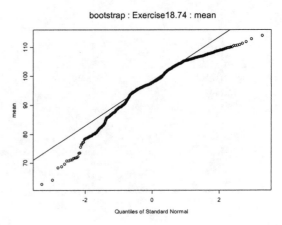

18.75 The study described in Exercise 18.74 is a one-sample problem. We have no methods for carrying out a permutation test in such one-sample problems (there is no obvious way to resample that is consistent with a one-sample test for a mean).

18.76 a) We are interested in whether the presentation causes an improvement in glove use. We must use a matched pairs method because the same nurses were recorded both times.

b) The *P*-value is 0.002 (the smallest possible for a two-sided test with 1000 resamples). This provides significant evidence that the presentation was helpful.

```
Exercise18.76 # variables Before and After
perm76 <- permutationTestMeans(Exercise18.76$Before,
                 data2 = Exercise18.76$After, paired=T,
                 alternative = "less", seed = 0)

perm76
plot(perm76)
```

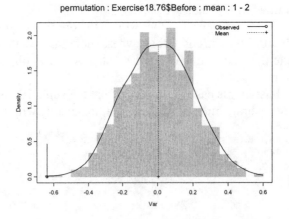

18.77 A 95% bootstrap *t* confidence interval for the mean change (after-before) is (0.41, 0.86). Zero is outside this interval, so the result is significant at the 0.05 level. We conclude that there is strong evidence that the mean change is different from 0, that is, positive.

```
boot77 <- bootstrap(Exercise18.76, mean(After)-mean(Before), seed=0)
plot(boot77)
qqnorm(boot77)
limits.t(boot77)
```

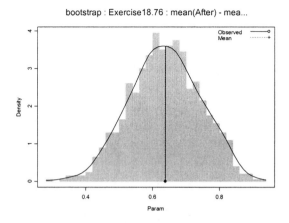

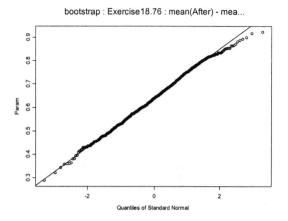

18.78 a) The distributions appear approximately Normal. Unemployment rates in 2002 are higher, with a larger spread.

b) The *P*-value for the two-sided alternative is 0.0001.

c) The *P*-value for the two-sided permutation test is 0.002 (the smallest possible for a two-sided test with 1000 replications). The average unemployment rate has increased, and the change is statistically significant.

```
Exercise18.78 # variables X2001 and X2002
par(mfrow=c(2,2))
hist(Exercise18.78$X2001, main="2001")
qqnorm(Exercise18.78$X2001, main="2001")
hist(Exercise18.78$X2002, main="2002")
qqnorm(Exercise18.78$X2002, main="2002")
par(mfrow=c(1,1))
t.test(Exercise18.78$X2001, Exercise18.78$X2002, paired=T)
perm78 <- permutationTestMeans(Exercise18.78$X2002,
                    data2 = Exercise18.78$X2001, paired=T, seed = 0)
perm78
permutationTestMeans(Exercise18.78$X2002, B = 99999,
                data2 = Exercise18.78$X2001, paired=T, seed = 0)
# P-value = 0.00006
plot(perm78)
```

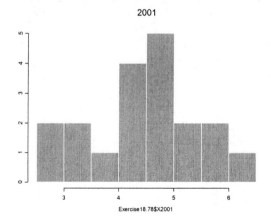

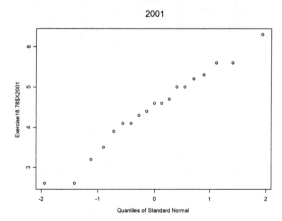

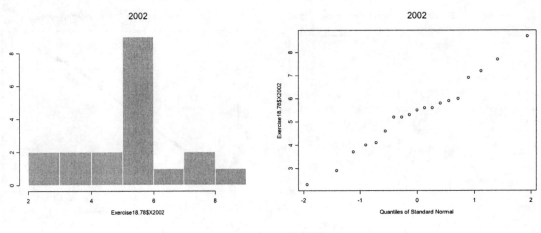

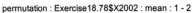

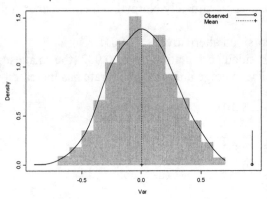

18.79 a) 80% for girls, and 66% for boys.

b) The *P*-value for a two-sided permutation test is 0.198. There is no strong evidence that there is a difference in the proportion of boys and girls who like chocolate ice cream.

```
Exercise18.79 # variables Sex (girls and boys) and Like (0 or 1)
40/50
30/45
perm79 <- permutationTestMeans(Exercise18.79, treatment=Sex, seed=0)
perm79
plot(perm79)
```

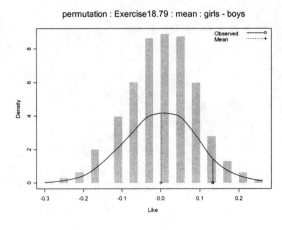

18.80 a) The histograms do not give the impression of Normality. However, the Normal quantile plots suggest that the underlying distributions could well be Normal; there are no outliers or systematic deviations from Normality. **b)** The bootstrap standard errors are 17.0 and 14.7 for the High and Medium groups, respectively. **c)** The bootstrap distributions appear very close to Normal. **d)** The percentile limits are (107.4, 173.7) and (93.3, 150.1), and the tilting intervals are (106.8, 171.1) and (94.6, 150.9). Using either confidence interval method, the intervals for the two groups overlap. This suggests that there may not be a statistically significant difference between the two groups. However, we should do a confidence interval for the difference to answer that question.
e) The 95% bootstrap percentile confidence interval for the difference is (−26, 62). This interval includes zero. The observed data do not provide strong evidence of a difference in mean word counts.

```
Exercise18.80 # variables WordCount and Education (High, Medium)
histogram(~WordCount | Education, data=Exercise18.80)
qqmath(~WordCount | Education, data=Exercise18.80)
groupMeans(Exercise18.80$WordCount, group=Exercise18.80$Education)
x80 <- split(Exercise18.80$WordCount, Exercise18.80$Education)
boot80a <- bootstrap(x80$High, mean, seed=0)
boot80b <- bootstrap(x80$Medium, mean, seed=0)
boot80a
boot80b
plot(boot80a)
qqnorm(boot80a)
plot(boot80b)
qqnorm(boot80b)
limits.percentile(boot80a)
limits.percentile(boot80b)
limits.tilt(boot80a)
limits.tilt(boot80b)
boot80c <- bootstrap2(Exercise18.80$WordCount, mean,
                treatment = Exercise18.80$Education, seed=0)
limits.percentile(boot80c)
```

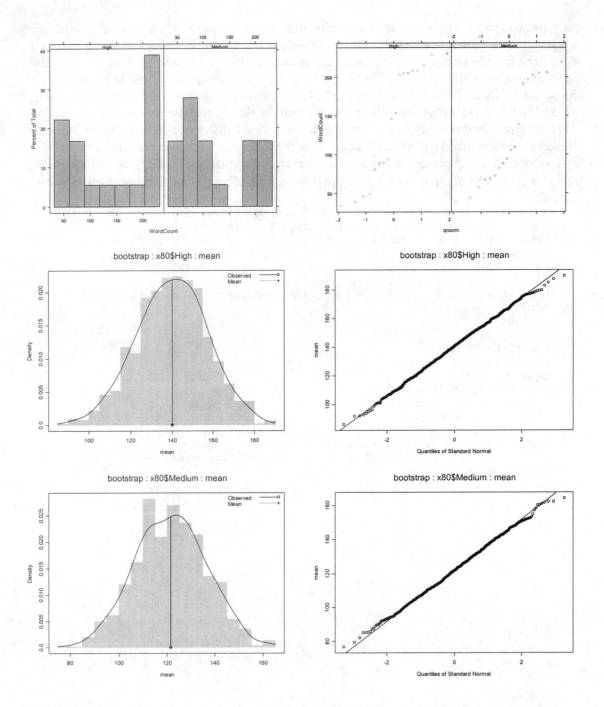

18.81 We test the hypotheses H_0: $\mu_1 = \mu_2$ vs. H_a: $\mu_1 \neq \mu_2$. The *P*-value is 0.212. Thus, there is not strong evidence that the mean word count is higher for ads placed in magazines aimed at people with high education levels than for ads placed in magazines aimed at people with medium education levels. The 95% confidence interval in Exercise 18.80 (d) for the difference in means contained 0. This suggests that there is not strong evidence of a difference in mean word counts. Here we conclude that there is not strong evidence that the mean word count is higher for ads placed in magazines aimed at people with high education levels than for ads placed in magazines aimed at people with medium education levels.

```
Exercise18.81 # variables
perm81 <- permutationTestMeans(Exercise18.80, treatment = Education, seed=0,
```

```
                                    alternative = "greater")
perm81
plot(perm81)
```

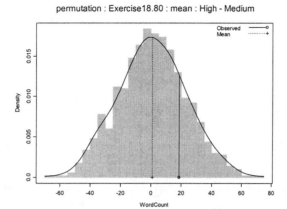

permutation : Exercise18.80 : mean : High - Medium

18.82 a) Roughly Normal.

b) The average number of burglaries was 64.3 before and 60.6 after the program began. A one-sided test, because we wish to test whether the program made an improvement. The *P*-value for the two-sample *t* test is 0.22.

c) The *P*-value for the permutation test is 0.22. This is the same (after rounding) as the formula *t* test.

d) The *P*-value is 0.788. This is testing whether the data provide strong evidence that burglaries have increased. That is the opposite of our goal, to determine whether the program has reduced burglaries. The *P*-value is more than 50% because the actual change was negative rather than positive; there is greater than a 50% chance that random chance would yield an increase greater than -3.7.

```
Exercise18.82 # variables Burglaries, When (Before and After)
groupMeans(Exercise18.82$Burglaries, Exercise18.82$When)
histogram(~Burglaries | When, data=Exercise18.82)
qqmath(~Burglaries | When, data=Exercise18.82)
x82 <- split(Exercise18.82$Burglaries, Exercise18.82$When)
t.test(x82$Before, x82$After, alternative="greater")
perm82a <- permutationTestMeans(Exercise18.82, treatment = When,
                    alternative = "greater", seed=0)
perm82a
plot(perm82a)
qqnorm(perm82a)
perm82b <- permutationTestMeans(Exercise18.82, treatment = When,
                    alternative = "less", seed=0)
perm82b
```

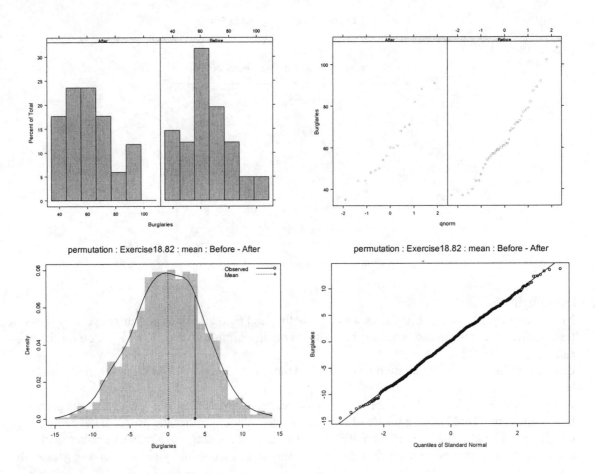

permutation : Exercise18.82 : mean : Before - After

permutation : Exercise18.82 : mean : Before - After

18.83 a) The bootstrap distribution appears to be approximately Normal.

b) The bootstrap standard error is 4.603. A 95% bootstrap *t* confidence interval using the conservative method for the degrees of freedom is (−13.4, 6.1). Using ($n_1 + n_2 - 2$) degrees of freedom gives a narrower interval (−12.9, 5.6).

c) A 95% bootstrap percentile interval is (−12.5, 5.6). This agrees closely with the second interval found in (b), so we conclude that the intervals are reasonably accurate. These intervals include 0 and so we would conclude that there is not strong evidence (at the 0.05 level) of a difference in the mean monthly burglary counts. The tests in Exercise 18.82 were one-sided tests and showed no strong evidence of a decrease in mean monthly burglaries (or of an increase in the case of part (d) of Exercise 18.82).

```
boot83 <- bootstrap2(Exercise18.82$Burglaries, mean,
                     treatment=Exercise18.82$When, seed=0)
plot(boot83)
qqnorm(boot83)
boot83
limits.t(boot83)
limits.t(boot83, df = (nrow(Exercise18.82)-2)) # degrees of freedom if pooling
t.test(x82$Before, x82$After)
limits.percentile(boot83)
```

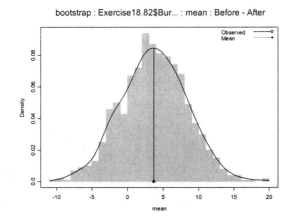

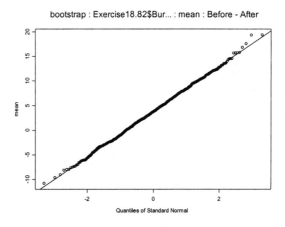